THE ALEXANDER SHAKESPEARE

General Editor

R. B. KENNEDY

King Henry IV Part I

Edited by

K. B. POTTEN and V. MILLINGTON

PREFATORY NOTE

This series of Shakespeare's plays uses the full
Alexander text which is recommended by many
Examining Boards. By keeping in mind the fact
that the language has changed considerably in four
hundred years, as have customs, jokes, and stage
conventions, the editors have aimed at helping the
modern reader – whether English is his mother
tongue or not – to grasp the full significance of these
plays. The Notes, intended primarily for examina-
tion candidates, are presented in a simple, direct
style. The needs of those unfamiliar with British
culture have been specially considered.

Since quiet study of the printed word is unlikely
to bring fully to life plays that were written directly
for the public theatre, attention has been drawn to
dramatic effects which are important in performance. The editors see Shakespeare's plays as living
works of art which can be enjoyed today on stage,
film and television in many parts of the world.

First Edition 1972
Revised Edition 1983
This Edition 1984

© Wm. Collins Sons and Co. Ltd.

ISBN 0 00 197314 2
ISBN 0 00 325252 3
Made and printed in Great Britain by
Wm. Collins Sons and Co. Ltd., Glasgow

2 3 4 5 6 7 8 9

Contents

THE THEATRE IN SHAKESPEARE'S DAY

On the face of it, the conditions in the Elizabethan theatre were not such as to encourage great writers. The public playhouse itself was not very different from an ordinary inn-yard; it was open to the weather; among the spectators there were often louts, pickpockets and prostitutes; some of the actors played up to the rowdy elements in the audience by inserting their own jokes into the authors' lines, while others spoke their words loudly but unfeelingly; the presentation was often rough and noisy, with fireworks to represent storms and battles, and a table and a few chairs to represent a tavern; there were no actresses, so boys took the parts of women, even such subtle and mature ones as Cleopatra and Lady Macbeth; there was rarely any scenery at all in the modern sense. In fact, a quick inspection of the English theatre in the reign of Elizabeth I by a time-traveller from the twentieth century might well produce only one positive reaction: the costumes were often elaborate and beautiful.

Shakespeare himself makes frequent comments in his plays about the limitations of the playhouse and the actors of his time, often apologizing for them. At the beginning of *Henry V* the Prologue refers to the stage as 'this unworthy scaffold' and to the theatre building (the Globe, probably) as 'this wooden O', and emphasizes the urgent need for imagination in making up for all the deficiencies of presentation. In introducing Act IV the Chorus goes so far as to say:

'. . . we shall much disgrace
With four or five most vile and ragged foils,
Right ill-dispos'd in brawl ridiculous,
The name of Agincourt.'   (lines 49–52)

In *A Midsummer Night's Dream* (Act V, Scene i) he seems to dismiss actors with the words:

'The best in this kind are but shadows.'

4

Yet Elizabeth's theatre, with all its faults, stimulated drama-
tists to a variety of achievement that has never been equalled
and, in Shakespeare, produced one of the greatest writers
in history. In spite of all his grumbles he seems to have been
fascinated by the challenge that it presented him with. It is
necessary to re-examine his theatre carefully in order to
understand how he was able to achieve so much with the
materials he chose to use. What sort of place was the
Elizabethan playhouse in reality?

The Development of the Theatre
up to Shakespeare's Time

For centuries in England noblemen had employed groups
of skilled people to entertain them when required. Under
Tudor rule, as England became more secure and united,
actors such as these were given more freedom, and they
often performed in public, while still acknowledging their
'overlords' (in the 1570s, for example, when Shakespeare
was still a schoolboy at Stratford, one famous company was
called 'Lord Leicester's Men'). London was rapidly becoming larger and more important in the second half of the
sixteenth century, and many of the companies of actors
took the opportunities offered to establish themselves at
inns on the main roads leading to the City (for example, the
Boar's Head in Whitechapel and the Tabard in Southwark)
or in the City itself. These groups of actors would come to an
agreement with the inn-keeper which would give them the
use of the yard for their performances after people had
eaten and drunk well in the middle of the day. Before long,
some inns were taken over completely by companies of
players and thus became the first public theatres. In 1574
the officials of the City of London issued an order which
shows clearly that these theatres were both popular and also
offensive to some respectable people, because the order
complains about 'the inordinate haunting of great multitudes of people, specially youth, to plays, interludes and
shows; namely occasion of frays and quarrels, evil practices

of incontinency in great inns . . .' There is evidence that, on public holidays, the theatres on the banks of the Thames were crowded with noisy apprentices and tradesmen, but it would be wrong to think that audiences were always undiscriminating and loud-mouthed. In spite of the disapproval of Puritans and the more staid members of society, by the 1590s, when Shakespeare's plays were beginning to be performed, audiences consisted of a good cross-section of English society, nobility as well as workers, intellectuals as well as simple people out for a laugh; also (and in this respect English theatres were unique in Europe), it was quite normal for respectable women to attend plays. So Shakespeare had to write plays which would appeal to people of widely different kinds. He had to provide 'something for everyone' but at the same time to take care to unify the material so that it would not seem to fall into separate pieces as they watched it. A speech like that of the drunken porter in *Macbeth* could provide the 'groundlings' with a belly-laugh, but also held a deeper significance for those who could appreciate it. The audience he wrote for was one of a number of apparent drawbacks which Shakespeare was able to turn to his and our advantage.

SHAKESPEARE'S LIFE AND TIMES

Very little indeed is known about Shakespeare's private life: the facts included here are almost the only indisputable ones. The dates of Shakespeare's plays are those on which they were first produced.

*   *   *

1558 Queen Elizabeth crowned.
1561 Francis Bacon born.
1564 Christopher Marlowe born.   William Shakespeare born, April 23rd, baptized April 26th.
1566   Shakespeare's brother, Gilbert, born.
1567 Mary, Queen of Scots, deposed.
James VI (later James I of England) crowned King of Scotland.
1572 Ben Jonson born.
Lord Leicester's Company (of players) licensed; later called Lord Strange's, then the Lord Chamberlain's, and finally (under James) The King's Men.
1573 John Donne born.
1574 The Common Council of London directs that all plays and playhouses in London must be licensed.
1576 James Burbage builds the first public playhouse, The Theatre, at Shoreditch, outside the walls of the City.
1577 Francis Drake begins his voyage round the world (completed 1580).
Holinshed's *Chronicles of England, Scotland and Ireland* published (which Shakespeare later used extensively).
1582   Shakespeare married to Anne Hathaway.

1583 The Queen's Company founded by royal warrant.

Shakespeare's daughter, Susanna, born.

1585

Shakespeare's twins, Hamnet and Judith, born.

1586 Sir Philip Sidney, the Elizabethan ideal 'Christian knight', poet, patron, soldier, killed at Zutphen in the Low Countries.

1587 Mary, Queen of Scots, beheaded.
Marlowe's *Tamburlaine* (*Part I*) first staged.

1588 Defeat of the Spanish Armada.
Marlowe's *Tamburlaine* (*Part II*) first staged.

1589 Marlowe's *Jew of Malta* and Kyd's *Spanish Tragedy* (a 'revenge tragedy' and one of the most popular plays of Elizabethan times).

1590 Spenser's *Faerie Queene* (Books I-III) published.

1592 Marlowe's *Doctor Faustus* and *Edward II* first staged. Witchcraft trials in Scotland.
Robert Greene, a rival playwright, refers to Shakespeare as 'an upstart crow' and 'the only Shake-scene in a country'.

Titus Andronicus
Henry VI, Parts I, II and III
Richard III

1593 London theatres closed by the plague.
Christopher Marlowe killed in a Deptford tavern.

Two Gentlemen of Verona
Comedy of Errors
The Taming of the Shrew
Love's Labour's Lost

1594 Shakespeare's company becomes The Lord Chamberlain's Men.

Romeo and Juliet

1595 Raleigh's first expedition to Guiana. Last expedition of Drake and Hawkins (both died).

Richard II
A Midsummer Night's Dream

8

1596 Spenser's *Faerie Queene* (Books IV-VI) published. James Burbage buys rooms at Blackfriars and begins to convert them into a theatre.

King John
The Merchant of Venice
Shakespeare's son Hamnet dies.
Shakespeare's father is granted a coat of arms.

1597 James Burbage dies; his son Richard, a famous actor, turns the Blackfriars Theatre into a private play-house.

Henry IV (Part I)
Shakespeare buys and redecorates New Place at Stratford.

1598 Death of Philip II of Spain.

Henry IV (Part II)
Much Ado About Nothing

1599 Death of Edmund Spenser. The Globe Theatre completed at Bankside by Richard and Cuthbert Burbage.

Henry V
Julius Caesar
As You Like It

1600 Fortune Theatre built at Cripplegate.
East India Company founded for the extension of English trade and influence in the East.
The Children of the Chapel begin to use the hall at Blackfriars.

Merry Wives of Windsor
Troilus and Cressida

1601

Hamlet
Twelfth Night

1602 Sir Thomas Bodley's library opened at Oxford.

1603 Death of Queen Elizabeth. James I comes to the throne. Shakespeare's company becomes The King's Men. Raleigh tried, condemned and sent to the Tower.

1604 Treaty of peace with Spain.

Measure for Measure
Othello
All's Well that Ends Well

1605 The Gunpowder Plot: an attempt by a group of Catholics to blow up the Houses of Parliament.

1606 Guy Fawkes and other plotters executed.

Macbeth
King Lear

1607 Virginia, in America, colonized.
A great frost in England.

Antony and Cleopatra
Timon of Athens
Coriolanus
Shakespeare's daughter, Susanna, married to Dr. John Hall.

1608 The company of the Children of the Chapel Royal (who had performed at Blackfriars for ten years) is disbanded.
John Milton born.
Notorious pirates executed in London.

Richard Burbage leases the Blackfriars Theatre to six of his fellow actors, including Shakespeare.
Pericles, Prince of Tyre

1609

Shakespeare's *Sonnets* published.

1610 A great drought in England.

Cymbeline

1611 Chapman completes his great translation of the *Iliad*, the story of Troy.
Authorized Version of the Bible published.

A Winter's Tale
The Tempest

1612 Webster's *The White Devil* first staged.

Shakespeare's brother, Gilbert, dies.

1613 Globe Theatre burnt down during a performance of *Henry VIII* (the firing of small cannon set fire to the thatched roof).
Webster's *Duchess of Malfi* first staged.

Henry VIII
Two Noble Kinsmen
Shakespeare buys a house at Blackfriars.

1614 Globe Theatre rebuilt 'in far finer manner than before'.

1616 Ben Jonson publishes his plays in one volume.
Raleigh released from the Tower in order to prepare an expedition to the gold mines of Guiana.

Shakespeare's daughter, Judith, marries Thomas Quiney.
Death of Shakespeare on his birthday, April 23rd.

1618 Raleigh returns to England and is executed on the charge for which he was imprisoned in 1603.

1623 Publication of the Folio edition of Shakespeare's plays.

Death of Anne Shakespeare (née Hathaway).

INTRODUCTION

The first part of *Henry IV* is one of a series of four plays that shows England developing out of a period of misrule and civil war to one of national triumph in war abroad and unity at home. These plays are *Richard II*, the two parts of *Henry IV* and *Henry V*. In the first play, Richard, an attractive but selfish and irresponsible figure, causes the vast majority of the aristocracy and of Englishmen in general to revolt against him in favour of his cousin, Henry Bolingbroke. Bolingbroke is proclaimed Henry IV and is at least indirectly responsible for the murder of Richard.

It is at this point that the play you are to study begins. Although one of a series, it is self-contained and can be enjoyed on its own. It is made up of two main stories, which link up in the second half. The first concerns Henry IV himself, an ageing and weary figure, trying to find peace for his country but forced to atone for his guilt in usurping the crown and in acquiescing in the death of his predecessor. One price that he pays is that of seeing his land torn by the rebellion against himself of a large group of powerful and ambitious noblemen, formerly his friends and allies but now distrustful of him and afraid for their own security.

The second story shows us Henry's son, Prince Hal, also a thorn in his father's flesh because of the irresponsible life he leads. In reality Prince Hal is finding his own way towards kingship, a way which he hopes will enable him to rule successfully, avoiding his predecessors' mistakes. It is Prince Hal who emerges in the final play of the series as the triumphant Henry V.

The language of the play

Henry IV, Part I is a play of action; it teems with incident at all levels. Rebels connive and muster armies, rival factions eye each other with suspicious hostility, travellers are robbed on the highway, reluctant men are pressed into service and armies clash on the battlefield. There is little time in this rapid succession of events for any thoughts that are either lyrical or profoundly contemplative, and the language of the play reflects this characteristic.

We can see two different kinds of expression within the play as a whole. Firstly, there is the solemn and weighty language of the historic plot. It is a language that has an increasingly pressing urgency behind it, dealing as it does with high affairs of state, bitter grievances, political scheming, and the strategies of war. It is a language that is often grand, impassioned or even lavish. Look for instance at Hotspur's speeches in Act I, Scene iii; at Glendower's utterances in Act III, Scene i; and at Vernon's description of Hal and his followers in Act IV, Scene i.

Secondly, we hear the unforgettably earthy prose of the comic scenes, which may reflect a leisurely, aimless way of life, but which nevertheless bubbles along with a racy wit and vivacity. It gives us the real flavour of the times, with numerous insights into the lives of ordinary people. It is here we learn of dank horse fodder, 'bots' (worms), fleas, 'jordans' (chamber pots) and 'chamber-lye' (urine). Scattered throughout are the typical expressions of the tavern – 'Lay by', 'Bring in', 'Play it off' and 'Dyeing scarlet'. Compared with the noble verse of the historic plot this is a much more colloquial language, full of puns, double meanings, popular quips and sayings. Because our language has altered since Elizabethan times, we may miss many of the subtleties of the verbal jokes, but the racy, earthy spirit of the language still comes across powerfully.

There are two strands of imagery which run through and unite the apparently very distinct language of both plots, giving them each great immediacy and impact. The first type of imagery is concerned with bodily, physical comparisons. For instance, Henry talks of the soil of England having lips which are thirsty for blood; Hotspur says he will 'pluck up drowned honour by the locks'; Northumberland's failure to join the rebels is seen as a sickness which 'doth infect the very lifeblood of our enterprise/A perilous gash, a very limb lopp'd off.' In the comic plot it is hardly surprising to find that this physical imagery is particularly associated with Falstaff. His bodily appetites are constantly emphasized and his sheer size gives rise to a very physical vein of abuse. Hal calls Falstaff 'fat-kidneyed rascal', a 'fat paunch', a 'huge hill of flesh', 'a swollen parcel of dropsies' and a 'stuffed cloak bag of guts'. Ironically, Falstaff abuses his victims at Gadshill by calling them 'gorbellied knaves' and 'bacon-fed knaves'.

Hand in hand with this physicality goes the second type of imagery: animal comparisons. Treason is described as being 'but trusted like the fox'; Hotspur is compared to a fighting cock which 'prunes himself and bristles up his crest' and, according to Kate, he is a 'mad-headed ape' and more angry than a weasel. In a very vivid speech, Vernon describes Hal and his soldiers as being 'plum'd like estridges', their plumes fluttering like eagles. He says they are 'wanton as youthful goats, wild as young bulls.' And in the comic plot Falstaff (who at one point had complained of being ' as melancholy as a gib cat or a lugg'd bear'), abuses Hal by calling him an 'eel-skin', a 'dried neat's-tongue', a 'bull's pizzle' and a 'stock-fish'. There are numerous examples of both these types of imagery; they give a powerful directness and immediacy to the verse and a great earthiness to the prose.

In the midst of all this turbulent activity and racy language, there is one notable moment of lyricism in Act III, Scene i, as Mortimer takes leave of his weeping wife (lines 200–227). One moment of profound reflection also occurs in Act V, Scene iv, when the dying Hotspur says,

> *But thoughts, the slaves of life, and life, time's fool*
> *And time that takes survey of all the world,*
> *Must have a stop.*

Such speeches, however, are exceptional in the play.

What we see in *Henry IV, Part I* is Shakespeare's ability to move with great assurance between earthy, colloquial prose and grandiloquent verse, always capturing exactly the right tone for each speaker, and weaving all the different elements into a rich and intensely dramatic whole.

Characterization

As the individual characters are dealt with quite fully in the 'Summing Up' on page 253, this section will concentrate on just one notable aspect of the characters in the play – the fact that Shakespeare presents us with people who have both strengths and weaknesses and therefore seem far more 'real' than characters who are either complete heroes or complete villains. Such convincing characterization can be clearly seen in the portrayal of Falstaff, Hotspur and King Henry.

There can be few dramatic creations as instantly and abidingly popular as Falstaff. What explanation can there be for the enormous popularity of a man who is described as a 'swollen parcel of dropsies' and a 'huge bombard of sack'; a man who is gluttonous and lecherous; a man who is a thief, a liar, a parasite and a cheat? Of course, we secretly revel in his anarchy and in his vices, as we do in the fact that everything he does is larger than life. But his popularity can also be explained by the fact that, as well as presenting his defects, Shakespeare shows us his enormous *positive* values – his tremendous zest for life, his warmth and joviality, his irrepressible wit and inventiveness, his verbal alacrity, his healthy scepticism and debunking mockery. We must obviously have grave reservations about a man who is capable of acting as ignominiously as he does towards the end of the play, and we fully see why Hal must reject him. Nevertheless, when the play is over, it is his attractive qualities that remain uppermost in our minds – his tireless energy and wit, his outrageous fantasies and his sheer love of life.

The other powerfully attractive character, Hotspur, is also presented in a similarly balanced way. His very nickname suggests his fiery temperament, yet he is also a man of great energy and commitment; a plain, outspoken soldier dedicated to the principle of honour. It is interesting to note that this last trait is presented both as a virtue and a defect. His sense of honour shines out in a treacherous world of shifting schemers and manipulators. Yet, at the same time, his vision of honour is shown to be too narrow and unbalanced and we can see clearly how it makes him fall a gullible prey to Worcester's cynical plotting. Other defects are clearly demonstrated, too; as well as being hot-headed, he is also immature, selfish, rude and arrogant. However, though we must admit the futility and wrong-headedness of much that he does in the play, we feel that his death is a tragedy. That is because we respond to his energy and zest, thrill to his often impressive speeches and respect the *positive* values he represents.

While not having the same impact on our imaginations as Falstaff and Hotspur, King Henry also exhibits strengths as well as defects. There *is* certainly much about him that justifies criticism. He has unlawfully seized a throne (a fact which is stressed time and again); he has betrayed those who helped him and he has schemed and manipulated to achieve his ambition. He is a survivor who will even stoop to the base and selfish tactic of having men disguised as himself on the battlefield in order to increase his chances of survival. On the positive side, he seems to feel remorse for his sins and he genuinely desires to rule over a peaceful and united kingdom. More important still is the fact that his very defects are also positive strengths. Henry may not be a saintly King, but his coolly calculating mind, his political cunning and his determination to hold on to power all prove to be powerful weapons against the rebels. And, in a world that feared political upheaval and the breakdown of law and order as much as the Elizabethans did, a strong, effective ruler, albeit a usurper, was positively to be welcomed. Henry *is* such a figure. He acts decisively and positively at every stage to secure the peace and stability his country so badly needs.

Shakespeare thus gives us a balanced picture of these three very different characters, showing us their good points as well as their bad and leaving us, at the end of the play, with their positive aspects uppermost in our minds. And, as we will see in the section on the dramatic structure of the play, this balanced view of Falstaff and Hotspur plays a vital part in what is, arguably, the central issue – the evolution and redemption of Hal.

Plot

The following summary highlights in broad terms the most significant aspects of each scene.

Act I   *Scene i:* Henry IV's hopes for peace and for the chance to fulfil his long-cherished dream of going on a Crusade are dashed by the news that Mortimer's army has been heavily defeated by Glendower in Wales, and that Hotspur has defeated the Scots under Douglas. Angered by Hotspur's arrogant refusal to hand over all but one of his prisoners, Henry nevertheless expresses envious admiration of Hotspur's valour, wishing that his own dishonoured son, Prince Hal, were such a man. Meanwhile Hotspur has been summoned to explain his disobedience at the next Council.

Scene ii: We now meet the insubordinate Hal in the exuberant and lawless company of Falstaff. Hal teases Falstaff about his idle life of gluttony and thieving and eventually, in mock remorse, Falstaff vows he will reform, only seconds later to claim it is no sin to labour in his vocation – purse-stealing! Poins enters with a proposal to rob a group of travellers the next morning. Hal refuses to take part but is later persuaded by Poins to play a trick on Falstaff whereby, when Falstaff and the others have carried out the robbery, the two of them, heavily disguised, will set upon them and seize the booty. The joke will lie in catching out Falstaff in the fantastic lies he will certainly tell about the incident. Alone at the end of the scene, Hal explains that he will allow his present company to 'smother up his beauty' for a while in order that his sudden reformation will astonish the world all the more.

Scene iii: Having dismissed the impudent Percy, Earl of Worcester, Henry sternly listens to his son Hotspur's explanation about the prisoners. To Hotspur's new demand that a ransom be paid for Mortimer in return for the prisoners, Henry angrily replies that he will never ransom a 'traitor'. He rejects Hotspur's outraged defence of Mortimer's loyalty and leaves, threatening the Percys with his displeasure unless they comply with his wishes. Worcester returns and explains to a furious Hotspur the reason for Henry's attitude to Mortimer – he fears him because he is Richard's rightful heir. Hotspur rages defiantly against Henry's ingratitude and against the dishonour that has fallen on them for having helped him to depose

Richard. Finally breaking through Hotspur's uncontrolled ravings, Worcester seizes this opportune moment to propose the rebellion against the King.

Act II *Scene i:* Gadshill, one of the thieves, fails to extract any information from the carriers about their goods and route. However his confederate, the chamberlain, gives him the information he requires, and is promised a share of the proceeds from the robbery.

Scene ii: On the highway, Falstaff curses his fellow thieves for hiding his horse. The others arrive and Hal and Poins move further off down the hill, ostensibly to catch any of the travellers who may escape the first attack. In noisy high spirits, Falstaff sets upon the travellers who are then robbed and tied up. Having briefly left the scene, the robbers return to share out the spoils, Falstaff complaining about the cowardice of Hal and Poins who, at that very moment, leap out on them. They all scatter. including Falstaff who puts up only a token resistance before running away, roaring!

Scene iii: All is not going well with the rebellion. An unnamed nobleman has excused himself from joining the rebels, saying their plot is dangerous and ill-conceived. Vehemently condemning such faintheartedness, Hotspur seeks reassurance in an over-confident appraisal of their plot and in plans for immediate departure. He ignores his wife's request to know the cause of all his recent agitation, concentrating instead on the matter of his horse. Eventually, however, he turns to her, saying he does not love her and that a soldier's business is war, not trifling with women. However, after an emotional plea from Kate, he swears he does indeed love her but says he will tell no woman where he is going or what he is doing. Her only consolation is to be allowed to follow him the next day.

Scene iv: At the Tavern, Hal is passing the time by poking fun at the serving men and at Francis in particular. At length, Falstaff arrives in a bad mood and cursing all cowards, especially Hal and Poins.

He gives an account of the robbery which is a pack of progressively more outrageous lies. When ultimately faced with the truth, the undaunted and resourceful Falstaff claims he had, of course, recognized the Prince and had naturally therefore refrained from striking him!

Harsh political reality at last intrudes into this topsy-turvy world when a summons arrives from the King for Hal, and with it news of the rebellion Falstaff and Hal now enact a practice interview, Falstaff playing the King and mimicking court rhetoric with great gusto. He deplores the Prince's disreputable life-style and companions, but makes an exception of the 'virtuous' Falstaff. Hal now takes on the role of King and castigates his 'son' for keeping company with Falstaff, whose vices he viciously exposes. Genuinely frightened for his own future, Falstaff urges the 'King' not to banish him from the company of Hal. Ominously Hal replies, 'I do, I will.'

The play is interrupted by the arrival of the sheriff who is searching for the thieves and their booty. Falstaff hides but Hal promises the sheriff he will come to him the next day. When the sheriff has gone, a search of the sleeping Falstaff's pockets reveals nothing but bills for food and drink. The scene ends with Hal intending to face his father, go to war, place Falstaff in charge of a company of foot soldiers, and repay the stolen money.

Act III *Scene i:* When the rebels meet to finalize their arrangements a clash of temperaments threatens to jeopardize their alliance. Hotspur childishly seeks every opportunity to deflate the conceited pretensions of Glendower. The division of England into three creates further dissension as Hotspur claims he has been cheated and demands that the River Trent be straightened to equalize his portion. Glendower emphatically refuses, only finally giving way to prevent a rift in the alliance. Hotspur is rebuked by Mortimer and Worcester for his rudeness and hot-tempered arrogance. The rebels (except for Glendower, who will follow later) have arranged to meet at Shrewsbury, and so Mortimer and Hotspur take leave of their wives.

Scene ii: The King's side against the rebels is now about to be significantly strengthened by his reconciliation with Hal. In a carefully calculated attack, Henry suggests that Hal is God's agent of punishment upon him and that he (Hal) is committing political suicide. He also says Hotspur, by virtue of his valour, is more fitted to rule than Hal, whose failure to support the King makes him no better than a traitor. Stung by these words, Hal vows to redeem himself by making Hotspur 'render every glory up'. He says he will die rather than break his vow. In recognition of this, Hal is to receive a position of high command. On this optimistic note, the King prepares to march to Bridgenorth.

Scene iii: Somewhat subdued by the failure of the robbery, Falstaff, like Hal, promises to reform. But *his* good intentions are very short-lived and he is soon complaining to an indignant Mistress Quickly that his pocket has been picked and a valuable ring taken. Accusations and abuse fly between them until, when Hal arrives, they both appeal to him. When Hal admits to being the pick-pocket, Falstaff's fury subsides and he magnanimously forgives the hostess! Hal reveals that Falstaff is to have a troop of infantry. Falstaff, however, shows little relish for war, wishing only to remain in the tavern.

Act IV *Scene i:* Problems beset the rebels. Northumberland is ill and can neither join them, nor muster his troops. Hotspur's reaction swings from gloom to unrealistic optimism. But Worcester, knowing on what shaky foundations their cause stands, fears Northumberland's absence will spread great apprehension. Vernon's description of Hal, magnificent and powerful at the head of his glittering troops, provokes Hotspur to vow angrily that he will fight Hal to the death. The final blow is that Glendower is also unable to raise his army. Despite Hotspur's brave assertion that their numbers may be adequate, pessimism is beginning to infect his mind. 'Doomsday is near; die all, die merrily.'

Scene ii: Having, typically, exploited his authority as an officer to benefit financially, Falstaff now leads a ragged band of soldiers drawn from the dregs of society. He cynically observes that they will 'fill a pit' just as well as their betters. On hearing that the armies are now encamped, he closes his mind to the battle ahead, preferring to think of the feasting that will follow

Scene iii: The rebel leaders disagree about the best time to go into battle – Hotspur inevitably favouring immediate action and choosing to ignore the strong arguments against it. Blunt arrives with a demand from Henry to know their grievances and an offer of absolute pardon. Hotspur replies sarcastically and reiterates all their grievances against the King. With a new-found sense of caution, however, he decides not to send such an unconsidered reply, promising to consider the offer and send word the following morning.

Scene iv: The Archbishop of York, fearing the depleted rebel army will not be successful against the King, despatches messages to his friends. He urges them to arm themselves in readiness to face the King, who intends to punish them

Act V   *Scene 1:* The King now rebukes Worcester and Vernon for attempting to overthrow the natural order of things. Once again, Worcester blames the King's ingratitude and treachery – reasons dismissed by the King as mere attempts to justify their actions to the weak-minded. In an attempt to minimize bloodshed, Hal offers to engage Hotspur in single combat, generously praising his opponent. The King repeats his offer of a full pardon, adding that he will not hesitate to administer 'dread correction' if the rebels do not yield. Finally alone, Falstaff scornfully rejects all this passionate pursuit of

'Honour' – in his eyes it is a futile concept, of benefit neither to the dead nor the living.

Scene ii: Worcester, rightly or wrongly refusing to trust the King he loathes, now draws upon his own head the final responsibility for the bloodshed by concealing the King's offer of mercy from Hotspur. Douglas sends a defiant answer to the King and Hotspur eagerly responds to the news of Hal's challenge. The pursuit of honour now dominates Hotspur's mind. In a fatalistic mood, he reasserts the justice of their cause and his belief that, whatever the outcome, what matters is to live and die honourably.

Scene iii: The battle has begun. Blunt, disguised in the King's colours, is slain by Douglas. Discovering the body, Falstaff observes, 'There's honour for you.' Such futile heroics are not for him; he has retired from the battle, having led his men into the thick of the battle and then abandoned them. When Hal enters, Falstaff claims to have killed Hotspur. He refuses to lend Hal the sword he requests when he learns that Hotspur is 'living to kill' him, but he offers his pistol instead. Finding nothing in the pistol case but a bottle of sack, Hal leaves, throwing the bottle at Falstaff in disgust. Alone again, Falstaff vows he will seek out Hotspur – honour such as Blunt now has is not for him.

Scene iv: Despite being wounded, Hal refuses to retire from the battle, urging the King to return to the field. Challenged by Douglas, the King fights and Hal, seeing him in danger, puts Douglas to flight. The climax of Hal's redemption is reached when he comes face to face with Hotspur and kills him. As Hotspur dies he laments only the dishonour of having to surrender his proud titles. Hal does not glory in his victory but pays generous tribute to Hotspur's great valour.

In a gross parody of this conflict, Falstaff has, meanwhile, fought with Douglas and feigned death. Hal now pauses over his 'body' lamenting the loss of Falstaff, for all that he did not love his follies. Hal leaves and the irrepressible Falstaff rises up. Fearing that Hotspur may also be feigning death, he ignominiously stabs him in the thigh. Hal returns and finds, to his astonishment, a resurrected Falstaff who claims to have killed Hotspur and demands a reward. He dismisses Hal's own claims as lies and, unabashed, exuberantly describes his encounter with Hotspur. Seeming to attach little importance to Falstaff's outrageous behaviour, Hal leaves to inspect the dead. Falstaff follows, bearing the body, in high hopes of a reward and promising to reform.

Scene v: The victorious King rebukes Worcester and sentences him to death along with Vernon. Hal begs that Douglas be freed in recognition of his valour. Finally, Henry prepares to deal with the rebels in York and in Wales, determined to suppress all rebellion and regain total control of his kingdom.

Dramatic structure

When we consider dramatic structure we are really asking whether there is an overall *shape* or *pattern* to be found in a play. In *Henry IV, Part One* a major theme – the evolution and redemption of Hal – provides us with one very clear pattern.

Two extreme and, in their different ways, equally attractive models of behaviour are presented to Hal in the shape of Falstaff and Hotspur. Superficially they seem to be rather like the Vice and Virtue of old morality plays – Falstaff, an idle, gluttonous and lecherous predator; Hotspur, a straightforward, honest and blunt man of action, dedicated to the pursuit of honour. The question would appear to be, which of these two 'models' will Hal choose to emulate?

At the beginning of the play, the King, who is in no doubt as to which of the two *he* would like his son to choose, is certain that Hal has made his choice and is beyond redemption. However, it soon becomes clear to *us* that, while Hal is fascinated by Falstaff and his world, he is also detached from it and is using it for his own ends. Indeed, we eventually see him reject the lawlessness of Falstaff, who becomes increasingly irrelevant to him, to assume his rightful place in the world and atone for his previous behaviour.

So has Hal totally rejected the Falstaff model in favour of the Hotspur model? Of course it isn't as simple as that, for Hotspur's character is no more ideal than Falstaff's is totally undesirable. Hotspur has many defects – his concept of life is too narrow, his idea of honour is too blinkered and unrealistic; he is intolerant, arrogant, reckless, selfish and immature. We would not want Hal to copy these defects and, ironically, it is his association with Falstaff which saves him from this. For, despite his gross faults and excesses, Falstaff offers Hal a great education in Life. He possesses vitality, warmth and gaiety; he is irreverent and scorns blinkered honour; he is a great debunker; and, above all, he loves enjoyment and Life itself. These things all make sufficient impact on Hal to ensure that, when he emerges at the end of the play as a true and honourable Prince, he is also a modest, affable and generous Prince who rejects the narrow extremes of Hotspur and who, above all, knows what life is about and understands his people. This evolution of Hal, whereby he absorbs the good qualities of his two models and rejects their faults and excesses, provides the moral 'structure' or pattern of the play.

A second pattern can be seen in the alternating plots – the comic and the historic – and it is easy to make the mistake of thinking they have little in common with each other. Indeed, the serious world of political intrigue and power struggles does seem, at first sight, far removed from the aimless debauchery and self-gratification of Falstaff's world; just as the politically calculating nobility seem to have nothing in common with the uneducated tapsters. And, as though to highlight the separateness of the plots, one is written in verse, the other in prose.

In fact, however, Shakespeare is offering us a comprehensive vision of the world and it soon becomes obvious that far more unites the plots than divides them. The situations, characters, themes and motifs in the two plots are complementary, frequently imitating each other. So, for instance, the national stability is not only threatened by the insurrection of the Percys but also by Hal's insubordination and

Falstaff's lawlessness and topsy-turvy morality. King Henry feels that Heaven is punishing him for usurping Richard's throne not only through the disobedience of the Percys but also through the disobedience of his son. The Percys are grasping and ambitious and so is Falstaff. The lying, cheating and trickery amongst the characters of the comic plot are little better than the treachery, deception and scheming that go on amongst the nobility. In the Gadshill robbery incidents we see the comic plot apeing the battle of Holmedon and the encounter between Mortimer and Glendower. Finally, Henry's interview with Hal (Act III, Scene ii) is beautifully parodied by Falstaff at the Boar's Head.

Just as the two plots often reinforce each other by imitation, so certain points are also emphasized by the use of contrast. For instance, Falstaff's contempt for the idea of honour is the perfect antithesis to Hotspur's dedication to its pursuit; Hal's unshakeable resolve to redeem the approval of others (Act III, Scene ii) is sharply contrasted with Falstaff's very fleeting good intentions in the following scene; Hotspur's noble death is thrown into sharp relief by the cowardly feigned 'death' of Falstaff.

Both plots gradually merge to unite finally on the battlefield, where we see the major issues or themes of the play resolved with the *redemption* of Hal, the defeat of *anarchy* and *ambition*, the restoration of *law* and *order* and the assertion of Henry's *kingship*.

LIST OF CHARACTERS

KING HENRY THE FOURTH
HENRY, PRINCE OF WALES ⎫
PRINCE JOHN OF LANCASTER ⎬ *sons of Henry IV*
EARL OF WESTMORELAND ⎫
SIR WALTER BLUNT ⎬ *friends of the King*
THOMAS PERCY, EARL OF WORCESTER
HENRY PERCY, EARL OF NORTHUMBERLAND
HENRY PERCY, *surnamed* HOTSPUR, *his son*
EDMUND MORTIMER, EARL OF MARCH
ARCHIBALD, EARL OF DOUGLAS
SCROOP, ARCHBISHOP OF YORK
SIR MICHAEL, *friend of the Archbishop*
OWEN GLENDOWER
SIR RICHARD VERNON
SIR JOHN FALSTAFF ⎫
POINS ⎪
BARDOLPH ⎬ *irregular humorists*
PETO ⎪
GADSHILL ⎭
LADY PERCY, *wife of Hotspur and sister of Mortimer*
LADY MORTIMER, *wife of Mortimer and daughter of Glendower*
HOSTESS QUICKLY, *of the Boar's Head, Eastcheap*
Lords, Officers, Attendants, Sheriff, Vintner, Chamberlain, Drawers, Carriers, Travellers

THE SCENE: *England and Wales*

25

NOTES

ACT ONE

SCENE I

A fanfare of trumpets and a procession might well open this formal scene. Henry IV would insist on splendour at the court to try to compensate for the difficulty of his position as a usurper. We find him expressing disappointment at the unruly behaviour of his son, the Prince of Wales (*Prince Hal*). Now that England's civil war is over, he expresses a wish to go on a Crusade, perhaps hoping that a religious war against the Muslims in Palestine (*the Holy Land*) will unite the country behind him. Hal is not present as his place on the Council has been given to his younger brother Prince John of Lancaster.

2-4. 'a breathing-space now gives us a chance of encouraging peace at home and discussing fresh wars in distant lands'.

3. *broils:* wars.

4. *strands afar remote:* distant shores (countries).

5-6. England is personified as a monster which, having eaten its children, has their blood smeared round its mouth.

6. *daub:* paint.

8-9. *armed . . . paces:* tramplings by the hooves of opposing cavalry.

5, 7. Here and in lines 15, 18, Henry stresses the phrase *No more*. Is he just making a statement or is he wishing desperately (perhaps even praying) that what he wants can come true?

9-18. Henry claims that in the future Englishmen will no longer destroy each other but will instead unite in a disciplined army to march together against a foreign enemy.

9. *opposed eyes.* The soldiers stare at each other in fear before they fight although they belong to the same nation; an unnatural state of affairs.

10. *like . . . heaven.* Meteors were feared by men because they did not follow a fixed path like other stars and therefore seemed to destroy the orderliness of the heavens and foretell unnatural events.

12. *intestine:* internal (adjective) i.e. a civil war.

13. *furious . . . butchery:* violent clash in which Englishmen massacre their fellow-countrymen.

14. *mutual well-beseeming:* united and orderly.

17-18. *like . . . master.* 'If you don't put a dagger back in its sheath correctly when you wear it, you yourself are likely to be cut by it.'

18-27. 'Therefore we shall now raise a united English army to fight against Christ's enemies in Palestine itself, where fourteen hundred years ago He was crucified for us.' Is this a clever plan of Henry's to enable him to make a permanent peace in England or do you feel from the way that Henry says this that he has sincere religious feelings? What sin has he committed for which he might feel desperately that he needs God's forgiveness?

21. *impressed:* called up to fight.

22. *power:* army.

ACT ONE

Enter the KING, LORD JOHN OF LANCASTER, EARL OF
WESTMORELAND, SIR WALTER BLUNT *and* Others

King

So shaken as we are, so wan with care,
Find we a time for frighted peace to pant
And breathe short-winded accents of new broils
To be commenc'd in strands afar remote.
No more the thirsty entrance of this soil   5
Shall daub her lips with her own children's blood;
No more shall trenching war channel her fields,
Nor bruise her flow'rets with the armed hoofs
Of hostile paces. Those opposed eyes
Which, like the meteors of a troubled heaven,   10
All of one nature, of one substance bred,
Did lately meet in the intestine shock
And furious close of civil butchery,
Shall now in mutual well-beseeming ranks
March all one way, and be no more oppos'd   15
Against acquaintance, kindred, and allies.
The edge of war, like an ill-sheathed knife,
No more shall cut his master. Therefore, friends,
As far as to the sepulchre of Christ—
Whose soldier now, under whose blessed cross   20
We are impressed and engag'd to fight—
Forthwith a power of English shall we levy,
Whose arms were moulded in their mothers' womb
To chase these pagans in those holy fields
Over whose acres walk'd those blessed feet   25

27

27. *For our advantage:* in order to redeem us.

28-30. *But . . . not now.* Henry now admits that this intention is not a recent one and that the others know of it already. You will need to read the rest of the scene carefully to decide whether Henry has just been trying to impress his nobles or whether he sincerely wishes to know what arrangements are made.

29. *bootless:* unnecessary.

30. *Therefore . . . now:* 'But it is not for this that we are now met.'

33. *dear expedience.* This phrase indicates the importance and urgency of the matter of the Crusade to Henry.

34. *hot in question:* discussed urgently.

35. *many . . . down:* many appointments to positions of command were decided on.

36. *all athwart.* The news from Wales interrupted the debate and was at cross purposes with the preparations for the Crusade.

37. The Welsh, though ruled by England, often caused trouble by rising under local chieftains.

38-46. Notice the words used to describe Glendower, the Welshwomen and their behaviour. Is this all fact, or is it part of a policy that attempts by this kind of publicity to blacken one's enemies? How would Westmoreland speak these lines and how would the court react to them? How does Hotspur describe the same battle in Act I, Scene iii? What impression of Glendower do you get in Act III, Scene i?

40. *irregular and wild:* unruly, uncivilized, possibly also suggesting the use of guerrilla tactics.

41. *rude:* violent.

42. Is *a thousand* a plausible figure?

43. *corpse:* corpses.

47-8. Henry seems to accept the news in a sad but resigned manner, almost as a man who knows that his hopes have been forlorn anyway.

51. *thus it did import:* this is what it amounted to.

52. *Holy-rood day:* the feast of the Holy Cross i.e. 14th September. *rood:* cross.

53-6. *brave . . . ever-valiant and approved . . . sad and bloody hour.* Westmoreland is unhappy that Archibald (the Earl of Douglas) whom he obviously admires should have decided to fight England.

54. *approved:* (three syllables) experienced in warfare.

Scot. Scotland was still an independent country with its own king and, when England was at war or was weak for other reasons, frequently attacked England from the north.

55. *Holmedon:* Humbleton in Northumberland.

56-61. News was first brought by a messenger who left while the battle was still at its height.

sad: usually meant grave or serious in Elizabethan times.

57-8. The sound of gunfire and the way things were going indicated the probability of great bloodshed.

59-60. *very . . . contention:* most violent peak of the battle.

Which fourteen hundred years ago were nail'd
For our advantage on the bitter cross.
But this our purpose now is twelvemonth old,
And bootless 'tis to tell you we will go;
Therefore we meet not now. Then let me hear   *30*
Of you, my gentle cousin Westmoreland,
What yesternight our Council did decree
In forwarding this dear expedience.

Westmoreland

   My liege, this haste was hot in question
And many limits of the charge set down   *35*
But yesternight, when all athwart there came
A post from Wales loaden with heavy news;
Whose worst was that the noble Mortimer,
Leading the men of Herefordshire to fight
Against the irregular and wild Glendower,   *40*
Was by the rude hands of that Welshman taken,
A thousand of his people butchered;
Upon whose dead corpse there was such misuse,
Such beastly shameless transformation,
By those Welshwomen done, as may not be   *45*
Without much shame re-told or spoken of.

King

   It seems then that the tidings of this broil
Brake off our business for the Holy Land.

Westmoreland

   This match'd with other did, my gracious Lord;
For more uneven and unwelcome news   *50*
Came from the north, and thus it did import:
On Holy-rood day, the gallant Hotspur there,
Young Harry Percy, and brave Archibald,
That ever valiant and approved Scot,
At Holmedon met,   *55*
Where they did spend a sad and bloody hour;
As by discharge of their artillery
And shape of likelihood the news was told;
For he that brought them, in the very heat

62-75. Since Henry already knows from Sir Walter Blunt the outcome of the battle, it seems as though he has deliberately waited until it suits him to announce it. This knowledge makes his earlier questions about the Crusade rather hypocritical. Is the King a tricky character to deal with? How would a producer reveal this?

63. *lighted:* dismounted.

64-5. 'Coated with samples of all the soils between Northumberland and London'.

66. *smooth and welcome.* Compare *uneven and unwelcome* in line 50.

67. *discomfited:* defeated.

68. Are these plausible figures?

69. *Balk'd . . . blood.* A balk is a ridge between furrows, so this suggests lines of blood-covered, dead soldiers.

74. *honourable spoil:* group of prisoners to be proud of (because they are noblemen).

74-7. What are Henry's feelings at the news? He seems to be overjoyed but perhaps he is talking himself into a feeling of triumph. And how do you interpret Westmoreland's reply? His use of the word *prince* might be a slip of the tongue, although he is probably complimenting Henry himself. At any rate, it certainly has the effect of making the King miserable.

78. *me . . . me.* Henry is now talking as a father, not as a king, and this explains why he no longer uses the royal 'we'.

78-9. *sin In envy.* This would suggest that Henry does have some sincere religious feelings.

81-3. Notice the phrases used by Henry to describe Hotspur whom he would like to be his own son.

81. *theme . . . tongue.* Honour is seen as a person who would prefer to talk about Hotspur than anyone else. This is the first emphatic mention of one of the play's chief themes.

82. *plant:* tree.

83. 'who is the favourite son of Fortune, her pride and joy'.

85. Possibly this is a reference to Bacchus, the Roman god of drinking and disorder. He was often shown with forehead stained by the juice of grapes that had been squashed on his head.

86. *O that:* if only.

87. *night-tripping:* who carries out her secret work at night.

89. *Percy . . . Plantagenet.* Percy was the family name of the Earls of Northumberland, and Harry Hotspur was the then Earl's son. Plantagenet was Henry's family name.

93. *surpris'd:* taken possession of.

And pride of their contention did take horse,   *60*
Uncertain of the issue any way.

King

Here is a dear, a true industrious friend,
Sir Walter Blunt, new lighted from his horse,
Stain'd with the variation of each soil
Betwixt that Holmedon and this seat of ours;   *65*
And he hath brought us smooth and welcome news.
The Earl of Douglas is discomfited:
Ten thousand bold Scots, two and twenty knights,
Balk'd in their own blood, did Sir Walter see
On Holmedon's plains; of prisoners, Hotspur took   *70*
Mordake, Earl of Fife and eldest son
To beaten Douglas; and the Earl of Athol,
Of Murray, Angus and Menteith.
And is not this an honourable spoil?
A gallant prize? Ha, cousin, is it not?   *75*

Westmoreland

In faith.
It is a conquest for a prince to boast of.

King

Yea, there thou mak'st me sad and mak'st me sin
In envy that my Lord Northumberland
Should be the father to so blest a son—   *80*
A son who is the theme of honour's tongue;
Amongst a grove, the very straightest plant;
Who is sweet Fortune's minion and her pride;
Whilst I, by looking on the praise of him,
See riot and dishonour stain the brow   *85*
Of my young Harry. O that it could be prov'd
That some night-tripping fairy had exchang'd
In cradle-clothes our children where they lay,
And call'd mine Percy, his Plantagenet!
Then would I have his Harry, and he mine.   *90*
But let him from my thoughts. What think you, coz,
Of this young Percy's pride? The prisoners
Which he in this adventure hath surpris'd

31

92-5. The current law allowed a victorious general to keep all his prisoners except those of royal blood, so, strictly, Hotspur is keeping to the letter of the law. Henry is probably enraged by his arrogant way of doing it.

97. Worcester is compared to a star whose influence on the earth is evil at all times, *in all aspects* (i.e. in whatever position it assumes in the sky). Astrology, still popular today, was a principal branch of learning in the sixteenth century, involving the belief that people's lives are ruled by the positions of the stars when they were born.

98-9. *prune . . . youth.* The joint opposition to Henry of Worcester and Hotspur seems here to be seen in terms of a fighting cock which preens itself and raises its crest in defiance.

100. *to answer this:* to give his reasons for this.

101-2. It is now clear that Henry has known from the beginning of the scene that the Crusade must be delayed.

105-7. The King, aware that the situation will need careful handling, orders Westmoreland to return quickly so that decisions can be made after his anger has cooled somewhat. Try to form some estimate of the sort of man Henry IV is on this first impression. He seems to be a complex character, a mixture of good and bad qualities. Is he a good leader, a man to be trusted? Does he rule his court well?

SCENE II

It is traditional to begin with Falstaff asleep on a bench as the Prince enters. In this scene should we see Falstaff as a friendly companion of the Prince, or as an evil influence preventing Hal from following his duty as heir to the throne, or as a combination of both?

2-12. Hal points out to Falstaff that since he spends his time in leading an irresponsible life he does not need to know the *time of day* (or the state of affairs). Notice the contrast of this with Scene i. The King was caught up in worries of past, present, and future; Falstaff seems to exist in a timeless world.

2. *fat-witted:* stupid.

sack: a popular kind of white wine.

4-5. *thou . . . know:* 'you have forgotten anything of real importance to you'.

To his own use he keeps; and sends me word,
I shall have none but Mordake Earl of Fife.   95
Westmoreland
This is his uncle's teaching, this is Worcester,
Malevolent to you in all aspects;
Which makes him prune himself, and bristle up
The crest of youth against your dignity.
King
But I have sent for him to answer this;   100
And for this cause awhile we must neglect
Our holy purpose to Jerusalem.
Cousin, on Wednesday next our council we
Will hold at Windsor—so inform the lords;
But come yourself with speed to us again,   105
For more is to be said and to be done
Than out of anger can be uttered.
Westmoreland
I will, my liege.

Exeunt

SCENE II—*London. The* PRINCE'S *lodging*

Enter the PRINCE OF WALES *and* SIR JOHN FALSTAFF

Falstaff
Now, Hal, what time of day is it, lad?
Prince
Thou art so fat-witted with drinking of old sack, and
unbuttoning thee after supper, and sleeping upon
benches after noon, that thou hast forgotten to
demand that truly which thou wouldest truly know.   5
What a devil hast thou to do with the time of the day?

7. *capons:* chicken, something of a delicacy then.

8. *bawds:* men or women who are in charge of prostitutes.

9. *leaping houses:* brothels.

10. *flame-coloured taffeta:* supposedly a fabric and colour worn by prostitutes.

11. *be so superfluous:* make such an unnecessary request.

13-15. Conversations between Hal and Falstaff are constant battles of wits. Falstaff dodges the Prince's insult by saying that, as he is a thief who steals by 'night,' the time of 'day' is certainly irrelevant.

13. *you come near me:* 'you have a point'.

14. *go by:* work by the light of.

moon . . . Phoebus. Phoebus, the sun, is a symbol of kingship. The moon is the guiding star of highwaymen (and also the emblem of the Percy family). Thus Hal, tempted by Falstaff, seems to be on the side of all law breakers.

16. *wag:* lad, particularly a mischievous one.

when . . . king: Falstaff hopes to become powerful on Hal's accession. As Hal's intention to reject Falstaff becomes obvious at the end of this scene, Falstaff's repetition of this phrase has an increasingly sad effect on the audience.

17-18. *for . . . none:* 'for you will have no royal dignity'.

20. *by my troth:* I swear it.

21. *egg and butter.* A very poor meal not worth saying grace for.

22. *roundly:* 'get to the point'.

23. *Marry:* an exclamation such as 'why, to be sure,' or 'indeed'.

23-9. Falstaff hopes that, when Hal is king, criminals will be treated as respectable men, and the laws will be turned upside down to make good evil and vice versa.

24. *squires . . . body:* gentlemen serving the lord of night; highwaymen.

25. *thieves . . . beauty:* ordinary thieves, or perhaps loafers, who waste day-time.

Diana: goddess of the moon, usually depicted as a huntress.

27-9. 'let men say we are law-abiding since we serve the moon who is our honourable mistress'.

30. *it holds well:* the comparison can be extended.

30-8. Pretending to agree, Hal in fact reminds Falstaff of the results of crime. Thieves' fortunes change like the tide, their profits are soon spent and they end up hanged.

36. *'Lay by':* 'Hand over your money'.

'Bring in': 'Let's have some wine'.

Unless hours were cups of sack, and minutes capons,
and clocks the tongues of bawds, and dials the signs of
leaping-houses, and the blessed sun himself a fair hot
wench in flame-coloured taffeta, I see no reason why   *10*
thou shouldst be so superfluous to demand the time
of the day.

Falstaff

Indeed, you come near me now, Hal; for we that
take purses go by the moon and the seven stars, and
not by Phœbus, he 'that wand'ring knight so fair'.   *15*
And, I prithee, sweet wag, when thou art a king, as,
God save thy Grace—Majesty, I should say; for grace
thou wilt have none—

Prince

What, none?

Falstaff

No, by my troth; not so much as will serve to be pro-   *20*
logue to an egg and butter.

Prince

Well, how then? Come, roundly, roundly.

Falstaff

Marry, then, sweet wag, when thou art king, let not
us that are squires of the night's body be called
thieves of the day's beauty; let us be Diana's foresters,   *25*
gentlemen of the shade, minions of the moon; and
let men say we be men of good government, being
governed, as the sea is, by our noble and chaste mistress the moon, under whose countenance we steal.

Prince

Thou sayest well, and it holds well too; for the for-   *30*
tune of us that are the moon's men doth ebb and flow
like the sea, being governed, as the sea is, by the
moon. As, for proof, now: a purse of gold most re-
solutely snatch'd on Monday night, and most dis-
solutely spent on Tuesday morning; got with swearing   *35*
'Lay by' and spent with crying 'Bring in'; now in as
low an ebb as the foot of the ladder, and by and by in

35

Saging he is one
of the robbers

39-40. Not liking to be reminded of this, Falstaff changes the subject.

41. *Hybla:* a Sicilian town renowned for its honey.
old . . . castle: a noisy reveller. There is also a pun on Oldcastle. The character of Falstaff is thought to be based on a tradition of dislike for the heretic Sir John Oldcastle.
42. *And . . . durance?* Refusing to be put off from his remarks about punishing crime Hal asks Falstaff if he will not enjoy wearing prison dress.
43. *quips:* jokes.
44. *quiddities:* quibbles.

46. Hal denies that he is immoral with women despite the evidence of his wild life.

48. Falstaff backs down and pretends that all he meant was that Hal has paid bills owed to her for drinks.

50-5. *Did . . . apparent.* Falstaff is forced to admit the Prince's generosity but continues the battle of wits by implying that Hal has spent his money in a disgraceful way.

55. *heir apparent:* official title for next in line to the throne.

57. *resolution:* courage (Falstaff means thieves' courage in robbing).
fubb'd: hindered.
58. *rusty . . . law.* Falstaff here draws a picture of law as a mad old man waving a sword with a rusty, and therefore useless, blade.

61. *rare:* splendid!

as high a flow as the ridge of the gallows.

Falstaff

By the Lord, thou say'st true, lad. And is not my hostess of the tavern a most sweet wench ?   *40*

Prince

As the honey of Hybla, my old lad of the castle. And is not a buff jerkin a most sweet robe of durance ?

Falstaff

How now, how now, mad wag! What, in thy quips and thy quiddities ? What a plague have I to do with a buff jerkin ?   *45*

Prince

Why, what a pox have I to do with my hostess of the tavern ?

Falstaff

Well, thou hast call'd her to a reckoning many a time and oft.

Prince

Did I ever call for thee to pay thy part ?   *50*

Falstaff

No; I'll give thee thy due, thou hast paid all there.

Prince

Yea, and elsewhere, so far as my coin would stretch; and where it would not, I have used my credit.

Falstaff

Yea, and so us'd it that, were it not here apparent that thou art heir apparent—but, I prithee, sweet wag,   *55* shall there be gallows standing in England when thou art King, and resolution thus fubb'd as it is with the rusty curb of old father antic the law ? Do not thou, when thou art king, hang a thief.

Prince

No; thou shalt.   *60*

Falstaff

Shall I ? O rare! By the Lord, I'll be a brave judge!

Prince

Thou judgest false already: I mean thou shalt have the

65-6. Being a hangman involves being too close to the gallows for Falstaff's comfort, but he has to make the best of it.
65. *jumps with my humour:* suits me.

67. *obtaining of suits.* Hal refers to the practice of lawyers of waiting in the courts hoping to be given cases to handle or courtiers waiting in the royal court to petition the king for favours. Falstaff refers to the favour given to hangmen of being allowed to keep the clothes of the dead man.
69. *no lean wardrobe:* (a) a great number of clothes; (b) very large garments for fat people like Falstaff.
69-74. This talk of death and hanging has made Falstaff miserable!
70. *gib cat:* tom cat.
lugg'd bear: a bear baited and attacked by dogs.
71. *lover's lute:* mournful romantic tune played on a lute (type of guitar).

73. *hare:* believed to be a miserable animal.
73-4. *melancholy . . . Ditch.* Elizabethan doctors believed that Melancholy was a disease of the blood causing depression. Moorditch was a ditch just outside the walls of London full of refuse and therefore foul-smelling. (The name is still used for a district near the City of London.)
75. *unsavoury similes:* unpleasant comparisons.
76. *comparative:* always making comparisons.
rascalliest: cheekiest.
77-93. A feature of Falstaff's character is to pretend that he is led astray and prevented by others from leading a good life.
78. *vanity:* worldly things.
78-9. *commodity . . . names:* good reputations.
80. *rated:* blamed.
81. *mark'd him not:* took no notice of him.

86-93. Falstaff uses Biblical language in order to sound holy, then pretends to be shocked when Hal does the same, and accuses him of being a devil, quoting scripture to lead Falstaff into sin.
84-5. *wisdom . . . regards it:* from the book of Proverbs (1, 20-24).
86. *damnable iteration:* evil power of quoting from the Bible.
89. *I knew nothing:* I was innocent.

hanging of the thieves, and so become a rare hangman.

Falstaff

Well, Hal, well; and in some sort it jumps with my 65
humour as well as waiting in the court, I can tell you.

Prince

For obtaining of suits?

Falstaff

Yea, for obtaining of suits, whereof the hangman
hath no lean wardrobe. 'Sblood, I am as melancholy
as a gib cat or a lugg'd bear. 70

Prince

Or an old lion, or a lover's lute.

Falstaff

Yea, or the drone of a Lincolnshire bagpipe.

Prince

What sayest thou to a hare, or the melancholy of
Moor Ditch?

Falstaff

Thou hast the most unsavoury similes, and art indeed 75
the most comparative, rascalliest, sweet young
prince. But, Hal, I prithee, trouble me no more with
vanity. I would to God thou and I knew where a commodity of good names were to be bought. An old
lord of the Council rated me the other day in the 80
street about you, sir, but I mark'd him not; and yet he
talk'd very wisely, but I regarded him not; and yet he
talk'd wisely, and in the street too.

Prince

Thou didst well; for wisdom cries out in the streets,
and no man regards it. 85

Falstaff

O, thou hast damnable iteration, and art indeed able
to corrupt a saint. Thou hast done much harm upon
me, Hal—God forgive thee for it! Before I knew thee,
Hal, I knew nothing; and now am I, if a man should
speak truly, little better than one of the wicked. I 90

92. *an:* if.
92-3. *I'll ... Christendom:* 'I will never allow any prince in the world to lead me to damnation.'

94. Hal can't resist poking fun at Falstaff's pious intentions.

95. *I'll make one:* 'I'll be one of the gang'.
96. *baffle me:* disgrace me in public (for not being a robber!). Falstaff seems to have forgotten all about his wish to reform.

97. *a good amendment:* 'a great improvement I must say!'

99-100. More religious vocabulary to defend his way of life!
100. *vocation:* occupation for which he is fitted by nature.

101. *Poins:* Like Falstaff and Hal, Poins is an educated man.
101-2. *set a match:* organized a robbery.
102-4. *O, if men ... man.* Falstaff here refers to an argument which divided various sects of the Christian Church. Is a man judged by his good deeds (*by merit*) or can he enter heaven by having faith alone? If the former position is the right one, then Poins has no hope of getting to heaven!
103-4. *omnipotent villain:* complete rogue.
104. *'Stand':* stand and deliver (your money).
true: honest.
106-10. Like Hal, Poins can't resist making fun of Falstaff.

108-10. *Jack ... leg:* 'How are you and the devil getting on since you sold your soul to him last Good Friday for a cup of wine and a chicken's leg?' (You may know the story of Faust who sold his soul to the devil in return for twenty-four years of life in which all power and knowledge would be given to him.)

114-16. Falstaff is sure to be damned—whether he keeps his promise and surrenders his soul to the devil or whether he cheats (*cozens*) the devil out of it. (Cheating is also a sin!)

must give over this life, and I will give it over. By
the Lord, an I do not I am a villain! I'll be damn'd for
never a king's son in Christendom.

Prince

Where shall we take a purse to-morrow, Jack?

Falstaff

Zounds, where thou wilt, lad: I'll make one. An I do   *95*
not, call me villain and baffle me.

Prince

I see a good amendment of life in thee—from praying
to purse-taking.

Falstaff

Why, Hal, 'tis my vocation, Hal; 'tis no sin for a man
to labour in his vocation.   *100*

Enter POINS

Poins!—Now shall we know if Gadshill have set a
match. O, if men were to be saved by merit, what hole
in hell were hot enough for him? This is the most omnipotent villain that ever cried 'Stand' to a true man.

Prince

Good morrow, Ned.   *105*

Poins

Good morrow, sweet Hal. What says Monsieur
Remorse? What says Sir John Sack and Sugar?
Jack, how agrees the devil and thee about thy soul,
that thou soldest him on Good Friday last for a cup
of Madeira and a cold capon's leg?   *110*

Prince

Sir John stands to his word—the devil shall have his
bargain; for he was never yet a breaker of proverbs;
he will give the devil his due.

Poins

Then art thou damn'd for keeping thy word with the
devil.   *115*

Prince

Else he had been damn'd for cozening the devil.

117. *But, my lads.* Joking stops for the time being. Serious matters must be attended to!

118. *Gadshill.* Poins means the place on the London to Canterbury road. The fact that there is also a character called Gadshill (line 101) is certainly confusing.

119. *offerings:* money, jewels to be placed at the shrine of St. Thomas à Becket in Canterbury Cathedral.

120. *fat:* full.

vizards: masks (for disguise).

121. *lies:* is staying.

122. *bespoke:* ordered.

123. *as . . . sleep:* as easy as winking.

124. *crowns:* gold coins in use at that time.

125. *tarry . . . hang'd:* 'stay at home and to hell with you'.

126-7. Falstaff threatens that, if he doesn't go, he will inform the authorities and have the others arrested and hanged!

128. *chops:* fat face.

130. Hal seems surprised at being expected to take part. After all that has been said, this virtuous tone seems rather smug.

131-3. More amusement as Falstaff claims that Hal will be a spoil-sport if he refuses to join them. Falstaff argues it will prove that Hal isn't a true and virtuous prince!

132-3. *blood royal, ten shillings:* a royal was a coin worth ten shillings in those days.

134. *madcap.* It seems to mean 'rogue', indicating that Hal has agreed to join in but it becomes obvious that he has not. How then are these two lines to be spoken?

137-8. This shows the tension underlying the superficial joking between Hal and Falstaff. Perhaps Falstaff fears that when Hal becomes king he will (as happens) be rejected. Perhaps Hal is annoyed temporarily with Falstaff's unruly conversation.

Poins

But, my lads, my lads, to-morrow morning, by four
o'clock early, at Gadshill! There are pilgrims going
to Canterbury with rich offerings, and traders riding
to London with fat purses. I have vizards for you all; *120*
you have horses for yourselves. Gadshill lies to-night
in Rochester; I have bespoke supper to-morrow night
in Eastcheap. We may do it as secure as sleep. If you
will go, I will stuff your purses full of crowns; if you
will not, tarry at home and be hang'd. *125*

Falstaff

Hear ye, Yedward: if I tarry at home and go not,
I'll hang you for going.

Poins

You will, chops?

Falstaff

Hal, wilt thou make one?

Prince

Who?—I rob, I a thief? Not I, by my faith. *130*

Falstaff

There's neither honesty, manhood, nor good fellowship in thee, nor thou cam'st not of the blood royal,
if thou darest not stand for ten shillings.

Prince

Well then, once in my days I'll be a madcap.

Falstaff

Why, that's well said. *135*

Prince

Well, come what will, I'll tarry at home.

Falstaff

By the lord, I'll be a traitor then, when thou art king.

Prince

I care not.

Poins

Sir John, I prithee, leave the Prince and me alone: I
will lay him down such reasons for this adventure *140*
that he shall go.

142-7. More mock-Biblical language as Falstaff again pretends to be virtuous in persuading Hal into crime. He seems to be trying to recover his self-respect after being snubbed.
143. *ears of profiting:* sense to see where his advantage lies.
144. *move:* persuade.
145. *for recreation sake:* He pretends that the robbery is just for fun. This is only partly true, as Falstaff stands for real disorder. It is also ironic as Falstaff's theft turns into Hal's joke.
146-7. *the poor . . . countenance:* criminal activities lack official support.
148-9. Two comments that suggest Falstaff has kept the energy of a young man despite his age.
All-hallown summer: a period of good weather in late autumn. All Hallows is the Feast of All Saints which is 1st November.

150-2. Only the thought of playing a trick on Falstaff persuades the Prince to take part in the robbery.
151. *a jest to execute:* a practical joke to carry out.

164. *habits:* clothes.
appointment: dress and equipment.

168. *cases of buckram:* garments made of coarse linen.
168-9. *for the nonce:* for this special occasion.
169. *inmask:* conceal.
noted: easily recognized.

Falstaff

Well, God give thee the spirit of persuasion, and him
the ears of profiting, that what thou speakest may
move, and what he hears may be believed; that the
true prince may, for recreation sake, prove a false *145*
thief; for the poor abuses of the time want countenance. Farewell; you shall find me in Eastcheap.

Prince

Farewell, thou latter spring! Farewell, All-hallown
summer!

Exit FALSTAFF

Poins

Now, my good sweet honey lord, ride with us to- *150*
morrow. I have a jest to execute that I cannot manage
alone. Falstaff, Bardolph, Peto, and Gadshill, shall
rob those men that we have already waylaid; yourself
and I will not be there; and when they have the booty,
if you and I do not rob them, cut this head off from my *155*
shoulders.

Prince

How shall we part with them in setting forth?

Poins

Why, we will set forth before or after them, and ap-
point them a place of meeting, wherein it is at our
pleasure to fail; and then will they adventure upon the *160*
exploit themselves; which they shall have no sooner
achieved but we'll set upon them.

Prince

Yea, but 'tis like that they will know us by our
horses, by our habits, and by every other appointment, to be ourselves. *165*

Poins

Tut! our horses they shall not see—I'll tie them in
the wood; our vizards we will change after we leave
them; and, sirrah, I have cases of buckram for the
nonce, to immask our noted outward garments.

45

170. *too hard:* too strong.

172. *turn'd back:* turned their backs (and ran away).
the third: Falstaff is not really a coward but a man who wishes to stay alive and who does not believe in being heroic if commonsense shows no chance of winning. Compare his outlook on life with Hotspur's. (Act I, Scene iii, lines 195-7)
174. *virtue:* point.
incomprehensible: beyond belief.

177. *wards:* defensive strokes in fencing.

178. *in . . . this:* in disproving this.

183-205. Hal's soliloquy reveals his motives in leading his present life. Two points are specially worth noting. First, he is deliberately learning about the people whom he will one day rule. Second, he intends to surprise everyone by reforming and ruling well when the time comes. Perhaps Falstaff's unruly vitality is more immediately attractive than Hal's cold calculation, but Falstaff's ways cause anarchy and Hal's tactics aim to avoid his father's mistakes and give his country peace and order.
183. *I know you all:* 'I know exactly what kind of people you are'.
184. *unyoked . . . idleness:* your uncontrolled and wild behaviour.
185. *sun.* Hal's mention of the symbol of royalty contrasts with his conversation with Falstaff in lines 9-38.
186. *contagious:* disease-carrying. People of that time believed that fogs and clouds carried disease.
188. *when . . . himself:* when the sun wishes to shine strongly.
189. *wonder'd at:* admired.
194. *they wish'd-for come:* 'everyone looks forward to them'.
195. *accidents:* happenings.
196. *loose behaviour:* wild way of life.
197. 'and become the good king my present life never suggested I could be'.
198. *word:* promise.
199. *falsify men's hopes:* prove men's expectations to be wrong.
200. *sullen ground:* dark background.

Prince

    Yea, but I doubt they will be too hard for us.   *170*

Poins

    Well, for two of them, I know them to be as true-bred
cowards as ever turn'd back; and for the third, if he
fight longer than he sees reason, I'll forswear arms.
The virtue of this jest will be the incomprehensible
lies that this same fat rogue will tell us when we meet *175*
at supper: how thirty, at least, he fought with; what
wards, what blows, what extremities he endured; and
in the reproof of this lives the jest.

Prince

    Well, I'll go with thee. Provide us all things necessary,
and meet me to-morrow night in Eastcheap; there I'll *180*
sup. Farewell.

Poins

    Farewell, my lord.

Exit POINS

Prince

    I know you all, and will awhile uphold
The unyok'd humour of your idleness;
Yet herein will I imitate the sun,   *185*
Who doth permit the base contagious clouds
To smother up his beauty from the world,
That, when he please again to be himself,
Being wanted, he may be more wonder'd at
By breaking through the foul and ugly mists   *190*
Of vapours that did seem to strangle him.
If all the year were playing holidays,
To sport would be as tedious as to work;
But when they seldom come, they wish'd-for come,
And nothing pleaseth but rare accidents.   *195*
So, when this loose behaviour I throw off
And pay the debt I never promised,
By how much better than my word I am,
By so much shall I falsify men's hopes;
And, like bright metal on a sullen ground,   *200*

[handwritten annotation: Below (1)]

[handwritten note: (1) Something thats gone for long is wanted more]

201. *glitt'ring . . . fault:* shining more brightly because of the background of my faults.
202. *goodly:* valuable.
202-3. 'be more remarkable than someone who has no faults to make his reformation shine more brightly by contrast'.
204. *to . . . skill:* to turn wrong-doing to my advantage.
205. *Redeeming time:* making amends for lost time. The idea of redemption occurs many times in the play and indicates the accepted connection between religion and the running of society.

SCENE III

The trouble hinted at in Hotspur's attitude concerning the prisoners that he captured at Holmedon has boiled over into a quarrel between the King and the Percy family sufficiently important to destroy Henry's plans for a crusade. In the last scene we met a group of ineffectual robbers and lawbreakers, here we see a group of potential rebels.
1-21. Henry probably moves about quite a lot in this scene to indicate his agitation at not being in full command of events.
1-3. *My . . . me:* 'By nature I have been too easy-going, too tolerant, unwilling to grow angry at your insults, and that is how you have come to look on me'.
1. *too . . . temperate:* The Elizabethans believed a man's character to be one of four basic kinds corresponding to the four humours – cold, hot, moist, dry. If a cold humour predominated over the others in a man's character it made him calm and unemotional.
4. *tread upon:* abuse.
4-9. *But . . . proud:* 'But without doubt I shall from now on act as a king should act, with the power to make men fear me, instead of continuing to behave in my usual, gentle way, which has lost me the respect of those who, being proud and strong, only respect men who are prouder and stronger than they are'.
6. *condition:* natural manner.
9. *but:* except.
10. *house:* family.
11. *scourge of greatness:* power of a king to punish those judged to be criminals.
13. *holp:* helped.
portly: fat, prosperous, important.
10-13. Far from being frightened, Worcester, Northumberland's brother and therefore Hotspur's uncle, refuses to pacify Henry. Remember that it was the Percy family who helped Henry when he returned from exile to claim his father's estates and that it was largely owing to their support that he became king. Now neither side can trust the other.
14. A vain attempt by Northumberland, not as strong-minded as Worcester, to prevent the King from losing his temper.

offend People Skilfully

My reformation, glitt'ring o'er my fault,
Shall show more goodly and attract more eyes
Than that which hath no foil to set it off.
I'll so offend to make offence a skill,
Redeeming time when men think least I will.   205

Exit

make amends
When no one expects it

SCENE III—*London. The palace*

Enter the KING, NORTHUMBERLAND, WORCESTER,
HOTSPUR, SIR WALTER BLUNT, *with* Others

King
My blood hath been too cold and temperate,
Unapt to stir at these indignities,
And you have found me; for accordingly
You tread upon my patience. But be sure
I will from henceforth rather be myself,   5
Mighty and to be fear'd, than my condition,
Which hath been smooth as oil, soft as young down,
And therefore lost that title of respect
Which the proud soul ne'er pays but to the proud.

Worcester
Our house, my sovereign liege, little deserves   10
The scourge of greatness to be us'd on it—
And that same greatness too which our own hands
Have holp to make so portly.

Northumberland
My lord—

King
Worcester, get thee gone; for I do see   15
Danger and disobedience in thine eye.

(3) I will look good when I drop all my bad habits (faults)

49

17-19. *your . . . brow:* your attitude is too over-bearing and a king cannot tolerate sullen opposition from his servants.

19. *frontier:* fort; advance defence.

20-1. Henry reacts with admirably strong action but in expelling Worcester from court he makes a dangerous enemy.
20. *good . . . us:* our freely-given permission to depart. Henry is in fact ordering him to go.
21. *your use and counsel:* your help and advice.

22-8. Northumberland, a cautious and crafty man, tries to calm Henry.

26. *delivered:* reported.
27. *envy:* jealousy, ill-will.
misprision: misunderstanding.

29-69. Hotspur's first speech shows him at his best, as the brave, victorious general, tired after the battle and annoyed with the pompous, official meddling of courtiers who have not fought but who try to order him about as soon as danger has passed. His sincerity and his outspokenness are attractive qualities; at the same time we should notice his intolerance of any point of view but his own.
31. *dry . . . toil:* exhausted by the ferocity of the battle.
33. *trimly dress'd:* in elegant, fashionable clothes.
34. *his . . . reap'd:* with his beard recently trimmed (whereas Hotspur had had no time for such niceties).
35. *like . . . home:* like a field from which the corn has just been reaped and removed to a granary.
36. *milliner:* a seller of scented gloves, luxurious articles of dress.
38. *pouncet-box.* Perfume container apparently used as a snuff-box.
ever and anon: every few seconds.
39-41. Snuff was (and is) a perfumed powder inhaled to produce a tingling sensation in the nose. Perhaps Hotspur is saying that the lord could not take snuff without sneezing but kept on taking it for the sake of appearances, or to disguise the smell of the dead bodies.
40. *Who:* his nose.
41. *Took it in snuff:* took it with resentment i.e. protested by sneezing. It was not good manners to sneeze when taking snuff.
43-5. *He call'd . . . his nobility:* he called the soldiers ignorant, loutish fellows for carrying corpses past him on the windward side (where he could smell them). Note the contrast between Hotspur's descriptions of the lord, *neat, trimly dress'd*, and the corpses, *slovenly, unhandsome*. Possibly Hotspur minces round the stage, mimicking the lord, to show his scorn of him.
46. *holiday . . . terms:* over-refined and effeminate language.
50. *pester'd with a popinjay:* tormented by such a gaudy chatterer (like a parrot).

O, sir, your presence is too bold and peremptory,
And majesty might never yet endure
The moody frontier of a servant brow.
You have good leave to leave us; when we need   *20*
Your use and counsel, we shall send for you.
              Exit WORCESTER
You were about to speak.
Northumberland   Yea, my good lord.
Those prisoners in your Highness' name demanded,
Which Harry Percy here at Holmedon took,
Were, as he says, not with such strength denied   *25*
As is delivered to your Majesty.
Either envy, therefore, or misprision
Is guilty of this fault, and not my son.
Hotspur
My liege, I did deny no prisoners.
But I remember when the fight was done,   *30*
When I was dry with rage and extreme toil,
Breathless and faint, leaning upon my sword,
Came there a certain lord, neat, and trimly dress'd,
Fresh as a bridegroom, and his chin new reap'd
Show'd like a stubble-land at harvest-home.   *35*
He was perfumed like a milliner,
And 'twixt his finger and his thumb he held
A pouncet-box, which ever and anon
He gave his nose and took't away again;
Who therewith angry, when it next came there,   *40*
Took it in snuff—and still he smil'd and talk'd—
And as the soldiers bore dead bodies by,
He call'd them untaught knaves, unmannerly,
To bring a slovenly unhandsome corse
Betwixt the wind and his nobility.   *45*
With many holiday and lady terms
He questioned me: amongst the rest, demanded
My prisoners in your Majesty's behalf.
I then, all smarting with my wounds being cold,
To be so pester'd with a popinjay,   *50*

51. 'because of the pain and my sense of grievance at being bothered by such a man'.
52. *neglectingly:* in an off-hand way.

55. *so like a waiting-gentlewoman:* 'in such a scared and silly way'. Hotspur loves to pretend that women are quite out of place in his life.
56. *God save the mark!* For Heaven's sake! (The expression was originally used as a kind of charm to avert an evil spell.)
57-8. *the sovereignest . . . bruise:* that the best cure for an internal bruise (caused presumably by a wound!) was the fat of a whale. Hotspur is, of course, still very sarcastic, trying to show how utterly ignorant of warfare (and medicine) the lord was.
58. *parmaceti:* spermaceti, a white, fatty substance found in the head of the sperm-whale.
60. *villainous saltpetre:* dreadful gun-powder.
62-3. *Which . . . cowardly:* which had killed so many fine young soldiers in such a cowardly fashion.

65. *bald . . . chat:* trivial, rambling remarks.

66. *indirectly:* in a careless way.

67. *beseech:* beg.
67-9. *let . . . Majesty:* 'don't let his report be accepted as a good reason for doubting my devotion to your Majesty'.
68. *current:* valid, with a pun on the root meaning of running.

70-6. Sir Walter Blunt is a fine, loyal servant of the King and later dies fighting for him at Shrewsbury.

74. *May reasonably die:* may be justifiably forgotten when the circumstances are considered.
75. *impeach:* accuse.
76. *so:* provided that.
77-80. Henry irritably points out that even now Hotspur has failed to surrender the prisoners.
77. *yet:* even now.
78. *But:* except.
with . . . exception: on condition.
79. *straight:* at once.
80. *Mortimer.* Mortimer, the Earl of March, had recently led an expedition to fight against the Welsh under Glendower. On being defeated in battle and taken prisoner, Mortimer married Glendower's daughter. Henry, for various reasons, refuses to follow the normal practice of securing a noble prisoner's release by paying a ransom to his captor.
81. *wilfully:* deliberately.
83. *great . . . Glendower.* Glendower was one of the great Welsh chieftains, renowned for his powers of magic and witchcraft.
85. *coffers:* the royal treasury.

Out of my grief and my impatience
Answer'd neglectingly I know not what—
He should, or he should not—for he made me mad
To see him shine so brisk, and smell so sweet,
And talk so like a waiting-gentlewoman   55
Of guns, and drums, and wounds—God save the mark!—
And telling me the sovereignest thing on earth
Was parmaceti for an inward bruise;
And that it was great pity, so it was,
This villainous saltpetre should be digg'd   60
Out of the bowels of the harmless earth,
Which many a good tall fellow had destroy'd
So cowardly; and but for these vile guns
He would himself have been a soldier.
This bald unjointed chat of his, my lord,   65
I answered indirectly, as I said;
And I beseech you, let not his report
Come current for an accusation
Betwixt my love and your high Majesty.

Blunt

The circumstance considered, good my lord,   70
Whate'er Lord Harry Percy then had said
To such a person, and in such a place,
At such a time, with all the rest re-told,
May reasonably die, and never rise
To do him wrong, or any way impeach   75
What then he said, so he unsay it now.

King

Why, yet he doth deny his prisoners,
But with proviso and exception—
That we at our own charge shall ransom straight
His brother-in-law, the foolish Mortimer;   80
Who, on my soul, hath wilfully betray'd
The lives of those that he did lead to fight
Against that great magician, damn'd Glendower,
Whose daughter, as we hear, that Earl of March
Hath lately married. Shall our coffers, then,   85

53

86. *redeem:* buy back.

87. *indent with fears:* come to an agreement with Mistrust (a kind of personification).

88. *When . . . themselves:* when they have no longer any right to our assistance.

77-92. Henry's speech needs careful study. There are two key facts: (i) Glendower is an enemy, and (ii) Mortimer was named heir to the throne by Richard II before Richard was deposed by Henry IV and murdered. The first fact partly explains why the King describes Glendower as an evil figure – Westmoreland used the same technique in his speech about the Welsh campaign in Act I, Scene i. The second fact explains Henry's insistence that Mortimer is a traitor. Notice the series of words with which he refers to Mortimer. Henry IV is clear-sighted about the dangers which threaten him and he knows that he has no legal claim to the throne. As a skilful politician, therefore, he uses every trick he knows to justify keeping Mortimer out of the country.

93-112. Hotspur's sense of honour refuses to accept such an accusation without proof. He consequently describes the battle between Mortimer and Glendower and both men in heroic terms that contrast with what we have read before.

94. *fall off:* betray his country. Mortimer's only fault, according to Hotspur, was that he had the bad luck to lose the battle.

97. *mouthed:* (two syllables) a strong image of Mortimer's wounds as mouths, loudly proclaiming his loyalty – for all these mouths only one tongue is needed.

99. Single combat was a renowned feature of medieval chivalry which, of course, Hotspur firmly believes in.

100. *confound:* contend.

101. *In . . . hardiment:* in prowess, in which each surpassed the other in turn.

102. *breath'd:* paused for breath.

104-7. To emphasize the heroism of the combat, Hotspur paints a picture of the ripples of the river, frightened by the appearance of the wounded champions, trying to hide themselves under the blood-stained river banks. It is a far-fetched image but this is typical of Hotspur when he gets worked up.

106. *crisp:* curly. Probably the pointed waves or ripples of the river are supposed to look like curls.

108. *base and rotten policy:* treacherous plotting.

109. *Colour her working:* disguise its activity. Note the pun on colour.

111-12. Mortimer would never have received so many wounds deliberately (*willingly*) just to disguise his purpose.

113-24. Henry does not wish to be involved in an embarrassing argument. He, therefore, uses his power to contradict Hotspur flatly, then changes the subject and ends on a threatening note.

113. *belie:* give a false impression of. Whose interpretation does the appearance of Mortimer support?

115. *I tell thee.* A very short effective line in which Henry angrily emphasizes every word.

116. *alone:* himself.

(margin notes: Bargain / Traitors)

Be emptied to redeem a traitor home?
Shall we buy treason, and indent with fears,
When they have lost and forfeited themselves?
No, on the barren mountains let him starve;
For I shall never hold that man my friend   90
Whose tongue shall ask me for one penny cost
To ransom home revolted Mortimer.

Hotspur

Revolted Mortimer!
He never did fall off, my sovereign liege,
But by the chance of war; to prove that true,   95
Needs no more but one tongue for all those wounds,
Those mouthed wounds, which valiantly he took
When on the gentle Severn's sedgy bank,
In single opposition hand to hand,
He did confound the best part of an hour   100
In changing hardiment with great Glendower.
Three times they breath'd, and three times did they drink,
Upon agreement, of swift Severn's flood;
Who then, affrighted with their bloody looks,
Ran fearfully among the trembling reeds   105
And hid his crisp head in the hollow bank
Bloodstained with these valiant combatants.
Never did base and rotten policy
Colour her working with such deadly wounds;
Nor never could the noble Mortimer   110
Receive so many, and all willingly.
Then let him not be slandered with revolt.

(margin note: Don't slander his)

King

Thou dost belie him, Percy, thou dost belie him;
He never did encounter with Glendower.
I tell thee   115
He durst as well have met the devil alone
As Owen Glendower for an enemy.
Art thou not asham'd? But, sirrah, henceforth
Let me not hear you speak of Mortimer;
Send me your prisoners with the speediest means,   120

(margin note: good name don't revolt him)

122-3. *My lord . . . son.* As with Worcester, the King virtually banishes them from the court.

Stage Direction. For the next hundred and twenty lines, Hotspur is uncontrollable in his rage that Mortimer has not had fair play. He paces up and down, listening to no one. This lack of self-control is a dangerous weakness in Hotspur. And we should ask at this stage which account of the battle seems likely to be true. Perhaps both Henry and Hotspur invent what they want to believe.

126. *I will after:* I will go after the king.
127. *ease my heart:* relieve my feelings.
128. 'although I risk being executed in the process'.
129. *choler:* anger. His father has to hold Hotspur back at this point.

131-2. *let . . . mercy:* let me be damned.

133-4. Notice Hotspur's typically extreme language.
133. *on his part:* on his behalf.

135. *But:* if I do not.

137. *ingrate:* ungrateful.
canker'd: malignant (cancerous).
Bolingbroke. Note the contemptuous use of Henry's family name.

139. *struck this heat up:* caused this fury.

142-4. Notice the words that indicate the King's fear.
143. *eye of death:* terror-struck look.

145-6. 'Richard, who is dead, officially named Mortimer his heir'. Note how Worcester reminds Hotspur of the usurpation.
146. *next of blood:* heir to the crown.

"is the next of blood?" means the next in line to the throne *[handwritten annotation]*

Or you shall hear in such a kind from me
As will displease you. My Lord Northumberland,
We license your departure with your son.
Send us your prisoners, or you will hear of it.
              Exeunt KING HENRY, BLUNT *and* Train

Hotspur
  An if the devil come and roar for them,   125
  I will not send them. I will after straight
  And tell him so; for I will ease my heart,
  Albeit I make a hazard of my head.

Northumberland
  What, drunk with choler? Stay and pause awhile.
  Here comes your uncle.

means drunk with anger *[handwritten annotation]*

              Re-enter WORCESTER

Hotspur   Speak of Mortimer!   130
  Zounds, I will speak of him; and let my soul
  Want mercy if I do not join with him.
  Yea, on his part I'll empty all these veins
  And shed my dear blood drop by drop in the dust,
  But I will lift the down-trod Mortimer   135
  As high in the air as this unthankful king,
  As this ingrate and canker'd Bolingbroke.

by god's Wounds *[handwritten]*   *I'm prepared to spill my blood* *[handwritten]*

Northumberland
  Brother, the King hath made your nephew mad.

Worcester
  Who struck this heat up after I was gone?

Hotspur
  He will, forsooth, have all my prisoners;   140
  And when I urg'd the ransom once again
  Of my wife's brother, then his cheek look'd pale,
  And on my face he turn'd an eye of death,
  Trembling even at the name of Mortimer.

of my wife's brother (Mortimer) *[handwritten annotation]*

Worcester
  I cannot blame him: was not he proclaim'd   145
  By Richard that dead is the next of blood?

Northumberland
  He was: I heard the proclamation;

means I'm not surprised *[handwritten annotation]*

148. *unhappy:* unlucky.

148-54. Northumberland's and Worcester's pity for Richard II and themselves seems hypocritical. Having made Bolingbroke king in hope of great rewards, which Henry has in fact not given them, they now wish to pretend to Hotspur, who does not know many of the true facts, that they were innocent.

149. *Whose . . . pardon!* Northumberland prays that God will forgive them for their part in deposing Richard II.

151. *intercepted:* being interrupted (by news of Bolingbroke's return from exile).

153-4. *we . . . spoken of:* we are falsely held to be guilty throughout the world.

155. *soft:* 'wait a moment'.

158-9. Hotspur obviously did not know of his brother-in-law's claim to the throne. As he gets more and more involved in the world of politics, he learns the trickeries of politicians fast and understands Henry's fear.

161. *forgetful:* who forgets whom he should be grateful to.

162-3. *wear . . . subornation:* have the hateful reputation of being men who helped to bring about murderous treachery.

164. *a world . . . undergo:* 'put up with being cursed by everyone'.

165-6. 'being the mere instruments through which Henry secured the murder of his predecessor'. Note the images – they were the despicable *cords, ladder, hangman,* that dispatched Richard (cf. Act I, Scene ii, lines 35-7).

168. *line:* low level.

predicament: difficult position.

169. *Wherein you range:* at which you rank.

this subtle king. Although Henry's character and actions are here being deliberately blackened by his enemies, we have seen enough to make us accept the word *subtle* (crafty, cunning).

171. *chronicles . . . come:* future history books.

173. *gage . . . :* employ both your *nobility and powers* in an unjust cause.

175-6. *Richard . . . Bolingbroke.* Notice how Hotspur's anger makes him see things in simple terms – Richard, in his eyes, seems utterly good, Henry utterly evil. The garden metaphor here is reminiscent of *Richard II,* Act III, Scene iv.

177. *in more shame:* in a still more shameful way.

180-2. *time . . . world again.* The word *redeem,* meaning 'buy back forgiveness for sins committed', occurs again. Hotspur is saying that his family should *redeem* themselves by deposing Henry IV in order to make amends for previously having deposed Richard. Prince Hal, in his soliloquy at the end of the previous scene, stated his intention of redeeming himself from his mis-spent youth by eventually supporting Henry IV and becoming an unexpectedly good king. Just as Hal and Hotspur were contrasted by Henry IV in Act I, Scene i, so they are contrasted here through their different plans for the future.

180. *yet time serves:* 'time is still available to you'.

And then it was when the unhappy King—
Whose wrongs in us God pardon!—did set forth
Upon his Irish expedition;   150
From whence he intercepted did return
To be depos'd, and shortly murdered.

Worcester

And for whose death we in the world's wide mouth
Live scandaliz'd and foully spoken of.

Hotspur

But soft, I pray you: did King Richard then   155
Proclaim my brother, Edmund Mortimer,
Heir to the crown?

Northumberland   He did: myself did hear it.

Hotspur

Nay, then I cannot blame his cousin king,
That wish'd him on the barren mountains starve.
But shall it be that you that set the crown   160
Upon the head of this forgetful man,
And for his sake wear the detested blot
Of murderous subornation—shall it be
That you a world of curses undergo,
Being the agents or base second means,   165
The cords, the ladder, or the hangman rather?
O, pardon me that I descend so low
To show the line and the predicament
Wherein you range under this subtle king!
Shall it, for shame, be spoken in these days   170
Or fill up chronicles in time to come,
That men of your nobility and power
Did gage them both in an unjust behalf—
As both of you, God pardon it! have done—
To put down Richard, that sweet lovely rose,   175
And plant this thorn, this canker, Bolingbroke?
And shall it, in more shame, be further spoken
That you are fool'd, discarded, and shook off,
By him for whom these shames ye underwent?
No; yet time serves wherein you may redeem   180

59

183. *disdain'd:* scornful.

184-6. *who studies . . . deaths:* 'who constantly plans to settle his debt to you by having you killed'.

187-93. Worcester, having waited patiently for Hotspur to reach this point, now feels that he will be responsive to suggestions of rebellion.
188. *unclasp a secret book:* reveal a secret plan.
189. *to your . . . discontents:* 'your dissatisfaction will make you quick to think up plans and give impetus to our action'.
190-3. Worcester deliberately uses the language of honour and danger which he knows will appeal to Hotspur.
192. *As to o'er-walk:* as it would take to cross.
current: river.

194. Hotspur's imagination is caught by this dangerous exploit. ('If you slip in such a situation, you will be drowned whether you sink at once or try to swim to the bank.') More important, he seems to have missed the point of Worcester's speech.
195-7. 'I don't care what dangers I meet or where they come from as long as I can meet them in an honourable battle'.
197-8. *O the blood . . . hare:* How much more exciting it is to live dangerously by hunting lions than safely by chasing hares.
199-200. Northumberland, talking quietly on one side to Worcester, points out, perhaps to soothe Worcester's impatience, that Hotspur, absorbed in his longing for danger, cannot listen patiently to other people's ideas.
201-7. These are famous lines that sum up Hotspur's attitude to life – a never-ending search for honour in all places. The idea is fresh and attractive, as is the language, but, once again, Hotspur goes to the wildest of extremes. Note that Falstaff also referred to the moon and the sea in connection with his activities (in Act I, Scene ii).
203. *deep:* sea.
204. *fathom-line:* line used for measuring the sea's depth.
205. *locks:* hair.
206-7. 'so that he who rescues honour (from the bottom of the sea) may be able to take it as his own without fear of being challenged for it'.
208. 'But away with this pretended friendship with the King'.
209-10. 'He is living in a world of dreams when he should be thinking of the realities of the situation'.

211. *give me audience:* listen to me.

Your banish'd honours, and restore yourselves
Into the good thoughts of the world again;
Revenge the jeering and disdain'd contempt
Of this proud king, who studies day and night
To answer all the debt he owes to you   185
Even with the bloody payment of your deaths.
Therefore I say—

Worcester   Peace, cousin, say no more.
And now I will unclasp a secret book,
And to your quick-conceiving discontents
I'll read you matter deep and dangerous,   190
As full of peril and adventurous spirit
As to o'er-walk a current roaring loud
On the unsteadfast footing of a spear.

Hotspur
If he fall in, good night, or sink or swim.
Send danger from the east unto the west,   195
So honour cross it from the north to south,
And let them grapple. O, the blood more stirs
To rouse a lion than to start a hare!

Northumberland
Imagination of some great exploit
Drives him beyond the bounds of patience.   200

Hotspur
By heaven, methinks it were an easy leap
To pluck bright honour from the pale-fac'd moon;
Or dive into the bottom of the deep,
Where fathom-line could never touch the ground,
And pluck up drowned honour by the locks;   205
So he that doth redeem her thence might wear
Without corrival all her dignities.
But out upon this half-fac'd fellowship!

Worcester
He apprehends a world of figures here,
But not the form of what he should attend.   210
Good cousin, give me audience for a while.

61

212. 'I beg your pardon.' Perhaps Hotspur realizes that he has been dominating the conversation. If so, his attempt to listen doesn't last long!

214-15. *Scot:* (a) Scotsman; (b) a small amount of money.

216. *start away:* lose the point in your wild outbursts.

219-26. Hotspur's two proposed ways of getting his own back on Henry are meant seriously. They would be very funny and also very childish.

228. 'I solemnly give up all interests and activities.'

229. *Save:* except.
gall: harm.
pinch: annoy.
Hotspur regards his wish to hurt the King as honourable, but the language which he uses is very petty compared with the heroic deeds he imagined earlier.

230. *sword-and-buckler:* weapons of a common man. Hotspur, of course, despises Hal on account of the low life he is leading.

231. *But that:* if it were not for the fact that.

232. *mischance:* accident.

233. *pot of ale:* Hotspur refers obliquely to Hal's drinking bouts with common people.

235. *attend:* pay attention.

237. *woman's mood:* a woman's wild and impotent words (in contrast to a man's deeds).

238. 'listening to nobody except yourself'.

Hotspur
  I cry you mercy.
Worcester   Those same noble Scots
  That are your prisoners—
Hotspur   I'll keep them all;
  By God, he shall not have a Scot of them;
  No, if a Scot would save his soul, he shall not.   *215*
  I'll keep them, by this hand.
Worcester   You start away,
  And lend no ear unto my purposes.
  Those prisoners you shall keep.
Hotspur   Nay, I will; that's flat.
  He said he would not ransom Mortimer;
  Forbad my tongue to speak of Mortimer;   *220*
  But I will find him when he lies asleep,
  And in his ear I'll holla 'Mortimer!'
  Nay,
  I'll have a starling shall be taught to speak
  Nothing but 'Mortimer', and give it him   *225*
  To keep his anger still in motion.
Worcester
  Hear you, cousin; a word.
Hotspur
  All studies here I solemnly defy,
  Save how to gall and pinch this Bolingbroke.
  And that same sword-and-buckler Prince of Wales— *230*
  But that I think his father loves him not
  And would be glad he met with some mischance—
  I would have him poison'd with a pot of ale.
Worcester
  Farewell, kinsman: I'll talk to you
  When you are better temper'd to attend.   *235*
Northumberland
  Why, what a wasp-stung and impatient fool
  Art thou to break into this woman's mood,
  Tying thine ear to no tongue but thine own!

240. *Nettled:* stung with nettles.
pismires: ants.
241. *politician:* crafty schemer. Hotspur's uncle, Worcester, is just as much a *politician* as the King is.
242-55. This is the first of several references to the way in which Bolingbroke became king. Hotspur's purpose is to show how hypocritical he was in winning support, how he promised rewards that he never gave his followers. You should compare this account with the others that occur later in the play (in Act III, Scene ii; Act IV, Scene iii and Act V, Scene i).
242-8. This lack of memory for detail is typical of Hotspur.
244. *the madcap . . . uncle.* This is the Duke of York who was appointed Regent during Richard II's absence in Ireland.
kept: lived.
246. *king of smiles.* An effective phrase, suggesting the falseness of Bolingbroke's friendliness.
248. *Ravenspurgh:* on the coast of Yorkshire where Bolingbroke landed when returning from exile.
251. *candy . . . courtesy:* sugar-sweet load of humble politeness.
252. *fawning greyhound:* flattering cur.

253. *infant fortune:* Bolingbroke's plans. 'Expect great things when my new-born plans become mature.'

255. *cozeners:* cheats. Notice the play on *cousin* in the previous line.
256. *I have done:* 'I've finished talking.'

257-8. Worcester is, of course, very sarcastic – but, at last, Hotspur has run out of words and will now listen.

259-62. Worcester's tactics seem clear. The son of Douglas is to be released, neither freely like the other prisoners nor in exchange for ransom money, but on condition that Douglas will bring an army to help the rebels.
259. *to:* to the subject of.
261. *Douglas' son:* see Act I, Scene i, lines 70-2.
261-2. *your . . . powers:* your only method of bargaining to raise troops.
divers: several.

266. *into the bosom creep:* worm your way into the confidence. The word *creep* (like a snake) emphasizes the underhand, illegal nature of Worcester's plans. He is keen to get a churchman on his side to give the plot outward respectability.

Hotspur

  Why, look you, I am whipt and scourg'd with rods,
  Nettled, and stung with pismires, when I hear   *240*
  Of this vile politician, Bolingbroke.
  In Richard's time—what do you call the place?—
  A plague upon it, it is in Gloucestershire—
  'Twas where the madcap duke his uncle kept—
  His uncle York—where I first bow'd my knee   *245*
  Unto this king of smiles, this Bolingbroke—
  'Sblood!
  When you and he came back from Ravenspurgh—

Northumberland

  At Berkeley Castle.

Hotspur

  You say true.   *250*
  Why, what a candy deal of courtesy
  This fawning greyhound then did proffer me!
  'Look when his infant fortune came to age'
  And 'gentle Harry Percy' and 'kind cousin'—
  O, the devil take such cozeners! God forgive me!   *255*
  Good uncle, tell your tale—I have done.

Worcester

  Nay, if you have not, to it again;
  We will stay your leisure.

Hotspur   I have done, i' faith.

Worcester

  Then once more to your Scottish prisoners:
  Deliver them up without their ransom straight,   *260*
  And make the Douglas' son your only mean
  For powers in Scotland; which, for divers reasons
  Which I shall send you written, be assur'd
  Will easily be granted. [*To* NORTHUMBERLAND] You,
     my lord,
  Your son in Scotland being thus employ'd,   *265*
  Shall secretly into the bosom creep
  Of that same noble prelate, well belov'd,
  The Archbishop.

271. *the Lord Scroop.* In fact, this was the Archbishop's cousin, the Earl of Wiltshire, not his brother. When Bolingbroke captured Bristol castle, he executed Scroop and other supporters of Richard II.

272. *in estimation:* by guesswork.

274. *ruminated:* carefully thought about.

275-6. 'and is only waiting for the right moment for it to be put into practice'.

277. *I smell it:* 'I get the idea.' Immediately, and without learning any details, Hotspur is all agog with excitement and confidence. Hence his father's cutting remark.

278. 'Even before we've started, off you go in your headstrong way.' Northumberland compares Hotspur to an over-eager hunter who lets his hounds loose before the quarry has been sighted.

279. *cannot choose but be:* 'can't help being'.

a noble plot: Hotspur at once assumes that the rebellion must be glorious, though there is little indication of honour in what Worcester suggests. We can see how Hotspur's lack of a sense of proportion can easily drag him down to the level of the cunning politicians he is associated with.

282. *well aim'd:* well planned.

283. 'and important reasons force us to hurry'.

283-4. Worcester's use of words allows of two meanings, both of which he probably intends: (i) to save our lives by raising an army (*head*) for our defence; (ii) to save our lives by destroying (*razing*) a king.

285-8. Worcester's words brilliantly state the impossibility of any real trust between the King and the Percy family, although we have no evidence that Henry IV intended to kill them. The fact that Henry owed much of his success to their support and the fact that he dared not reward them fully for fear of weakening his position must lead to the 'guessing-game' about each other that Worcester describes here. In such a situation open hostility seems inevitable sooner or later.

285. 'for, however tactfully we behave . . .'

286. *him:* himself.

288. *pay us home:* discharge the debt in full, i.e. kill us.

290. To withdraw his affection.

295. *steal:* go secretly. This also shows the illegal cunning of Worcester.

Hotspur
  Of York, is it not?
Worcester
  True; who bears hard   *270*
  His brother's death at Bristow, the Lord Scroop.
  I speak not this in estimation,
  As what I think might be, but what I know
  Is ruminated, plotted, and set down,
  And only stays but to behold the face   *275*
  Of that occasion that shall bring it on.
Hotspur
  I smell it. Upon my life, it will do well.
Northumberland
  Before the game is afoot thou still let'st slip.
Hotspur
  Why, it cannot choose but be a noble plot.
  And then the power of Scotland and of York   *280*
  To join with Mortimer, ha?
Worcester   And so they shall.
Hotspur
  In faith, it is exceedingly well aim'd.
Worcester
  And 'tis no little reason bids us speed,
  To save our heads by raising of a head;
  For, bear ourselves as even as we can,   *285*
  The King will always think him in our debt,
  And think we think ourselves unsatisfied,
  Till he hath found a time to pay us home.
  And see already how he doth begin
  To make us strangers to his looks of love.   *290*
Hotspur
  He does, he does. We'll be reveng'd on him.
Worcester
  Cousin, farewell. No further go in this
  Than I by letters shall direct your course.
  When time is ripe, which will be suddenly,
  I'll steal to Glendower and Lord Mortimer;   *295*

296. *at once:* all at the same time.

297. *fashion:* arrange.

298-9. 'to defend by our own efforts our threatened safety'.

300. *I trust.* This indicates Northumberland's worry and doubt.

302. *fields:* battle fields.
applaud our sport: the clash of arms and the groans of dying men shall be our applause. Is this another indication of Hotspur's lack of maturity? Is war just a game to him to be applauded by an audience? Is a reference to applause appropriate at the end of an act?

Where you and Douglas and our pow'rs at once,
As I will fashion it, shall happily meet,
To bear our fortunes in our own strong arms,
Which now we hold at much uncertainty.

Northumberland

Farewell, good brother. We shall thrive, I trust.   *300*

Hotspur

Uncle, adieu. O, let the hours be short
Till fields and blows and groans applaud our sport!

Exeunt

ACT TWO

SCENE I

Shakespeare seems to see the two carriers in their suspicion of strangers as representative of humble working-class men, the inevitable victims of lawlessness in the state both at the political level through the Percy rebellion and at the social level through Falstaff's activities. Darkness with pools of light cast by lanterns carried by the men would create an appropriate atmosphere.

1. 'I'm damned if it isn't already four in the morning'. Time is important to this man who has a definite job to do.

2. *Charles' wain:* the Great Bear constellation, from whose position in the sky the carrier tells the time.

3. *ostler:* stable-boy.

4. *Anon:* Coming. Originally the word meant 'at once' but here it is probably equivalent to the modern 'presently', or 'in a little while'.

5. *beat Cut's saddle:* 'smooth out the padding of Cut's (his horse's) saddle'.

flocks: tufts of wool.

6. *point:* pommel.

poor jade: miserable nag.

wrung . . . withers: sore from the rubbing of the saddle.

6-7. *out . . . cess:* extremely, utterly.

8. *Peas and beans:* the second carrier's fodder.

dank: wet.

9. *the next . . . bots:* 'the quickest way of giving wretched horses worms' (an intestinal disease).

9-10. *this house . . . died.* The second carrier says that since the death of the previous landlord the inn has been badly managed. Shakespeare may intend the audience to see in this a reference to the state of the country. In this case *Robin Ostler* might refer to a past king, perhaps Edward III.

11. *never . . . rose:* 'never enjoyed life after the price of oats increased'. Shakespeare's audiences would know about the problems of shortages and rising prices.

13. *villainous:* dreadful.

14. *stung like a tench.* The fresh water fish, tench and loach, are frequently infested by a kind of louse. Also the spots on a tench look rather like small bites.

15-17. *By the mass:* a common mode of swearing.

there . . . cock: 'no Christian king could have been bitten more times than I have been since midnight'.

Despite the king's claim, as the greatest man in society, to experience things more fully than anyone else, the carrier has been *better bit* than any king. This suggests a theme of this play that the life of the ordinary man has value despite the fact that the nobles, rebels, and courtiers alike, treat ordinary folk as mere pawns in the game and finally as cannon-fodder.

ACT TWO

Enter a CARRIER *with a lantern in his hand*

First Carrier

Heigh-ho! an it be not four by the day, I'll be hang'd;
Charles' wain is over the new chimney, and yet our
horse not pack'd. What, ostler!

Ostler [*Within*]

Anon, anon.

First Carrier

I prithee, Tom, beat Cut's saddle; put a few flocks   5
in the point; poor jade is wrung in the withers out of
all cess.

Enter another CARRIER

Second Carrier

Peas and beans are as dank here as a dog, and that is
the next way to give poor jades the bots; this house
is turned upside down since Robin Ostler died.   10

First Carrier

Poor fellow never joyed since the price of oats rose; it
was the death of him.

Second Carrier

I think this be the most villainous house in all
London road for fleas; I am stung like a tench.

First Carrier

Like a tench! By the mass, there is ne'er a king christen   15
could be better bit than I have been since the first
cock.

71

18. *jordan:* chamber-pot.

19. *leak in your chimney:* urinate in the fireplace.
chamber-lye: urine.

19-20. *breeds fleas like a loach.* This probably means 'produces as many fleas as a loach produces fry (small fish)'.

22. *razes:* roots.

23. *Charing Cross.* Then, a village separate from the city of London through which the carrier must travel.

25. *starved:* numb with cold.

26-8. *An . . . villain:* 'The only thing you're good for is to be cracked on the head.'

28-9. *Hast . . . thee?:* 'Can't anyone rely on you?'

Stage Direction. *Enter Gadshill.* The carriers, not expecting to see this man, a well-to-do fellow, are at once suspicious. We know, from Act I, Scene ii, that he is the planner of the robbery.

31. *two o'clock:* The carrier wishes to mislead Gadshill concerning the time. Why?

32-3. Why does Gadshill want the carrier's lantern?

34. *Soft!:* Not so fast.
I know . . . that: 'I know all about tricks like that.'

37. *Ay . . . tell?:* 'Wouldn't you just like to know when I'll give it to you?'
quoth 'a: says he.

Second Carrier

Why, they will allow us ne'er a jordan; and then we
leak in your chimney; and your chamber-lye breeds
fleas like a loach. 20

First Carrier

What, ostler! come away, and be hang'd; come away.

Second Carrier

I have a gammon of bacon and two razes of ginger,
to be delivered as far as Charing Cross.

First Carrier

God's body! the turkeys in my pannier are quite
starved. What, ostler! A plague on thee! hast thou 25
never an eye in thy head? Canst not hear? An 'twere
not as good deed as drink to break the pate on thee,
I am a very villain. Come, and be hang'd! Hast no
faith in thee?

Enter GADSHILL

Gadshill

Good morrow, carriers. What's o'c'ock? 30

First Carrier

I think it be two o'clock.

Gadshill

I prithee lend me thy lantern to see my gelding in the
stable.

First Carrier

Nay, by God! Soft! I know a trick worth two of that,
i' faith. 35

Gadshill

I pray thee lend me thine.

Second Carrier

Ay, when, canst tell? Lend me thy lantern, quoth 'a?
Marry, I'll see thee hang'd first.

Gadshill

Sirrah carrier, what time do you mean to come to
London? 40

41. *Time . . . candle:* In time to go to bed tonight.
warrant: assure.
42-4. The carriers announce loudly for Gadshill's benefit that they will journey in company with another group who are travelling with much money and will therefore welcome the safety of added numbers.

46. *At hand:* Just coming.
quoth pick-purse: a common play on the word *hand.*

47. *That's . . . as:* 'That's just the same as saying'.

48-9. *thou variest . . . labouring:* 'you're just as responsible for the crime of robbery as the foreman of a group of workers is for the job he directs his men to do'.
49-50. *thou . . . how:* 'you're the organizer of our crimes.'

51-2. *It . . . yesternight:* 'What I told you last night is quite true.'

52. *franklin:* wealthy owner of free-hold land.
Wild: Weald.

53. *marks:* a mark was worth 13s.4d.

55. *auditor:* government treasury official.
55-6. *abundance of charge:* a very large sum of money.

57. *eggs and butter:* breakfast.

58. *presently:* immediately.

59. *Saint Nicholas' clerks:* highwaymen, Saint Nicholas being the patron saint of travellers.
60. *I'll give thee this neck:* 'you can chop my head off'.

61. *I'll none of it:* 'I don't want it'.
I pray . . . hangman: a grimly humorous reference to the penalty for robbery.
63. *as truly . . . may:* as honestly as a criminal can.

64. *What:* why.

65. *fat:* This suggests that Gadshill is similar in size and shape to Falstaff.
66-7. *starveling:* skinny fellow.
67-8. *Troyans . . . of:* 'good chaps that you can't even imagine'.

Second Carrier

    Time enough to go to bed with a candle, I warrant
thee. Come, neighbour Mugs, we'll call up the gentlemen; they will along with company, for they have
great charge.

Exeunt CARRIERS

Gadshill

    What, ho! chamberlain!   45

Chamberlain [*Within*]

    At hand, quoth pick-purse.

Gadshill

    That's even as fair as—at hand, quoth the chamber-
lain; for thou variest no more from picking of purses
than giving direction doth from labouring; thou
layest the plot how.   50

Enter CHAMBERLAIN

Chamberlain

    Good morrow, Master Gadshill. It holds current that
I told you yesternight: there's a franklin in the Wild
of Kent hath brought three hundred marks with him
in gold; I heard him tell it to one of his company last
night at supper, a kind of auditor; one that hath abun- 55
dance of charge too—God knows what. They are up
already and call for eggs and butter; they will away
presently.

Gadshill

    Sirrah, if they meet not with Saint Nicholas' clerks,
I'll give thee this neck.   60

Chamberlain

    No, I'll none of it; I pray thee keep that for the hang-
man; for I know thou worshippest Saint Nicholas
as truly as a man of falsehood may.

Gadshill

    What talkest thou to me of the hangman? If I hang,
I'll make a fat pair of gallows; for if I hang, old Sir 65
John hangs with me; and thou knowest he is no star-
veling. Tut! there are other Troyans that thou

75

69. *to do . . . grace:* to honour the profession (by joining in a robbery). This is, of course, a reference to Hal.

69-70. *if . . . into:* 'if the authorities should get nosy'.

70. *for . . . sake:* because of their reputation.

71. *make all whole:* make everything look legal. Just as Worcester wished to use the good name of the Archbishop of York, Gadshill wishes to take advantage of Hal's position as Prince of Wales to make his activities look honourable.

71. *foot landrakers:* tramps or wandering foot-pads.

72. *long-staff . . . strikers:* robbers who would knock a man down with a long stick just to rob him of sixpence.

72-3. *mad . . . malt-worms:* violent, moustached, purple-faced drunkards. Gadshill seems to compete with Falstaff in lurid eloquence as well as in physical bulk.

74. *tranquillity:* men who live in easy comfort.

burgomasters: councillors and aldermen.

oneyers: treasury officials.

75. *hold in:* remain loyal to each other.

77. *zounds:* by God's wounds, a common mode of swearing.

77-85. *for they . . . invisible:* Gadshill and the Chamberlain align themselves with the forces of lawlessness in their wish for a society in which criminals can flourish undetected and unpunished. These lines give a picture of the corruption of the country at all levels which Hal will have to overcome if he is to give England the peace and order it needs.

79. *prey on her:* (as highwaymen and rebels).

80. *boots:* booty, plunder.

81. *boots:* footwear.

81-2. *Will . . . way ?:* 'Will she (your country) protect you (as a criminal) in time of trouble?'

83. *liquor'd:* made drunk.

83-4. *We . . . cocksure:* 'So corrupt is the state of the country that we criminals have nothing to fear from the law'.

84-5. *receipt of fern-seed:* recipe for obtaining fern-seed, which was believed to make its possessor invisible probably because it is itself so microscopic as to be almost invisible. Gadshill claims that there is so much corruption that their small gang of robbers won't be noticed.

86. *are more beholding:* ought to be more grateful to.

89. *purchase:* proceeds of robbery.

90-3. The Chamberlain cunningly does not believe that Gadshill's offer to shake his hand will guarantee him his share of the profits. Gadshill replies that robbers and honest folk are all men, whether *false* or *true* in the eyes of the world.

93. *muddy:* stupid.

This scene ends the first section of the play. The picture of disorder at all levels of society is now complete as the lawless gangs move into action.

dream'st not of, the which for sport sake are content
to do the profession some grace; that would, if matters should be look'd into, for their own credit sake, *70*
make all whole. I am joined with no foot landrakers,
no long-staff sixpenny strikers, none of these mad
mustachio purple-hu'd malt-worms; but with nobility
and tranquillity, burgomasters and great oneyers,
such as can hold in, such as will strike sooner than *75*
speak, and speak sooner than drink, and drink sooner
than pray. And yet, zounds, I lie; for they pray contin-
ually to their saint, the commonwealth; or, rather,
not pray to her, but prey on her; for they ride up and
down on her, and make her their boots. *80*

Chamberlain

What, the commonwealth their boots? Will she hold
out water in foul way?

Gadshill

She will, she will; justice hath liquor'd her. We steal
as in a castle, cocksure; we have the receipt of fern-
seed, we walk invisible. *85*

Chamberlain

Nay, by my faith, I think you are more beholding to
the night than to fern-seed for your walking invisible.

Gadshill

Give me thy hand: thou shalt have a share in our
purchase, as I am a true man.

Chamberlain

Nay, rather let me have it, as you are a false thief. *90*

Gadshill

Go to; 'homo' is a common name to all men. Bid
the ostler bring my gelding out of the stable. Farewell, you muddy knave.

Exeunt

SCENE II

Act II, Scene ii, together with Act II, Scene iv, provides one of the most famous comic incidents in Shakespeare. Falstaff, although tricked and eventually exposed in his lies, is at his greatest – a vast figure, revelling in disorder, with the high spirits of a young man, enjoying a life that escapes from the dullness of routine. He is undoubtedly a menace whom Hal will have to reject, but there can be no doubt that of all the characters in this play (most of whom are cunning, down-to-earth, and unemotional) Falstaff is the dominating force in terms of energy, vitality, and sheer love of living.

1. *shelter:* hide yourself.
2. *frets:* (i) complains, (ii) wears away (velvet was sometimes stiffened with gum, but this rubbed away quickly).
3. *Stand close:* get under cover.

5-6. Hal probably jumps out at Falstaff in the dark, deliberately startling him.

10. *I am accursed:* 'It's just my rotten luck, I am doomed'.

12. *by the squier:* measured by the footrule, and therefore 'exactly'.

13. *break my wind:* become utterly breathless.
13-15. *Well . . . rogue:* 'I deserve to die peacefully in my bed if I can restrain myself from killing that rogue.'
15. *forsworn:* vowed to avoid.
16-19. *and yet . . . hanged:* Falstaff, typically blaming others absurdly for his wicked ways, pretends that Poins has given him magic love-potions. This would explain why Falstaff has not been able to do without Poins' company!

21-4. *I'll . . . tooth.* This is another of Falstaff's comic moods of repentance that occur when things are not going so well.
21. *starve:* die.
23. *veriest varlet:* most complete rascal.

SCENE II—*The highway, near Gadshill*

Enter the PRINCE OF WALES *and* POINS

Poins
Come, shelter, shelter; I have remov'd Falstaff's
horse, and he frets like a gumm'd velvet.
Prince
Stand close.

Enter FALSTAFF

Falstaff
Poins! Poins! And be hang'd! Poins!
Prince
Peace, ye fat-kidney'd rascal; what a brawling dost   5
thou keep!
Falstaff
Where's Poins, Hal?
Prince
He is walk'd up to the top of the hill; I'll go seek
him.
Falstaff
I am accurs'd to rob in that thief's company; the ras-   10
cal hath removed my horse, and tied him I know not
where. If I travel but four foot by the squier further
afoot, I shall break my wind. Well, I doubt not but
to die a fair death for all this, if I scape hanging for
killing that rogue. I have forsworn his company   15
hourly any time this two and twenty years, and yet
I am bewitch'd with the rogue's company. If the
rascal have not given me medicines to make me love
him, I'll be hang'd. It could not be else: I have drunk
medicines. Poins! Hal! A plague upon you both!   20
Bardolph! Peto! I'll starve ere I'll rob a foot further.
An 'twere not as good a deed as drink to turn true
man, and to leave these rogues, I am the veriest varlet
that ever chewed with a tooth. Eight yards of uneven
ground is three-score and ten miles afoot with me;   25

27-8. *A plague . . . another:* 'What a state of affairs when thieves can't be loyal to each other!'

28. *Whew!* The Prince and Poins whistle to each other in the dark in order to scare or confuse Falstaff.

32. *list:* listen.

34. *Have . . . down?* In reply to Hal's teasing suggestion that Falstaff should lie down, Falstaff makes a joke at the expense of his own great weight.

35. *'Sblood:* another swear-word (by Christ's blood).

37. *colt:* make a fool of.

38. *uncolted:* without your horse.

41. *ostler:* groom, stable-boy.

42. *Hang . . . garters.* Falstaff's joke is based on the fact that as heir to the crown Hal was automatically a member of the Order of the Garter.

43. *ta'en:* arrested.

peach: 'blab'. To get revenge Falstaff threatens to betray his accomplices to the authorities.

ballads: In the Elizabethan period ballads were popular songs sometimes describing famous events, sometimes the activities of criminals and other notorious characters.

45. *so forward:* so well advanced.

47. *Stand!* Gadshill and his companions might jump out at Falstaff, pretending to be about to rob him. Falstaff, however, is not deceived; he replies with a joke playing on the other meaning of *stand*, as opposed to 'sit'.

49. *setter:* organizer of the robbery.

51. *Case:* Put on your masks.

and the stony-hearted villains know it well enough.
A plague upon it, when thieves cannot be true one to
another! [*They whistle*] Whew! A plague upon you all!
Give me my horse, you rogues; give me my horse,
and be hang'd.   30

Prince

Peace, ye fat-guts! lie down; lay thine ear close to
the ground, and list if thou canst hear the tread of
travellers.

Falstaff

Have you any levers to lift me up again, being down?
'Sblood, I'll not bear mine own flesh so far afoot   35
again for all the coin in thy father's exchequer. What
a plague mean ye to colt me thus?

Prince

Thou liest: thou art not colted, thou art uncolted.

Falstaff

I prithee, good Prince Hal, help me to my horse, good
king's son.   40

Prince

Out, ye rogue! shall I be your ostler?

Falstaff

Hang thyself in thine own heir-apparent garters. If I
be ta'en, I'll peach for this. An I have not ballads made
on you all, and sung to filthy tunes, let a cup of sack
be my poison. When a jest is so forward, and afoot   45
too!—I hate it.

           Enter GADSHILL, BARDOLPH *and* PETO *with him*

Gadshill

Stand!

Falstaff

So I do, against my will.

Poins

O, 'tis our setter: I know his voice. Bardolph, what
news?   50

Bardolph

Case ye, case ye; on with your vizards: there's money

81

51-3. *there's . . . exchequer.* This would probably be a group of tax collectors, taking the money to the royal treasury in London.

54. *King's tavern.* Falstaff means the inn where the Prince and his companions drink.

55. *to make us all:* to make us all rich.

56. In his present bad mood Falstaff can't resist reminding the others of the penalty for robbery.

57. *front:* attack.

58. *lower:* further down the lane.

62. *will . . . us:* See note on Act I, Scene ii, line 177.

63. *Paunch:* Fat Stomach; hence Falstaff's reference to *Gaunt.*

64. *John of Gaunt:* a great nobleman and soldier in the reign of Richard II.

70. Falstaff regrets that if he is arrested he will not be able to get his revenge on Poins for taking his horse.

of the King's coming down the hill; 'tis going to the
King's exchequer.
Falstaff
You lie, ye rogue; 'tis going to the King's tavern.
Gadshill
There's enough to make us all.   55
Falstaff
To be hang'd.
Prince
Sirs, you four shall front them in the narrow lane;
Ned Poins and I will walk lower; if they scape from
your encounter, then they light on us.
Peto
How many be there of them?   60
Gadshill
Some eight or ten.
Falstaff
Zounds, will they not rob us?
Prince
What, a coward, Sir John Paunch?
Falstaff
Indeed, I am not John of Gaunt, your grandfather;
but yet no coward, Hal.   65
Prince
Well, we leave that to the proof.
Poins
Sirrah Jack, thy horse stands behind the hedge: when
thou need'st him, there thou shalt find him. Farewell,
and stand fast.
Falstaff
Now cannot I strike him, if I should be hang'd.   70
Prince [*Aside to* POINS]
Ned, where are our disguises?
Poins [*Aside*]
Here, hard by; stand close.

Exeunt the PRINCE *and* POINS

73. *happy . . . dole:* good luck to everyone. Falstaff's bad mood changes to one of excited enjoyment the moment the action begins.

81. *whoreson caterpillars:* filthy parasites.
bacon-fed: fat.
These are marvellous phrases for Falstaff, of all people, to use. He is playing his favourite role of being virtuous.
81-2. *They hate us youth.* Very funny, but also, more grimly, a common cry of all revolutionaries.
82. *fleece:* rob, strip.
83. *undone:* ruined.
84. *gorbellied:* pot-bellied.
85. *chuffs:* miserly, wealthy landowners.
store: total wealth.
87. *grand-jurors:* respectable and important citizens.
we'll jure ye: 'we'll give you a hiding'.
80-7. In view of the number of travellers stated in line 61, Falstaff probably dances round the outside of the struggling group while yelling his war-cries, at least until he sees that there is no opposition.

90. *argument:* topic of conversation.

Falstaff
　Now, my masters, happy man be his dole, say I; every
　man to his business.
Enter the TRAVELLERS

First Traveller
　Come, neighbour; the boy shall lead our horses　　*75*
　down the hill; we'll walk afoot awhile, and ease our
　legs.

Thieves
　Stand!

Travellers
　Jesus bless us!

Falstaff
　Strike; down with them; cut the villains' throats.　　*80*
　Ah, whoreson caterpillars! bacon-fed knaves! They
　hate us youth. Down with them; fleece them.

Travellers
　O, we are undone, both we and ours for ever!

Falstaff
　Hang ye, gorbellied knaves, are ye undone? No, ye
　fat chuffs; I would your store were here. On, bacons,　　*85*
　on! What, ye knaves! young men must live. You are
　grand-jurors, are ye? We'll jure ye, faith.

Here they rob them and bind them
Exeunt
Re-enter the PRINCE *and* POINS *in buckram*

Prince
　The thieves have bound the true men. Now, could
　thou and I rob the thieves and go merrily to London,
　it would be argument for a week, laughter for a　　*90*
　month, and a good jest for ever.

Poins
　Stand close; I hear them coming.
Enter the THIEVES *again*

Falstaff
　Come, my masters, let us share, and then to horse

85

95. *arrant:* absolute.
there's . . . stirring: there's no justice anywhere. It is typical that Falstaff should appeal to law and order at such a time.

99. The second stage direction is important. Notice that Falstaff alone does put up some slight resistance but, true to his philosophy of life, will not continue to fight when the odds are against him.

102. In the darkness each of the thieves mistakes the others for officers of the law.
103-4. A wonderfully exaggerated picture of Falstaff miserably tramping along with waves of sweat rolling off him and soaking the ground.

SCENE III

Plans for the rebellion are not developing as smoothly as the Percy family hoped. The refusal of the anonymous lord to join the plot clearly disgusts Hotspur, but this scene also reveals much of Hotspur's own inner uncertainty though he will not admit such weakness to himself.

solus: alone.

3. *your house:* your family.

7-8. *why . . . drink.* Hotspur is, of course, very sarcastic.

before day. An the Prince and Poins be not two
arrant cowards, there's no equity stirring. There's   95
no more valour in that Poins than in a wild duck.
    As they are sharing, the PRINCE *and* POINS *set upon them*

Prince

Your money!

Poins

Villains!

    [*They all run away, and* FALSTAFF, *after a blow or
    two, runs away too, leaving the booty behind them*]

Prince

Got with much ease. Now merrily to horse.
The thieves are all scattered, and possess'd with fear   100
So strongly that they dare not meet each other;
Each takes his fellow for an officer.
Away, good Ned. Falstaff sweats to death
And lards the lean earth as he walks along.
Were't not for laughing, I should pity him.   105

Poins

How the fat rogue roar'd!

                                    Exeunt

SCENE III—*Warkworth Castle*

Enter HOTSPUR *solus, reading a letter*

Hotspur

'But, for mine own part, my lord, I could be well
contented to be there, in respect of the love I bear
your house.' He could be contented—why is he not,
then? In respect of the love he bears our house—he
shows in this he loves his own barn better than he   5
loves our house. Let me see some more. 'The purpose
you undertake is dangerous'—why, that's certain:
'tis dangerous to take a cold, to sleep, to drink; but I
tell you, my lord fool, out of this nettle, danger, we

12. *unsorted:* inappropriate, ill-advised.
12-13. *too light . . . opposition:* 'too weak to have a chance of measuring up to such powerful opposition'.

15. *hind:* slave.

14-21. Hotspur's first reaction to the points of the letter is simply to insult the writer and to repeat in vague terms what an excellent plot it is. Does this perhaps suggest that Hotspur has inner doubts of his own?
15-16. *lack-brain:* stupid fool.
18. *full of expectation:* with excellent chances of success.
19. *frosty-spirited:* cowardly.
20. *commends:* praises (but does not fight at Shrewsbury).

23-8. *Is . . . already?* Why does Hotspur feel it necessary to mention each name?

28. *pagan:* unbelieving.
29. *infidel:* person lacking faith.
29-30. *in . . . heart:* in extreme fear.
30. *lay open:* betray.
31-2. *O, I . . . buffets:* 'I could kick myself'.
32-3. *for moving . . . action!:* 'for trying to persuade such a cowardly wretch to take part in such a glorious campaign'. It would appear as though Hotspur has foolishly ignored Worcester's instruction in Act I, Scene iii, lines 292-3.

35-117. In a play in which there are hardly any strong emotional relationships (since it presents a world of politicians and self-seekers) Lady Percy's mature love for her husband stands out remarkably. Hotspur's attitude to her is more difficult to work out. Although he is very immature, even childish at times, and although his idea of manliness makes him pretend to despise women and love as weak, certain lines, particularly 114-116, can be interpreted as indicating deep love for his wife. Hotspur's vitality and emotional responses and Falstaff's love of life make them both stand out in this play.
37. *thus alone:* The fact that Hotspur has been deliberately avoiding company indicates his worry.
41. *stomach:* appetite.
golden: precious. Inability to sleep is often presented by Shakespeare as a sign of lack of peace of mind.
42. *bend . . . earth:* stare at the ground.
43. *start:* jump in fear.

pluck this flower, safety. 'The purpose you undertake   *10*
is dangerous; the friends you have named uncertain;
the time itself unsorted; and your whole plot too
light for the counterpoise of so great an opposition.'
Say you so, say you so? I say unto you again, you are
a shallow, cowardly hind, and you lie. What a lack-   *15*
brain is this! By the Lord, our plot is a good plot as
ever was laid; our friends true and constant—a good
plot, good friends, and full of expectation; an excellent plot, very good friends. What a frosty-spirited
rogue is this! Why, my Lord of York commends the   *20*
plot and the general course of the action. Zounds, an
I were now by this rascal, I could brain him with his
lady's fan. Is there not my father, my uncle, and myself; Lord Edmund Mortimer, my Lord of York, and
Owen Glendower? Is there not, besides, the Douglas?   *25*
Have I not all their letters to meet me in arms by the
ninth of the next month, and are they not some of
them set forward already? What a pagan rascal is this!
an infidel! Ha! you shall see now, in very sincerity of
fear and cold heart, will he to the King and lay open   *30*
all our proceedings. O, I could divide myself and go
to buffets for moving such a dish of skim milk with so
honourable an action! Hang him; let him tell the
King: we are prepared. I will set forward to-night.

Enter LADY PERCY

How now, Kate! I must leave you within these two   *35*
hours.

Lady Percy

O my good lord, why are you thus alone?
For what offence have I this fortnight been
A banish'd woman from my Harry's bed?
Tell me, sweet lord, what is't that takes from thee   *40*
Thy stomach, pleasure, and thy golden sleep?
Why dost thou bend thine eyes upon the earth,
And start so often when thou sit'st alone?
Why hast thou lost the fresh blood in thy cheeks,

45. 'and refused the delight of your loving company due to me as your wife'.

46. 'for the sake of tired pondering and hateful worries'.

47. *faint slumbers:* light sleep.
watch'd: stayed awake.

48. *iron:* cruel.

49. *terms of manage:* commands.

51. *sallies and retires:* charges and retreats.

52. *palisadoes:* strong positions defended by stakes.
frontiers: ramparts.

53. *basilisks:* cannons; *culverin:* small gun. Both these names for weapons come from words for venomous reptiles.

55. *currents . . . fight:* changing fortunes of a fierce battle.

57. *bestirr'd:* disturbed.

59. *late:* recently.

60. *motions:* expressions.

62. *On . . . hest:* when suddenly confronted with some crucial responsibility.
portents: signs, symptoms.

63. *heavy business:* difficult problem.

65. *What, ho!* Hotspur calls for his servant. Has Hotspur not heard his wife, or is he just pretending not to have heard her? How would Hotspur behave during her speech?
packet: letters.

68. *even now:* a moment ago.

69. *crop-ear:* a horse whose ears had been trimmed short.

71. *back:* ride.
straight: at once.
O esperance!: 'Hope!' This was the Percy family motto.

72. *park:* paddock.

And given my treasures and my rights of thee   45
To thick-ey'd musing and curs'd melancholy?
In thy faint slumbers I by thee have watch'd,
And heard thee murmur tales of iron wars;
Speak terms of manage to thy bounding steed;
Cry 'Courage! To the field!' And thou hast talk'd   50
Of sallies and retires, of trenches, tents,
Of palisadoes, frontiers, parapets,
Of basilisks, of cannon, culverin,
Of prisoners' ransom, and of soldiers slain,
And all the currents of a heady fight.   55
Thy spirit within thee hath been so at war,
And thus hath so bestirr'd thee in thy sleep,
That beads of sweat have stood upon thy brow
Like bubbles in a late disturbed stream;
And in thy face strange motions have appear'd,   60
Such as we see when men restrain their breath
On some great sudden hest. O, what portents are these?
Some heavy business hath my lord in hand,
And I must know it, else he loves me not.

Hotspur
  What, ho!

Enter a SERVANT
  Is Gilliams with the packet gone?   65

Servant
  He is, my lord, an hour ago.
Hotspur
  Hath Butler brought those horses from the sheriff?
Servant
  One horse, my lord, he brought even now.
Hotspur
  What horse? A roan, a crop-ear, is it not?
Servant
  It is, my lord.
Hotspur   That roan shall be my throne.   70
  Well, I will back him straight. O esperance!
  Bid Butler lead him forth into the park.

91

74. Hotspur is deliberately off-hand with his wife.

75. Lady Hotspur means 'What is the matter with you?' Hotspur misunderstands her on purpose. Probably his reasons are complicated. He does not believe that women should be interested in such matters but also perhaps, if he loves his wife, he wishes to protect her from worry and is being 'cruel to be kind'.
77. *mad-headed ape:* crazy fool.

78-9. *A weasel . . . with:* 'Not even a weasel is as bad-tempered as you are.'
In faith: Honestly.

81-2. *doth . . . title:* 'is making trouble concerning his claim to the throne'. An intelligent guess on her part.

83. *To line his enterprise:* To support his ambition.

84. An amusing line that suggests an affectionate protest as Lady Hotspur tries to stop Hotspur leaving to ride his horse. He has probably been walking round the room trying to shake her off.
85. *paraquito:* chatterer, literally a parrot (see Act II, Scene iv, lines 96-7).
87. This dialogue, despite its very real seriousness, suggests a certain playfulness. Kate may have pushed Hotspur into a chair and, to prevent his escape, firmly seized his little finger.

89. *Away:* Hotspur, exasperated, pushes his wife off and seems to rebuff her finally. How far does he really mean what he says in lines 90-1?
90. *trifler:* time-waster.
92. *mammets:* dolls.
tilt: charge against an enemy in a tournament. Hotspur even talks about kissing in warlike terms.
93. *crack'd crowns:* (a) wounded heads; (b) beaten kings; (c) damaged coins.
94. *pass them current:* treat them as legal coins. The idea of using damaged money as good money suggests that, unconsciously, Hotspur feels that the rebellion is not as honourable as he would like to think.
96-9. The force of her husband's words seems to make Kate suddenly doubt her husband's love. It is a most moving, unhappy speech.

Exit SERVANT

Lady Percy
  But hear you, my lord.
Hotspur
  What say'st thou, my lady?
Lady Percy
  What is it carries you away?   75
Hotspur
  Why, my horse, my love, my horse.

← *Hotspur making a joke*

Lady Percy
  Out, you mad-headed ape!
  A weasel hath not such a deal of spleen
  As you are toss'd with. In faith,
  I'll know your business, Harry, that I will.   80
  I fear my brother Mortimer doth stir
  About his title and hath sent for you
  To line his enterprise; but if you go—
Hotspur
  So far afoot, I shall be weary, love.
Lady Percy
  Come, come, you paraquito, answer me   85
  Directly unto this question that I ask.
  In faith, I'll break thy little finger, Harry,
  An if thou wilt not tell me all things true.
Hotspur
  Away.
  Away, you trifler! Love, I love thee not,   90
  I care not for thee, Kate; this is no world
  To play with mammets and to tilt with lips:
  We must have bloody noses and crack'd crowns,
  And pass them current too. God's me, my horse!
  What say'st thou, Kate? what wouldst thou have with
      me?   95
Lady Percy
  Do you not love me? Do you not, indeed?
  Well, do not, then; for since you love me not,
  I will not love myself. Do you not love me?

100-12. Sensing her misery, Hotspur's mood changes to one of tenderness though he still cannot bring himself to reveal his secrets.
101-2. *And . . . infinitely.* This might be interpreted to mean that he is only in love with her when he is away from her. But it is instead, I think, a revelation of Hotspur's almost tragic position. He loves his wife very much, but is so obsessed with the worries of the campaign and with his exaggerated search for honour and action that he cannot relax to enjoy a settled married life.

107-8. *no farther . . . wife:* 'no wiser than you can be as a woman, although you are my wife.'
constant: reliable.

110. *closer:* more trustworthy.
110-11. *for . . . know:* this is an old joke against a woman's supposed inability to keep a secret.

117. *It must, of force:* 'I haven't any choice in the matter.' Again we feel Hotspur's limitations, this time in not having the intelligence to see his wife's real quality. It is still a happy marriage, but Hotspur insists on isolating himself from offered support.

SCENE IV

To pass the time while awaiting the arrival of Falstaff and his cronies, Hal has been talking to the serving men at the inn. To modern ears he sounds callous and condescending in the way he makes fun of them. To Elizabethans, however, it may not have sounded like this at all. Hal's preparation for kingship by learning something of all levels of the population would be a strong point in his favour – and a prince was almost universally accepted as far better than any working man. So his attitude might have seemed quite natural.
At the same time Hal seems to feel little emotion. Compared with Falstaff and Hotspur he is a cold figure. Or has he determined to control rigidly any feelings that rise in him?
1. *fat room:* stuffy place (the main bar probably, from which we should hear noise and laughter).
1-2. *lend . . . hand:* help me.
4. *loggerheads:* block-heads.
5. *hogsheads:* barrels. Hal has been in the cellar with the serving men.
5-6. *I . . . humility:* 'I have humbled myself completely.'

Nay, tell me if you speak in jest or no.
Hotspur
  Come, wilt thou see me ride?   *100*
  And when I am o' horseback, I will swear
  I love thee infinitely. But hark you, Kate:
  I must not have you henceforth question me
  Whither I go, nor reason whereabout.
  Whither I must, I must; and, to conclude,   *105*
  This evening must I leave you, gentle Kate.
  I know you wise, but yet no farther wise
  Than Harry Percy's wife; constant you are,
  But yet a woman; and for secrecy,
  No lady closer; for I well believe   *110*
  Thou wilt not utter what thou dost not know,
  And so far will I trust thee, gentle Kate.
Lady Percy
  How, so far?
Hotspur
  Not an inch further. But hark you, Kate:
  Whither I go, thither shall you go too;   *115*
  To-day will I set forth, to-morrow you.
  Will this content you, Kate?
Lady Percy   It must, of force.
                Exeunt

SCENE IV—*Eastcheap. The Boar's Head Tavern*

        Enter the PRINCE *and* POINS

Prince
  Ned, prithee, come out of that fat room and lend me
  thy hand to laugh a little.
Poins
  Where hast been, Hal?
Prince
  With three or four loggerheads amongst three or
  fourscore hogsheads. I have sounded the very base-   5

95

7. *leash:* originally a term meaning three dogs fastened together with leather thongs, but here a reference to the lowest class of society from which the drawers come.
drawers: barmen.
8-10. 'They swear that although I am not yet a king I am already the greatest, kindest and most polite of men'.
11. *Jack:* low-bred fellow.
12. *Corinthian:* 'good chap'.
mettle: spirit.

15-17. Hal makes fun of the barmen's slang.

16. *breathe . . . watering:* 'pause for breath while you drink'.
'*hem!*' 'clear your throat!'
17. *play it off:* 'drink it up'.
so . . . proficient: so expert.
19. Tinkers drank heavily and had their own dialect.

20-1. *thou . . . action.* Hal is either being sarcastic or sincerely means that he finds a sense of honour in mixing with the uneducated classes of society. In any case this line and all the Prince's actions here contrast strongly with Hotspur's ways of seeking *honour* in *action*. What would Hotspur think of Hal's behaviour?
22-3. *pennyworth of sugar.* Small amounts of sugar wrapped in paper were sold to those who bought sack.
23-4. *under-skinker:* pot-boy, the humblest of all workers at the inn.
25-7. Hal probably mimics the unbroken voice of the pot-boy.

27. *Score:* put on the bill.
bastard: sweet Spanish wine.
Half-moon. The name of a room in the inn and perhaps a deliberate reference to the crest of the Percy family.
29. *by-room:* adjoining room.
30. *puny:* young.
to what end: why.
31. *leave:* stop.
31-2. *that . . . 'Anon':* so that he will constantly have to call out 'Coming'.
33. *a precedent:* 'how to do it'.

35. *Thou art perfect:* 'That's exactly right'.

string of humility. Sirrah, I am sworn brother to a
leash of drawers and can call them all by their
christen names, as Tom, Dick, and Francis. They take
it already upon their salvation that though I be but
Prince of Wales yet I am the king of courtesy; and   *10*
tell me flatly I am no proud Jack, like Falstaff, but a
Corinthian, a lad of mettle, a good boy—by the Lord,
so they call me—and when I am King of England I
shall command all the good lads in Eastcheap.
They call drinking deep, dyeing scarlet; and when   *15*
you breathe in your watering, they cry 'hem!' and bid
you play it off. To conclude, I am so good a proficient
in one quarter of an hour that I can drink with any
tinker in his own language during my life. I tell thee,
Ned, thou hast lost much honour that thou wert not   *20*
with me in this action. But, sweet Ned—to sweeten
which name of Ned, I give thee this pennyworth of
sugar, clapp'd even now into my hand by an under-
skinker, one that never spake other English in his life
than 'Eight shillings and sixpence' and 'You are wel-   *25*
come' with this shrill addition, 'Anon, anon, sir!
Score a pint of bastard in the Half-moon' or so. But,
Ned, to drive away the time till Falstaff come, I
prithee, do thou stand in some by-room, while I
question my puny drawer to what end he gave me the   *30*
sugar; and do thou never leave calling 'Francis!' that
his tale to me may be nothing but 'Anon'. Step aside,
and I'll show thee a precedent.

Exit POINS

Poins [*Within*]
  Francis!
Prince
  Thou art perfect.   *35*
Poins [*Within*]
  Francis!

Enter FRANCIS

37-8. *Look . . . Ralph:* Francis shouts this instruction back into the room from which he has just come.
Pomgarnet: another room in the inn, perhaps one decorated with a design of pomegranates.
39. *hither:* here.

41. *How . . . serve?:* 'How much more of your apprenticeship do you have to serve?'

42. *five years:* If Francis was serving, as was usual, a seven-year apprenticeship, he would probably be about fourteen.

45. *by'r lady!:* by Our Lady (the Virgin Mary).
lease: contract.
46-8. *darest . . . it?:* 'do you dare to break your contract and run away?' Is the Prince thinking of his neglect of his duties at court?

49. *books:* Bibles.
50. *I could . . . heart:* 'I would love to do so', (but, perhaps, dare not).

Francis
Anon, anon, sir. Look down into the Pomgarnet,
Ralph.
Prince
Come hither, Francis.
Francis
My lord?   *40*
Prince
How long hast thou to serve, Francis?
Francis
Forsooth, five years, and as much as to—
Poins [*Within*]
Francis!
Francis
Anon, anon, sir.
Prince
Five year! by'r lady, a long lease for the clinking of *45*
pewter. But, Francis, darest thou be so valiant as to
play the coward with thy indenture and show it a fair
pair of heels and run from it?
Francis
O Lord, sir, I'll be sworn upon all the books in
England, I could find in my heart—   *50*
Poins [*Within*]
Francis!
Francis
Anon, sir.
Prince
How old art thou, Francis?
Francis
Let me see, about Michaelmas next I shall be—
Poins [*Within*]
Francis!   *55*
Francis
Anon, sir. Pray stay a little, my lord.
Prince
Nay, but hark you, Francis: for the sugar thou gavest

64-6. *Anon, . . . wilt:* Hal pretends that *Anon, anon* is in answer to his offer of a thousand pounds.

68. *jerkin:* a kind of coat.

69. *knot-pated:* with very short hair.
puke: greyish-black.
caddis-garter: worsted tape.
70. *smooth-tongue:* oily.
Spanish-pouch: the vintner is probably wearing a Spanish leather purse.
71. Hal is talking about Francis's employer, the vintner, who enters in a moment. Francis may realise this only too well but be frightened of losing his job.
72-4. Very difficult lines to understand. The Prince may be deliberately talking nonsense or he may be saying that if Francis hasn't the courage to rob his master and run away he will have a miserable life.
74. *sully:* get dirty.
In Barbary: centre of sugar trade on North African coast. Hal seems to be reverting to the cost of the sugar (see lines 57-8).

77. Is Hal making fun of Francis in a pleasant way, or is he dismissing him curtly, being now bored with the conversation?

me—'twas a pennyworth, was't not?

Francis

O Lord, I would it had been two!

Prince

I will give thee for it a thousand pound; ask me when 60
thou wilt, and thou shalt have it.

Poins [*Within*]

Francis!

Francis

Anon, anon.

Prince

Anon, Francis? No, Francis; but to-morrow, Francis;
or, Francis, o' Thursday; or indeed, Francis, when 65
thou wilt. But, Francis—

Francis

My lord?

Prince

Wilt thou rob this leathern jerkin, crystal-button,
knot-pated, agate-ring, puke-stocking, caddis-garter,
smooth-tongue, Spanish-pouch— 70

Francis

O Lord, sir, who do you mean?

Prince

Why, then, your brown bastard is your only drink;
for, look you, Francis, your white canvas doublet will
sully. In Barbary, sir, it cannot come to so much.

Francis

What, sir? 75

Poins [*Within*]

Francis!

Prince

Away, you rogue! Dost thou not hear them call?
Here they both call him; FRANCIS *stands amazed, not
knowing which way to go*
Enter VINTNER

Vintner

What, stand'st thou still, and hear'st such a calling?

101

82. *Let . . . awhile:* 'Let them stand outside for a few minutes'.

86. *Shall . . . merry?* 'Shall we have some fun (at their expense)?'

87-8. *what . . . drawer?* 'what's the point of making such a fool of the barman?'

90. *I am now of all humours.* There are two possible interpretations of this important phrase: (i) I now understand all the various types of human nature and human beings or (ii) I am now ready to be in any frame of mind you wish. The first suggestion fits the Prince's preparation for kingship and contrasts him with Hotspur whom he talks about a few lines lower down, but primarily Hal seems to be enjoying amusing company and he is certainly slightly drunk. It is interesting to note that, even so, themes of honour and state affairs are not far from his mind.
91-3. *since . . . midnight:* since the world began.

96-7. *That . . . woman:* 'Isn't it incredible that Francis should have so little to say and yet be a human being?' Kate also called her husband a *paraquito* – Shakespeare seems to be comparing Hotspur and Francis in their mutual narrow-mindedness.
97-9. *His . . . reckoning:* 'All he does is run up and down stairs (with drinks) and all he talks about is bills.'
99. *I . . . mind:* 'I can't see the point of Hotspur's narrow ambition'.
100-6. *he . . . trifle:* Hal is, of course, very sarcastic at Hotspur's expense, but notice how closely these lines resemble the atmosphere of the previous scene between Hotspur and his wife.
101. *at a breakfast:* for breakfast.
washes his hands: carries on as if he has performed a routine action.
102. *Fie upon:* 'I hate'.

Look to the guests within. [*Exit* FRANCIS] My lord,
old Sir John, with half-a-dozen more, are at the door.   *80*
Shall I let them in?

Prince

Let them alone awhile, and then open the door. [*Exit*
VINTNER] Poins!

Re-enter POINS

Poins

Anon, anon, sir.

Prince

Sirrah, Falstaff and the rest of the thieves are at the   *85*
door. Shall we be merry?

Poins

As merry as crickets, my lad. But hark ye: what cunning match have you made with this jest of the drawer?
Come, what's the issue?

Prince

I am now of all humours that have showed them-   *90*
selves humours since the old days of goodman Adam
to the pupil-age of this present twelve o'clock at
midnight.

Re-enter FRANCIS

What's o'clock, Francis?

Francis

Anon, anon, sir.

Exit

answer
to question
95

Prince

That ever this fellow should have fewer words than a
parrot, and yet the son of a woman! His industry is
upstairs and downstairs; his eloquence the parcel of
a reckoning. I am not yet of Percy's mind, the
Hotspur of the north; he that kills me some six or   *100*
seven dozen of Scots at a breakfast, washes his hands,
and says to his wife 'Fie upon this quiet life! I want
work'. 'O my sweet Harry,' says she 'how many hast
thou kill'd to-day?' 'Give my roan horse a drench'
says he; and answers 'Some fourteen,' an hour after,   *105*

103

106-8. *I'll . . . wife:* This piece of play-acting does not take place.
108. *'Rivo!':* an expression associated with drunkards: the exact meaning is not known.
108-9. *Call in ribs . . . tallow:* 'Call in fat guts.'

Stage Direction. *Enter Falstaff etc.* A very important entry to which this scene has been leading up. Falstaff, of course, is in a bad mood after the fiasco of the robbery; Poins and Hal act very innocently, possibly standing behind him when he slumps on to a stool.

111-16. Falstaff prepares to accuse Hal and Poins of cowardice. Also, as always when things go wrong, he is in one of his repentant moods.
113. *nether stocks:* stockings. He claims that he will give up his wicked ways and take up the harmless occupation of knitting stockings, mending them, then wearing them mended, each of these actions being more humiliating than the previous one.
115-16. *Is . . . extant?:* 'Isn't courage and loyalty to be found anywhere?' This is another instance of Falstaff's wishing to turn standards upside down.

117-19. *Didst . . . sun's:* Titan is the sun. Hal compares Falstaff's huge red face buried in a tankard of sack to the sun's rays melting a dish of butter. He may also be referring to the perspiration still rolling off Falstaff's face.
119. *behold that compound:* 'look at that fat lump'.
120. *lime:* sometimes put in wine by cheating inn-keepers to increase their customers' thirst. Falstaff probably finishes his before pretending to notice it in the hope of getting a free drink!
120-30. In all these references to cowards, Falstaff pretends to ignore Hal and Poins while subtly making it clear about whom he is talking.
123-4. *Go . . . wilt:* 'nobody cares about me any longer so I might as well die any time'.
124. *manhood:* courage and manliness.
125-6. *shotten herring:* a herring that is thin after spawning.
126. *good men unhang'd:* Since in Falstaff's view it is virtuous to be a highwayman, the wicked men who insist on law and order have hanged the good men!
128. *the while:* these evil times.
128-9. *I would . . . anything:* Weavers often sang at their work and many of them were Puritans who loved psalms. The Puritans were an increasing minority of Protestant extremists who were frequently mocked for their piety during Elizabeth's reign.
131. *woolsack:* Hal's first speech since Falstaff's entry ridicules his fatness and wish to become a weaver.
132-5. *A king's . . . Wales!* Falstaff, furious at the Prince's 'cowardice', says that when Hal becomes king he and his subjects will be so weak that Falstaff will be able to drive them out with a wooden dagger (*lath*).

'a trifle, a trifle'. I prithee call in Falstaff; I'll play
Percy, and that damn'd brawn shall play Dame Mortimer his wife. 'Rivo!' says the drunkard. Call in ribs,
call in tallow.

Enter FALSTAFF, GADSHILL, BARDOLPH *and* PETO;
followed by FRANCIS *with wine*

Poins

    Welcome, Jack. Where hast thou been? 110

Falstaff

    A plague of all cowards, I say, and a vengeance too!
Marry and amen! Give me a cup of sack, boy. Ere I
lead this life long, I'll sew nether-stocks, and mend
them and foot them too. A plague of all cowards!
Give me a cup of sack, rogue. Is there no virtue 115
extant?

He drinks

Prince

    Didst thou never see Titan kiss a dish of butter,
pitiful-hearted Titan, that melted at the sweet tale of
the sun's? If thou didst, then behold that compound.

Falstaff

    You rogue, here's lime in this sack too! There is 120
nothing but roguery to be found in villainous man;
yet a coward is worse than a cup of sack with lime in
it. A villainous coward! Go thy ways, old Jack; die
when thou wilt; if manhood, good manhood, be not
forgot upon the face of the earth, then am I a shotten 125
herring. There lives not three good men unhang'd in
England, and one of them is fat and grows old. God
help the while! A bad world, I say. I would I were a
weaver; I could sing psalms or anything. A plague of
all cowards, I say still. 130

Prince

    How now, woolsack! What mutter you?

Falstaff

    A king's son! If I do not beat thee out of thy kingdom
with a dagger of lath, and drive all thy subjects afore

136. *whoreson:* literally 'son of a whore', and therefore 'bastard'.
round: fat and outspoken.

141-6. Confronted by Poins, Falstaff at once swears that he hasn't called him a coward – but then insinuates that he is one!

143-4. *you . . . back:* 'you don't mind who looks at that handsome back' but also 'you don't care from whom you run away'.

145. *backing:* sticking up for.

146. *backing:* turning your back.

150. *All . . . that:* Never mind that.

155. Hal seems to be innocently excited and quite carried away, for a while.

thee like a flock of wild geese, I'll never wear hair on
my face more. You Prince of Wales!   135

Prince

Why, you whoreson round man, what's the matter?

Falstaff

Are not you a coward? Answer me to that—and
Poins there?

Poins

Zounds, ye fat paunch, an ye call me coward, by the
Lord, I'll stab thee.   140

Falstaff

I call thee coward! I'll see thee damn'd ere I call thee
coward; but I would give a thousand pound I could
run as fast as thou canst. You are straight enough in
the shoulders—you care not who sees your back.
Call you that backing of your friends? A plague   145
upon such backing! Give me them that will face me.
Give me a cup of sack; I am a rogue if I drunk to-day.

Prince

O villain! thy lips are scarce wip'd since thou drunk'st
last.

Falstaff

All is one for that. [*He drinks*] A plague of all   150
cowards, still say I.

Prince

What's the matter?

Falstaff

What's the matter! There be four of us here have
ta'en a thousand pound this day morning.

Prince

Where is it, Jack? Where is it?   155

Falstaff

Where is it! taken from us it is: a hundred upon poor
four of us.

Prince

What, a hundred, man?

159-215. No doubt stimulated by all the sack, Falstaff now launches into a superb set of lies, with impromptu details, although he clearly planned something of the sort. The absurd contradictions are probably deliberate – Falstaff almost certainly knows that he will not be believed and does not want to be believed, perhaps even realising the trick that has been played on him. The escape into the delightful world of make-believe is what fascinates him and his imagination bubbles over into a masterpiece of comic story-telling. As his invention gets under way, his energy and enthusiasm will make him dominate the stage by his movements.

159. *at half-sword:* at close quarters.

162. *hose:* close-fitting tights.

buckler: shield.

163-4. *ecce signum:* 'behold the sign'. These words, used in the ritual of raising the Cross, are a daring piece of irreverence on Falstaff's part as he probably raises his sword like a cross.

164. *dealt:* fought.

164-5. *all . . . do:* 'all my efforts were not enough'.

167. *sons of darkness:* followers of Satan, because they lie.

174. *Ebrew Jew:* a thorough-going Jew.

175-6. Even Gadshill exaggerates, wishing their defeat to seem as blameless as possible.

177. *other:* other men.

180. *radish:* a symbol of leanness.

183. The Prince plays up to Falstaff's lies superbly.

Falstaff

I am a rogue if I were not at half-sword with a dozen
of them two hours together. I have scap'd by miracle. *160*
I am eight times thrust through the doublet, four
through the hose; my buckler cut through and
through; my sword hack'd like a hand-saw—ecce
signum! I never dealt better since I was a man—all
would not do. A plague of all cowards! Let them *165*
speak; if they speak more or less than truth, they are
villains and the sons of darkness.

Prince

Speak, sirs; how was it?

Gadshill

We four set upon some dozen—

Falstaff

Sixteen at least, my lord.   *170*

Gadshill

And bound them.

Peto

No, no, they were not bound.

Falstaff

You rogue, they were bound, every man of them; or
I am a Jew else, an Ebrew Jew.

Gadshill

As we were sharing, some six or seven fresh men set *175*
upon us—

Falstaff

And unbound the rest, and then come in the other.

Prince

What, fought you with them all?

Falstaff

All! I know not what you call all, but if I fought not
with fifty of them, I am a bunch of radish. If there were *180*
not two or three and fifty upon poor old Jack, then
am I no two-legg'd creature.

Prince

Pray God you have not murder'd some of them.

184. *pepper'd:* killed.
185. *paid:* finished off.

187. *horse:* ass.
my old ward: my favourite guard (in fencing). At this point Falstaff
starts to demonstrate his prowess.
188. *here . . . point:* 'this was how I stood and how I held my sword'.

193. *mainly:* strongly.

195. *target:* shield.

199. *hilts:* a sword-hilt, in the shape of a cross, was frequently used
for taking oaths.

202. *mark:* (i) pay careful attention to. (ii) keep count (of the number
of men in buckram).

Falstaff

Nay, that's past praying for: I have pepper'd two of
them; two I am sure I have paid—two rogues in buck- *185*
ram suits. I tell thee what, Hal, if I tell thee a lie, spit
in my face, call me horse. Thou knowest my old ward:
here I lay, and thus I bore my point. Four rogues in
buckram let drive at me—

Prince

What, four? Thou saidst but two even now. *190*

Falstaff

Four, Hal; I told thee four.

Poins

Ay, ay, he said four.

Falstaff

These four came all afront, and mainly thrust at me.
I made me no more ado but took all their seven
points in my target, thus. *195*

Prince

Seven? Why, there were but four even now.

Falstaff

In buckram.

Poins

Ay, four, in buckram suits.

Falstaff

Seven, by these hilts, or I am a villain else.

Prince [Aside to POINS]

Prithee, let him alone; we shall have more anon. *200*

Falstaff

Dost thou hear me, Hal?

Prince

Ay, and mark thee too, Jack.

Falstaff

Do so, for it is worth the list'ning to. These nine in
buckram that I told thee of—

Prince

So, two more already. *205*

206. *points:* (i) tips of swords. (ii) laces attaching hose to the doublet.

209. *came . . . hand:* pressed hard on them, sword in hand.
with a thought: as quick as thought.

212. *misbegotten:* bastard.

213. *Kendal green:* coarse green cloth, first made in Westmorland and usually worn by foresters and some servingmen.

216-74. The Prince has had enough of Falstaff's lies and delights in exposing them, hoping to embarrass Falstaff. However, not only does Falstaff's invention seem to gain the upper hand, he also brilliantly evades Hal's attempt to show him up. Behind the apparent playfulness there is considerable tension between the two men.
216-17. *These . . . palpable:* Hal likens Falstaff to the devil, who is known as the 'father of lies'.
palpable: obvious.
216. *begets:* invents.
218. *knotty-pated:* thick-headed.
219. *tallow-catch:* lump of grease.
220-1. It is Falstaff's turn to pretend innocence.

224. *your reason:* why you spin such a yarn.

227-31. With a brilliant stroke, Falstaff claims the right of the individual to freedom and poses as a hero in defence of that right.
231. *upon compulsion?* This is a reference to the use of torture to extort confessions. Hal and Poins are bearing in on Falstaff, probably cornering him in a threatening manner.
228. *strappado:* A Spanish military punishment in which the victim was tied round the body, hauled up by a pulley and allowed to fall part of the way to the ground, so that bones and joints cracked.
230. *reasons:* also suggests 'raisins'.

Falstaff
  Their points being broken—
Poins
  Down fell their hose.
Falstaff
  Began to give me ground; but I followed me close,
  came in foot and hand, and with a thought seven of
  the eleven I paid.   *210*
Prince
  O monstrous! eleven buckram men grown out of two!
Falstaff
  But, as the devil would have it, three misbegotten
  knaves in Kendal green came at my back and let
  drive at me—for it was so dark, Hal, that thou couldest
  not see thy hand.   *215*
Prince
  These lies are like their father that begets them—
  gross as a mountain, open, palpable. Why, thou clay-
  brain'd guts, thou knotty-pated fool, thou whoreson,
  obscene, greasy tallow-catch—
Falstaff
  What, art thou mad? art thou mad? Is not the truth *220*
  the truth?
Prince
  Why, how couldst thou know these men in Kendal
  green, when it was so dark thou couldst not see thy
  hand? Come, tell us your reason; what sayest thou
  to this?   *225*
Poins
  Come, your reason, Jack, your reason.
Falstaff
  What, upon compulsion? Zounds, an I were at the
  strappado, or all the racks in the world, I would not
  tell you on compulsion. Give you a reason on compulsion! If reasons were as plentiful as blackberries, *230*
  I would give no man a reason upon compulsion, I.

232. *I'll . . . sin:* Possibly the Prince means that he wants to hear no more of the robbery and the lies associated with it.

232-4. *this sanguine . . . flesh:* It is perhaps a sign of Falstaff's victory that he can make the Prince resort to this abuse.

sanguine: red-faced, whereas cowards were normally pale and white.

235. *Starveling.* This and all the following metaphors emphasize the Prince's slightness as compared with the massive Falstaff.

236. *neat's-tongue:* ox tongue.

bull's pizzle: the dried penis of a bull was sometimes used as a whip.

stock fish: dried cod.

238. *yard:* rule.

238-9. *standing tuck:* thin sword on legs.

240-52. Hal lets Falstaff have the last word and produces the truth in the hope that this will reduce him to confusion.

241. *base comparisons.* In fact it was Hal who started this.

246. *put you down:* expose your lies.

247. *out-fac'd:* bluffed.

250. *dexterity:* agility.

254. *starting-hole:* hiding-place.

256. *apparent:* obvious.

258-66. Although apparently driven to admit the fact, Falstaff once again turns the situation to advantage by claiming he knew Hal *on instinct.* He now poses as a courageous patriot and man of honour.

261. *Hercules:* hero of Greek legends and famous for feats of strength.

Prince

I'll be no longer guilty of this sin; this sanguine coward, this bed-presser, this horse-back-breaker, this huge hill of flesh—

Falstaff

'Sblood, you starveling, you eel-skin, you dried 235 neat's-tongue, you bull's pizzle, you stock-fish—O for breath to utter what is like thee!—you tailor's yard, you sheath, you bow-case, you vile standing tuck!

Prince

Well, breathe awhile, and then to it again; and when 240 thou hast tired thyself in base comparisons, hear me speak but this.

Poins

Mark, Jack.

Prince

We two saw you four set on four, and bound them and were masters of their wealth. Mark now, how a 245 plain tale shall put you down. Then did we two set on you four; and, with a word, out-fac'd you from your prize, and have it; yea, and can show it you here in the house. And, Falstaff, you carried your guts away as nimbly, with as quick dexterity, and 250 roar'd for mercy, and still run and roar'd, as ever I heard bull-calf. What a slave art thou to hack thy sword as thou hast done, and then say it was in fight! What trick, what device, what starting-hole, canst thou now find out to hide thee from this open and 255 apparent shame?

Poins

Come, let's hear, Jack; what trick hast thou now?

Falstaff

By the Lord, I knew ye as well as he that made ye. Why, hear you, my masters: was it for me to kill the heir-apparent? Should I turn upon the true prince? 260 Why, thou knowest I am as valiant as Hercules; but

262-3. *lion . . . prince:* It was believed that a lion would recognize instinctively a king or a prince and would not harm him. Falstaff thus ends with a compliment to Hal.

266-7. *But . . . money:* Triumphantly Falstaff returns to the world of reality.
267. *clap to:* lock.
268. *Watch . . . pray.* Falstaff mocks the phrase 'Watch and pray'. He in fact means 'Stay up tonight while the money lasts and pray for forgiveness tomorrow when it's spent'.

271. *play extempore:* an improvised play.

272. *argument:* plot.

278-80. It is ironical that, at the moment of Falstaff's great triumph, the outside world of harsh reality should interrupt the scene. It is the beginning of the pressure that the King, the Court, law and order will put on the Prince to make him lead a conventional life. Thus the arrival of the nobleman signifies eventual doom for Falstaff.

281-2. Hal's first reaction is to ignore the demands of the outside world.
281. *a royal man.* A play on words – a royal was a coin then worth fifty pence, a noble thirty-three pence.
282. *back again to my mother:* a meaningless phrase used simply to balance *comes from your father.*

285. *What . . . midnight?* Again Falstaff makes fun of the world of law and order.
gravity: serious-mindedness.

beware instinct—the lion will not touch the true
prince. Instinct is a great matter: I was now a
coward on instinct. I shall think the better of myself
and thee during my life—I for a valiant lion, and 265
thou for a true prince. But, by the Lord, lads, I am
glad you have the money. Hostess, clap to the doors.
Watch to-night, pray to-morrow. Gallants, lads,
boys, hearts of gold, all the titles of good fellowship
come to you! What, shall we be merry? Shall we have 270
a play extempore?

Prince

Content—and the argument shall be thy running
away.

Falstaff

Ah, no more of that, Hal, an thou lovest me!

Enter HOSTESS

Hostess

O Jesu, my lord the Prince! 275

Prince

How now, my lady the hostess! What say'st thou to
me?

Hostess

Marry, my lord, there is a nobleman of the court at
door would speak with you; he says he comes from
your father. 280

Prince

Give him as much as will make him a royal man, and
send him back again to my mother.

Falstaff

What manner of man is he?

Hostess

An old man.

Falstaff

What doth gravity out of his bed at midnight? Shall 285
I give him his answer?

Prince

Prithee do, Jack.

289-316. The Prince takes advantage of Falstaff's absence to drag the rather sordid background details from his companions. Somehow – which is no doubt the Prince's intention – this takes the glamour from Falstaff's triumph and reminds the audience of his unscrupulous nature.
289. *fair:* a marvellous fight. Hal is very sarcastic.

300. *spear-grass:* couch-grass. The leaves have sharp and rough edges.

302-.3 *I . . . before:* 'I did things that I haven't done for the last seven years'.

304. *monstrous devices:* outrageous tricks.

305-16. These lines concerning Bardolph's appearance depend on the current belief that a person's character was revealed by his features and facial expression.
306. *taken with the manner:* caught in the act.
307. *extempore:* spontaneously. Bardolph's face is fiery red in colour, especially his nose. He is also covered with pimples, carbuncles, boils. *fire:* Bardolph's face.

310-11. Bardolph points to his face.

313. *portend:* tell of my character.

Falstaff
Faith, and I'll send him packing.
Exit
Prince
Now, sirs: by'r lady, you fought fair; so did you,
Peto; so did you, Bardolph. You are lions too: you *290*
ran away upon instinct; you will not touch the true
prince; no, fie!
Bardolph
Faith, I ran when I saw others run.
Prince
Faith, tell me now in earnest, how came Falstaff's
sword so hack'd? *295*
Peto
Why, he hack'd it with his dagger, and said he would
swear truth out of England but he would make you
believe it was done in fight; and persuaded us to do
the like.
Bardolph
Yea, and to tickle our noses with spear-grass to make *300*
them bleed, and then to beslubber our garments with
it, and swear it was the blood of true men. I did that
I did not this seven year before—I blush'd to hear his
monstrous devices.
Prince
O villain! Thou stolest a cup of sack eighteen years *305*
ago, and wert taken with the manner, and ever since
thou hast blush'd extempore. Thou hadst fire and
sword on thy side, and yet thou ran'st away; what
instinct hadst thou for it?
Bardolph
My lord, do you see these meteors? do you behold *310*
these exhalations?
Prince
I do.
Bardolph
What think you they portend?

119

314. 'Too much drinking and no money.'

315. 'A hot temper, my lord, if I am correctly understood.'

316. Hal's answer plays on the word 'collar' in answer to Bardolph's *choler* and on the second meaning of *rightly taken* (legally arrested). He therefore grimly jokes that Bardolph is likely to hang one day.
317. *bare-bone:* skin and bones.
318. *creature of bombast:* (a) sack of cotton wool; (b) teller of tall stories.
318-19. *How . . . knee?* Since his conversation with Bardolph and Peto, Hal seems to be in a better – and more witty – mood.
322. *thumb-ring:* often worn by men of importance.
322-3. *A plague . . . bladder:* A marvellous inversion of 'Laugh and grow fat', and of the idea that sorrow was supposed to make a person waste away.
323-65. *There's villainous . . . answer:* Falstaff may not just be making fun of the rebellion. Possibly he is a little worried by what Hal's reaction to the news will mean for him personally. He is always very concerned to safeguard his own future, a fact which does not match his 'live for the day' attitude. The truth is that there is a sad side to him which emerges clearly later on.
324. *villainous:* dreadful.
abroad: made public.
325. *must to:* must go to.
327. *he . . . bastinado:* As a magician Glendower was believed to have the power of beating devils.
bastinado: cudgel.
Amaimon: a principal devil.
328. *and . . . cuckold.* Lucifer is the lord of Hell. A cuckold is a man whose wife is unfaithful; both were supposed to wear horns.
328-9. *swore . . . liegeman:* 'made the devil swear to be his loyal servant'.
329. *upon . . . hook.* Since the bill-hook has no cross-hilt, the magician Glendower tricked the devil.
334-9. *that runs . . . sparrow:* Between them, Hal and Falstaff make fun of the deeds of skill and daring that such soldiers as Hotspur and Douglas are renowned for, just as Falstaff has mocked Glendower's powers.

338. *You have hit it:* 'You have described it exactly.'

Prince

  Hot livers and cold purses.

Bardolph

  Choler, my lord, if rightly taken.   *315*

Prince

  No, if rightly taken, halter.

            Re-enter FALSTAFF

  Here comes lean Jack, here comes bare-bone. How
now, my sweet creature of bombast! How long is't
ago, Jack, since thou sawest thine own knee?

Falstaff

  My own knee! When I was about thy years, Hal, I *320*
was not an eagle's talon in the waist: I could have
crept into any alderman's thumb-ring. A plague of
sighing and grief! it blows a man up like a bladder.
There's villainous news abroad. Here was Sir John
Bracy from your father: you must to the court in the *325*
morning. That same mad fellow of the north, Percy,
and he of Wales that gave Amaimon the bastinado,
and made Lucifer cuckold, and swore the devil his
true liegeman upon the cross of a Welsh hook—what
a plague call you him?   *330*

Poins

  O, Glendower.

Falstaff

  Owen, Owen—the same; and his son-in-law Mortimer, and old Northumberland, and that sprightly
Scot of Scots, Douglas, that runs o' horseback up a
hill perpendicular—   *335*

Prince

  He that rides at high speed and with his pistol kills
a sparrow flying?

Falstaff

  You have hit it.

Prince

  So did he never the sparrow.

340. *rascal.* A deer that was poor sport to hunt because it refused to run away from its hunters. Falstaff is making fun of Douglas again.

344. *cuckoo.* Hal has repeated Falstaff's words.

348. *blue-caps:* Scottish soldiers. A scornful remark since blue caps were worn by servants in England.

350-1. *land . . . mack'rel:* In times of crisis people often sell quickly and the price of property drops suddenly.
352. *like:* likely.
352-3. *and . . . hold:* 'and if this rebellion takes place'.
353-4. *we shall . . . hundreds:* 'women will be easy to come by'. This is a reference to the likelihood of a drop in moral standards in times of disturbance.

356. *good trading:* successful business.
357. *horrible afeard:* horribly frightened.

360-1. *Doth . . . at it?:* 'Don't you tremble at the thought of it?'

363. *chid:* told off, scolded.
366-469. This play-acting is in part very close to the actual interview that takes place between Hal and Henry IV in Act III, Scene ii. Much of it is foolery and yet we feel that Falstaff, frightened about his future, is desperately trying to convince Hal that he is indispensable. He fails, and the scene ends on a grim note that anticipates the rejection of Falstaff by Hal at the end of *Henry IV Part II.*
366. *Do . . . for:* You take the part of.

Falstaff

Well, that rascal hath good mettle in him; he will not *340*
run.

Prince

Why, what a rascal art thou, then, to praise him so
for running!

Falstaff

O' horseback, ye cuckoo; but afoot he will not budge
a foot. *345*

Prince

Yes, Jack, upon instinct.

Falstaff

I grant ye, upon instinct. Well, he is there too, and
one Mordake, and a thousand blue-caps more. Worcester is stol'n away to-night; thy father's beard is
turn'd white with the news; you may buy land now as *350*
cheap as stinking mack'rel.

Prince

Why, then, it is like, if there come a hot June, and
this civil buffeting hold, we shall buy maidenheads as
they buy hob-nails, by the hundreds.

Falstaff

By the mass, lad, thou sayest true: it is like we shall *355*
have good trading that way. But tell me, Hal, art not
thou horrible afeard. Thou being heir-apparent,
could the world pick thee out three such enemies again
as that fiend Douglas, that spirit Percy, and that devil
Glendower? Art thou not horribly afraid? Doth not *360*
thy blood thrill at it?

Prince

Not a whit, i' faith; I lack some of thy instinct.

Falstaff

Well, thou wilt be horribly chid to-morrow when
thou comest to thy father. If thou love me, practise
an answer. *365*

Prince

Do thou stand for my father, and examine me upon

368. *state:* throne of state.

370-2. Hal means that Falstaff makes a clown of a king.
370. *taken for:* considered to be.
join'd-stool: a stool made by a joiner, therefore usually a reliable piece of furniture.

373-4. *an . . . moved:* 'if you haven't quite lost all finer feelings you will now be deeply moved (by your father's unhappiness)'.

376-7. *in King Cambyses' vein. Cambyses* was a well-known melodramatic tragedy of the time, and in Hal's and Falstaff's manner of speech Shakespeare seems to be making fun of a style of writing popular during his life-time. He does so in other plays, too, such as *Hamlet* (the First Player's speeches in Act II, Scene ii).
378. *my leg:* my bow.

379. *Stand aside, nobility.* Falstaff addresses the hostess, Bardolph and Peto, with a kind of pompous sarcasm.

382. *O, the father:* a mildly profane oath ('God the Father!').
how . . . countenance! 'what a solemn expression he has on his face!'
383. *tristful:* sorrowing.

385-6. *harlotry players:* good-for-nothing actors.

387. *tickle-brain:* feather brain.

390. *camomile:* a medicinal herb. Falstaff uses an irrelevant illustration of his argument (as King) that the more Hal wastes his youth, the sooner he will grow old.

the particulars of my life.

Falstaff

Shall I? Content! This chair shall be my state, this
dagger my sceptre, and this cushion my crown.

Prince

Thy state is taken for a join'd-stool, thy golden 370
sceptre for a leaden dagger, and thy precious rich
crown for a pitiful bald crown!

Falstaff

Well, an the fire of grace be not quite out of thee, now
shalt thou be moved. Give me a cup of sack to make
my eyes look red, that it may be thought I have wept; 375
for I must speak in passion, and I will do it in King
Cambyses' vein.

Prince

Well, here is my leg.

Falstaff

And here is my speech. Stand aside, nobility.

Hostess

O Jesu, this is excellent sport, i' faith!   380

Falstaff

Weep not, sweet queen, for trickling tears are vain.

Hostess

O, the father, how he holds his countenance!

Falstaff

For God's sake, lords, convey my tristful queen;
For tears do stop the floodgates of her eyes.

Hostess

O Jesu, he doth it as like one of these harlotry 385
players as ever I see!

Falstaff

Peace, good pint-pot; peace, good tickle-brain.—
Harry, I do not only marvel where thou spendest thy
time, but also how thou art accompanied; for though
the camomile, the more it is trodden on the faster it 390
grows, yet youth, the more it is wasted the sooner
it wears. That thou art my son I have partly thy

394. *trick:* expression.

395. *nether:* lower.
that doth . . . me: 'that provides evidence that I am your father'.

397. *art thou . . . at?:* 'have you made yourself so common?'
397-8. *sun of heaven:* Falstaff refers to the sun as the emblem of royalty. Cf. Act I, Scene ii, lines 185-91.
398. *micher:* truant.

402-3. *This pitch . . . defile:* This is another of Falstaff's Biblical references (*Ecclesiasticus* xiii, 1).

408. *noted:* noticed.

410. *an it like:* if it please.

411. *portly:* well-built.

413. *a most noble carriage:* a dignified demeanour.

415-16. *lewdly given:* fond of wickedness.

417-19. *If then . . . Falstaff.* More scripture. Falstaff compares his honest face to the fruit, his good character to the tree.
418. *peremptorily:* positively, emphatically.

420. *naughty varlet:* bad lad.

423. Again Falstaff has turned the 'interview' into a comic triumph for himself. The Prince insists on reversing roles to remedy the situation.
424. *Depose.* Falstaff, feeling pleased with himself, dares to use this dangerous word. (Hal's father was himself a usurper.)
dost it: i.e. play the part of the king.
425. *in word and matter:* in how you speak and in what you say.

mother's word, partly my own opinion, but chiefly
a villainous trick of thine eye, and a foolish hanging
of thy nether lip, that doth warrant me. If then thou *395*
be son to me, here lies the point: why, being son to
me, art thou so pointed at? Shall the blessed sun of
heaven prove a micher and eat blackberries? A question not to be ask'd. Shall the son of England prove a
thief and take purses? A question to be ask'd. There is *400*
a thing, Harry, which thou hast often heard of, and it
is known to many in our land by the name of pitch.
This pitch, as ancient writers do report, doth defile;
so doth the company thou keepest; for, Harry, now I
do not speak to thee in drink, but in tears; not in *405*
pleasure, but in passion; not in words only, but in
woes also. And yet there is a virtuous man whom I
have often noted in thy company, but I know not his
name.

Prince

What manner of man, an it like your Majesty? *410*

Falstaff

A goodly portly man, i' faith, and a corpulent; of a
cheerful look, a pleasing eye, and a most noble carriage; and, as I think, his age some fifty, or, by 'r
lady, inclining to three-score. And now I remember
me, his name is Falstaff. If that man should be lewdly *415*
given, he deceiveth me; for, Harry, I see virtue in his
looks. If then the tree may be known by the fruit, as
the fruit by the tree, then, peremptorily I speak it,
there is virtue in that Falstaff: him keep with, the rest
banish. And tell me now, thou naughty varlet, tell *420*
me, where hast thou been this month?

Prince

Dost thou speak like a king? Do thou stand for me,
and I'll play my father.

Falstaff

Depose me? If thou dost it half so gravely, so majes-
tically, both in word and matter, hang me up by the *425*

426. *rabbit-sucker:* skinned young rabbit.
poulter's hare: hare on display in a poulterer's shop.

427. How will Hal feel at acting a part which he will one day have to play in earnest?

432-3. *I'll tickle . . . prince:* 'My acting of the part of a young prince will amuse you'.

434-48. As Prince of Wales (perhaps as a result of being reminded of his eventual duty by Sir John Bracy's visit) and as 'King', Hal sees behind the humour and liveliness of Falstaff the essential menace to law and order that he represents. In terms of traditional evil characters that Shakespeare's audiences would be familiar with from the church's morality plays, Falstaff is described cruelly but realistically, and his later downfall is brought one stage nearer.
434. *ungracious:* ill-mannered.
434-5. *ne'er look on me:* 'don't dare to look me in the face again'.
435-6. *carried away from grace:* led astray.
437. *tun:* large wine-cask.
438. *trunk of humours:* huge body full of crude feelings.
439. *bolting-hutch:* a bin into which flour is sifted.
439-40. *parcel of dropsies.* Dropsy is a disease in which the body is puffed up with fluid.
440. *bombard:* leather tankard.
441. *Manningtree ox:* At Manningtree in Essex whole oxen were roasted at the annual fair.
442. *reverend vice:* hypocritical devil.
442-3. *grey iniquity:* dignified sinner (*vice* and *iniquity* were both names for the buffoon-like devil in the morality plays).
443. *vanity in years:* foolishly proud old man.
444. *Wherein is he good . . . ?:* What is he good for . . . ?
445. *cleanly:* skilful.
446. *cunning:* able.
449. *I . . . you:* 'I wish I knew whom your Grace was talking about'.

452. *white-bearded:* innocent-looking.

heels for a rabbit-sucker or a poulter's hare.
Prince
Well, here I am set.
Falstaff
And here I stand. Judge, my masters.
Prince
Now, Harry, whence come you?
Falstaff
My noble lord, from Eastcheap.   430
Prince
The complaints I hear of thee are grievous.
Falstaff
'Sblood, my lord, they are false. Nay, I'll tickle ye
for a young prince, i' faith.
Prince
Swearest thou, ungracious boy? Henceforth ne'er
look on me. Thou art violently carried away from 435
grace; there is a devil haunts thee in the likeness of
an old fat man; a tun of man is thy companion. Why
dost thou converse with that trunk of humours, that
bolting-hutch of beastliness, that swoll'n parcel of
dropsies, that huge bombard of sack, that stuff'd 440
cloak-bag of guts, that roasted Manningtree ox with
the pudding in his belly, that reverend vice, that grey
iniquity, that father ruffian, that vanity in years?
Wherein is he good, but to taste sack and drink it?
wherein neat and cleanly, but to carve a capon and 445
eat it? wherein cunning, but in craft? wherein crafty,
but in villainy? wherein villainous, but in all things?
wherein worthy, but in nothing?
Falstaff
I would your Grace would take me with you; whom
means your Grace?   450
Prince
That villainous abominable misleader of youth,
Falstaff, that old white-bearded Satan.

455-69. Falstaff's masterly defence of himself in pretending to speak as the Prince is unexpectedly moving, especially in the chant-like repetition of *banish not him thy Harry's company*.

458. *saving your reverence:* 'if your reverence will pardon the expression'.

whoremaster: one who employs prostitutes and makes money out of them.

462. *Pharaoh's lean kine.* A reference to the famous story in Genesis (chapter 41) in which the cattle (*lean kine*) seen by the Pharaoh of Egypt in a dream represented years of famine.

468-9. *Banish plump . . . world:* 'To banish plump Jack would be to turn your back on life itself.'

470. *I do, I will:* 'I do banish plump Jack, I will banish the world (of the common people).' This is a grim reply for Falstaff to hear, because Hal almost certainly says it in serious tones which do not fit into this apparently comic situation.

Stage Direction. *A knocking heard.* This dramatic sound from off stage breaks in on Falstaff's self-defence – it is the political world recalling Hal to his duty. The effect of the Sheriff's visit, although Hal protects Falstaff, is to cause the stolen money to be returned and to make him announce his intention of going to the wars.

471-2. *most monstrous watch:* unusually large number of watchmen.

473-4. Falstaff dislikes the interruption and, perhaps fearing the significance of the Sheriff's visit, wants more time to defend himself. Is he frightened that Hal may betray him?

476. *the devil . . . fiddle-stick:* what a fuss!

Falstaff
My lord, the man I know.
Prince
I know thou dost.
Falstaff
But to say I know more harm in him than in myself *455*
were to say more than I know. That he is old—the
more the pity—his white hairs do witness it; but that
he is—saving your reverence—a whoremaster, that I
utterly deny. If sack and sugar be a fault, God help
the wicked! If to be old and merry be a sin, then *460*
many an old host that I know is damn'd; if to be fat
be to be hated, then Pharaoh's lean kine are to be
loved. No, my good lord: banish Peto, banish Bardolph, banish Poins; but, for sweet Jack Falstaff,
kind Jack Falstaff, true Jack Falstaff, valiant Jack *465*
Falstaff— and therefore more valiant, being, as he is,
old Jack Falstaff—banish not him thy Harry's company, banish not him thy Harry's company. Banish
plump Jack, and banish all the world.
Prince
I do, I will. [*A knocking heard*] *470*
   Exeunt HOSTESS, FRANCIS *and* BARDOLPH
    Re-enter BARDOLPH, *running*

Bardolph
O, my lord, my lord! the sheriff with a most mon-
strous watch is at the door.
Falstaff
Out, ye rogue! Play out the play: I have much to say
in the behalf of that Falstaff.
    Re-enter the HOSTESS

Hostess
O Jesu, my lord, my lord! *475*
Prince
Heigh, heigh! the devil rides upon a fiddle-stick;
what's the matter?

480-2. *Never . . . seeming so.* This is a difficult passage but Falstaff probably means 'Don't make the mistake of taking me for a false friend when I am really most loyal to you; you, too, although you don't give that impression, are a true Prince who will not, therefore, betray his subjects.'

484. *I deny your major:* I deny your main statement.
484-5. *If you . . . enter:* Falstaff, putting a brave face on it, pretends not to care whether the Sheriff comes in or not.
485. *cart:* vehicle used to take men to their place of execution. Falstaff is therefore saying 'I can die as nobly as anyone else'.

488. *arras:* wall-curtain.
488-9. *up above.* What part of the Elizabethan stage would they use?

491. *date:* time-limit. Feeling more secure, Falstaff can afford to joke again.

494. *what . . . me ?:* 'what do you want with me?'

495. *hue and cry:* a public chase after thieves or other criminals.

Hostess

The sheriff and all the watch are at the door; they are
come to search the house. Shall I let them in?

Falstaff

Dost thou hear, Hal? Never call a true piece of gold *480*
a counterfeit. Thou art essentially made, without
seeming so.

Prince

And thou a natural coward, without instinct.

Falstaff

I deny your major. If you will deny the sheriff, so;
if not, let him enter. If I become not a cart as well as *485*
another man, a plague on my bringing up! I hope I
shall as soon be strangled with a halter as another.

Prince

Go, hide thee behind the arras; the rest walk up
above. Now, my masters, for a true face and good
conscience.   *490*

Falstaff

Both which I have had; but their date is out, and
therefore I'll hide me.

        Exeunt all but the PRINCE *and* PETO

Prince

Call in the sheriff.

        Enter SHERIFF *and the* CARRIER

Now, master sheriff, what is your will with me?

Sheriff

First, pardon me, my lord. A hue and cry   *495*
Hath followed certain men unto this house.

Prince

What men?

Sheriff

One of them is well known, my gracious lord—
A gross fat man.

Carrier

As fat as butter.   *500*

501-14. Notice how Shakespeare puts this passage into verse as Hal conducts the interview in an official and business-like way.

503. *engage my word:* promise.

508-14. What will the Sheriff's attitude to the Prince be? Does this conversation about the time suggest that Hal is mocking the Sheriff by stressing the fact that it is the early hours of the morning when the Prince should be asleep, or is this an indication that, as he returns to the world of the court, Hal becomes as interested in time as we saw Henry IV to be in Act I, Scene i?

515. *Paul's:* St. Paul's Cathedral.

517-18. Falstaff has probably fallen asleep in relief at his escape.

521. *Nothing but papers:* 'Only bills.'

Prince

    The man, I do assure you, is not here,
    For I myself at this time have employ'd him.
    And, sheriff, I will engage my word to thee
    That I will, by to-morrow dinner-time,
    Send him to answer thee, or any man,   *505*
    For any thing he shall be charg'd withal;
    And so let me entreat you leave the house.

Sheriff

    I will, my lord. There are two gentlemen
    Have in this robbery lost three hundred marks.

Prince

    It may be so; if he have robb'd these men   *510*
    He shall be answerable; and so, farewell.

Sheriff

    Good night, my noble lord.

Prince

    I think it is good morrow, is it not?

Sheriff

    Indeed, my lord, I think it be two o'clock.

            Exeunt SHERIFF *and* CARRIER

Prince

    This oily rascal is known as well as Paul's. Go, call *515*
    him forth.

Peto

    Falstaff! Fast asleep behind the arras, and snorting
    like a horse.

Prince

    Hark how hard he fetches breath. Search his pockets.

    [*He searcheth his pocket, and findeth certain papers*]

    What hast thou found?   *520*

Peto

    Nothing but papers, my lord.

Prince

    Let's see what they be: read them.

526. *Anchovies:* a snack to increase one's hunger and thirst.

527. *ob.:* a halfpenny (abbreviation of 'obolus', a small Greek coin).

529-30. *keep close:* hide.

530. *at more advantage:* at a more convenient time.

532-3. *thy place . . . honourable:* 'you shall have officer's rank'.

533. *a charge of foot:* a position of command over foot-soldiers.

534. *his death . . . twelve-score:* 'it will kill him to march a couple of hundred yards'.

535. *with advantage:* with interest.

536. *betimes:* early.

Peto [*Reads*]

Item, A capon	-	-	-	-	-	-	2s. 2d.
Item, Sauce	-	-	-	-	-	-	4d.
Item, Sack, two gallons	-	-	-	-	-	5s. 8d.	*525*
Item, Anchovies and sack after supper	-	2s. 6d.
Item, Bread	-	-	-	-	-	-	ob.

Prince

O monstrous! but one halfpennyworth of bread to
this intolerable deal of sack! What there is else, keep
close; we'll read it at more advantage. There let him *530*
sleep till day. I'll to the court in the morning. We
must all to the wars, and thy place shall be honourable. I'll procure this fat rogue a charge of foot; and I
know his death will be a march of twelve-score. The
money shall be paid back again with advantage. Be *535*
with me betimes in the morning; and so, good
morrow, Peto.

Peto

Good morrow, good my lord.

Exeunt

The scene
ends with Hal
make preparations
for the fight
against
the
rebellion

ACT THREE

SCENE I

The first two scenes of Act III show preparations for the campaign by the rebels and by the King. For the rebels the outlook is disquieting since the meeting reveals further serious deficiencies of character in Hotspur and to some extent in Glendower. The relationship between the two men is far from harmonious and only remarkable self-control on Glendower's part prevents an open breach.

1. *These promises:* promises of help from various nobles. Mortimer is reading documents as he enters.

parties sure: 'members of the plot are reliable'.

2. *induction:* beginning.

6. It is typical of Hotspur to forget a key document like this.

6-10. Glendower takes command of proceedings as the host, and pays Hotspur an exaggerated compliment.

11-12. Hotspur finds it impossible not to make fun of Glendower's elaborate courtesy.

13-17. People believed at that time that violent events and signs in the sky foretold marvels or disasters on earth.

14. *front:* face.

15. *burning cressets:* flaming torches.

18-20. Glendower's pompous attitude meets with cynical scorn from Hotspur and already we can see the clash of temperament between these two men.

18. *season:* time.

19. *but:* simply.

ACT THREE

SCENE I—*Wales. Glendower's castle*
  Enter HOTSPUR, WORCESTER, MORTIMER *and*
      GLENDOWER

Mortimer
 These promises are fair, the parties sure,
 And our induction full of prosperous hope.
Hotspur
 Lord Mortimer, and cousin Glendower,
 Will you sit down?
 And uncle Worcester—a plague upon it!   *5*
 I have forgot the map.
Glendower   No, here it is.
 Sit, cousin Percy; sit, good cousin Hotspur,
 For by that name as oft as Lancaster
 Doth speak of you, his cheek looks pale, and with
 A rising sigh he wisheth you in heaven.   *10*
Hotspur
 And you in hell, as oft as he hears
 Owen Glendower spoke of.
Glendower
 I cannot blame him: at my nativity
 The front of heaven was full of fiery shapes,
 Of burning cressets; and at my birth   *15*
 The frame and huge foundation of the earth
 Shaked like a coward.
Hotspur
 Why, so it would have done at the same season
 if your mother's cat had but kitten'd, though your-
 self had never been born.   *20*
Glendower
 I say the earth did shake when I was born.

22-3. 'and I say that the earthquake's occurrence was no indication that the world was fearful at your birth'.

25-6. Another sarcastic reply by Hotspur to Glendower's boasts.

27-33. *Diseased . . . towers:* It was formerly believed that earthquakes were caused when winds that had been locked below the ground tried to burst their way out. It is also, unconsciously on Hotspur's part, a telling account of the process of rebellion.
28. *eruptions:* outbursts.
teeming: productive.
29. *colic:* severe pains in the intestines.
31. *for enlargement striving:* in its attempt to escape.
32. *beldam:* grandmother.
33-5. *At . . . shook.* Hotspur cleverly implies that Glendower's birth produced a windbag!
34. *distemp'rature:* sickness.
35-49. Glendower's temper rises, but he manages to control it.

36. *crossings:* contradictions.

38. Does the exact repetition of line 14 suggest that this is a set speech which Glendower has carefully learnt in order to impress his listeners?

40. *clamorous to:* noisy in.

42. *courses:* events.

44. *clipp'd in:* surrounded.
45. *chides:* chafes, worries away at.
46. 'Who knows more than I do or has taught me anything?'

48-9. '(who) can follow me in the difficult processes of magic and keep pace with me in carrying out mysterious experiments in alchemy?' Alchemy, the form of chemistry practised in Shakespeare's day and earlier, had a large element of magic in it.
50. Hotspur's reply to Glendower's pompous but strangely impressive rhetoric once again shows up his lack of tact, his refusal to see or be patient with anybody else's point of view.
better Welsh: 'such utter rubbish'.

Hotspur
   And I say the earth was not of my mind,
   If you suppose as fearing you it shook.
Glendower
   The heavens were all on fire, the earth did tremble.
Hotspur
   O, then the earth shook to see the heavens on fire,   *25*
   And not in fear of your nativity.
   Diseased nature oftentimes breaks forth
   In strange eruptions; oft the teeming earth
   Is with a kind of colic pinch'd and vex'd
   By the imprisoning of unruly wind   *30*
   Within her womb; which, for enlargement striving,
   Shakes the old beldam earth, and topples down
   Steeples and moss-grown towers. At your birth,
   Our grandam earth, having this distemp'rature,
   In passion shook.   *35*
Glendower   Cousin, of many men
   I do not bear these crossings. Give me leave
   To tell you once again that at my birth
   The front of heaven was full of fiery shapes,
   The goats ran from the mountains, and the herds
   Were strangely clamorous to the frighted fields.   *40*
   These signs have mark'd me extraordinary;
   And all the courses of my life do show
   I am not in the roll of common men.
   Where is he living, clipp'd in with the sea
   That chides the banks of England, Scotland, Wales,   *45*
   Which calls me pupil or hath read to me?
   And bring him out that is but woman's son
   Can trace me in the tedious ways of art
   And hold me pace in deep experiments.
Hotspur
   I think there's no man speaks better Welsh. I'll to   *50*
   dinner.
Mortimer
   Peace, cousin Percy; you will make him mad.

53-69. With increasing solemnity Glendower lays claim to awesome powers; each time his pretensions are unceremoniously debunked until Glendower, to save face and avoid a furious quarrel, takes refuge in more practical matters.
53. *vasty deep:* vast sea.

58-9. *to shame . . . devil:* If the devil is the father of lies, then truth must shame him.

63. *unprofitable chat:* pointless banter.

64. *made head:* led an army.

67. *Bootless:* unsuccessful, without profit.
weather-beaten. Glendower implies that he raised by magic art the storms that drove Henry back.
68. *boots.* Hotspur, of course, puns on the word.
69. 'How the devil did he manage to avoid catching a fever?'
agues: fevers.
70. *Come . . . map:* We can feel the effort that Glendower makes at this point to keep control of himself.
our right: England, which is ours by right.
71. *our . . . ta'en:* 'the distribution which the three of us have agreed to'.
72. *Archdeacon.* According to Holinshed, the historian from whom Shakespeare gained much of the material for this play, this was the Archdeacon of Bangor.
73. *limits:* areas.
74. *hitherto:* to this point. Mortimer is indicating to the others the proposed boundaries on the map.
77. *bound:* boundary.
78. *coz:* cousin. They were, in fact, brothers-in-law, but the term 'cousin' could apply to various family relationships, and also to close friends.
79. *lying off:* stretching away.
80-1. The three copies of the agreement are to be signed by each of the rebels.
80. *drawn:* drawn up.

Glendower
    I can call spirits from the vasty deep.
Hotspur
    Why, so can I, or so can any man;
    But will they come when you do call for them?   *55*
Glendower
    Why, I can teach you, cousin, to command
    The devil.
Hotspur
    And I can teach thee, coz, to shame the devil
    By telling truth: tell truth, and shame the devil.
    If thou have power to raise him, bring him hither,   *60*
    And I'll be sworn I have power to shame him hence.
    O, while you live, tell truth, and shame the devil!
Mortimer
    Come, come, no more of this unprofitable chat.
Glendower
    Three times hath Henry Bolingbroke made head
    Against my power; thrice from the banks of Wye   *65*
    And sandy-bottom'd Severn have I sent him
    Bootless home and weather-beaten back.
Hotspur
    Home without boots, and in foul weather too!
    How scapes he agues, in the devil's name?
Glendower
    Come, here is the map; shall we divide our right   *70*
    According to our threefold order ta'en?
Mortimer
    The Archdeacon hath divided it
    Into three limits very equally:
    England, from Trent and Severn hitherto,
    By south and east is to my part assign'd;   *75*
    All westward, Wales beyond the Severn shore,
    And all the fertile land within that bound,
    To Owen Glendower; and, dear coz, to you
    The remnant northward lying off from Trent.
    And our indentures tripartite are drawn;   *80*

82. *execute:* finalize.

86. *As . . . us:* as we have been instructed.

89. *Within that space:* In that length of time.

92. *conduct:* keeping.

93-5. Glendower's romantic view of life demands that there should be great show of emotion between husband and wife. How does the relationship of Hotspur and Kate compare with Glendower's ideas?
93. *and take no leave:* with no formal farewell.
94. *a world of water shed:* much weeping. This is a beautiful but typically exaggerated phrase of Glendower's.
96-141. Hotspur has been peering discontentedly at the map. On discovering that he has, as he thinks, been cheated of his fair share, he again threatens to wreck the rebellion through a quarrel, this time for the sake of his 'honour'.
96. *moiety:* share, portion.
98. *comes . . . in:* curves into my territory.
100. *monstrous cantle:* enormous slice. The disputed area was probably in Lincolnshire and Nottinghamshire.
102. *here.* Hotspur indicates on the map his proposed new course for the river.
smug: smooth.

105. *so rich a bottom:* such fertile land.

107-11. Mortimer attempts to pacify Hotspur by pointing out that what he loses in one place he gains in another.
108. *bears:* follows.

110-11. 'cutting into my land across the river from you just as much as, further along its course, it cuts into yours'.

Which being sealed interchangeably,
A business that this night may execute,
To-morrow, cousin Percy, you and I
And my good Lord of Worcester will set forth
To meet your father and the Scottish power, *85*
As is appointed us, at Shrewsbury.
My father Glendower is not ready yet,
Nor shall we need his help these fourteen days.
To GLENDOWER
Within that space you may have drawn together
Your tenants, friends, and neighbouring gentlemen. *90*

Glendower
A shorter time shall send me to you, lords;
And in my conduct shall your ladies come,
From whom you now must steal and take no leave;
For there will be a world of water shed
Upon the parting of your wives and you. *95*

Hotspur
Methinks my moiety, north from Burton here,
In quantity equals not one of yours.
See how this river comes me cranking in,
And cuts me from the best of all my land
A huge half-moon, a monstrous cantle out. *100*
I'll have the current in this place damm'd up,
And here the smug and silver Trent shall run
In a new channel, fair and evenly;
It shall not wind with such a deep indent
To rob me of so rich a bottom here. *105*

Glendower
Not wind! It shall, it must; you see it doth.

Mortimer
Yea, but
Mark how he bears his course and runs me up
With like advantage on the other side,
Gelding the opposed continent as much *110*
As on the other side it takes from you.

112-14. Worcester, speaking for the first time, supports Hotspur. Why has he not attempted to control his nephew's tongue? Do Hotspur and Worcester put themselves and family pride before the success of the rebellion?
112. *a little . . . here:* a small effort will enable the river to be re-channelled at this point.

116-20. These short jerky lines give the feeling of tempers rising dangerously.

121-6. Glendower's pride, stung by Hotspur's insult, tries to put Hotspur in his place – by suggesting that Hotspur, although an English nobleman, is little more than a barbarian.
123. *being but young:* while still very young.
123-5. *I framed . . . ornament:* 'I set musical accompaniments on the harp to many beautiful English songs and in this way added to the beauty of the language'.
126. *virtue:* accomplishment.

127-35. Hotspur, priding himself on being a thoroughly masculine type, claims that he despises such cultural stuff.

130. *metre ballad-mongers:* hack song-writers.
131. *a brazen . . . turn'd:* the noise of a brass candlestick being shaped on a lathe.
134. *mincing:* namby-pamby.
135. 'It's like the dragging steps of a hobbled horse.' An appropriate comparison for Hotspur to make.
136. Again Glendower swallows his pride and gives way in order to save the situation. How does his behaviour tally with what is suggested of him in Act I, Scene i?
137. *I do not care:* Having got his own way, Hotspur pretends it doesn't matter.
137-8. *I'll . . . friend.* His reply to Glendower's generosity is another insult.

Worcester
    Yea, but a little charge will trench him here,
    And on this north side win this cape of land,
    And then he runs straight and even.
Hotspur
    I'll have it so; a little charge will do it.   *115*
Glendower
    I'll not have it alter'd.
Hotspur   Will not you?
Glendower
    No, nor you shall not.
Hotspur   Who shall say me nay?
Glendower
    Why, that will I.
Hotspur
    Let me not understand you, then; speak it in Welsh.   *120*
Glendower
    I can speak English, lord, as well as you,
    For I was train'd up in the English court;
    Where, being but young, I framed to the harp
    Many an English ditty lovely well,
    And gave the tongue a helpful ornament—   *125*
    A virtue that was never seen in you.
Hotspur
    Marry,
    And I am glad of it with all my heart!
    I had rather be a kitten and cry mew
    Than one of these same metre ballad-mongers;   *130*
    I had rather hear a brazen canstick turn'd,
    Or a dry wheel grate on the axle-tree;
    And that would set my teeth nothing on edge,
    Nothing so much as mincing poetry.
    'Tis like the forc'd gait of a shuffling nag.   *135*
Glendower
    Come, you shall have Trent turn'd.
Hotspur
    I do not care; I'll give thrice so much land

139-40. 'But when it's a matter of an agreement, do you hear, I'll stand up for my rights over the minutest of details'.

143. *I'll . . . writer:* 'I'll tell the clerk who is copying out the agreements to hurry'.
144. *Break with:* tell.

146. *doteth on:* adores.

147. *cross:* antagonize.

148. *I cannot choose:* 'I can't help it.'
148-55. *Sometimes . . . faith.* There was believed to be a prophecy stating that Henry IV was the *moldwarp* (mole), accursed by God, and that his kingdom would be shared by the *dragon, lion* and wolf, who represent in order Glendower, Percy and Mortimer. Glendower has obviously been trying unsuccessfully to convince Hotspur that their rebellion is in accordance with magical omens.
150. *Merlin:* the famous magician of Welsh legends.
152. *moulten:* whose feathers have moulted.
153. *couching, ramping:* Hotspur mocks the heraldic terms 'couchant' and 'rampant' which describe the appearance of animals used as symbols on a coat-of-arms or a shield etc.
154. *skimble-skamble stuff:* nonsense.
155. *As . . . faith:* As is beyond belief.
158. *lackeys:* slaves.
158-9. *I cried . . . word.* On the previous night Hotspur thought he had managed to avoid being rude to Glendower. Does his reference to this conversation partially excuse his rudeness during this scene?
159. *mark'd . . . word:* paid no attention at all.
160. *railing:* nagging.
161-4. 'I would much rather live in a windmill in an atmosphere of cheese and garlic than feed on delicacies and have him talking to me in any comfortable summer-house in the Christian world.'

165-9. *In faith . . . India:* Far from being bored, Mortimer is greatly impressed by his father-in-law. Are both men partially right in their judgement, or do you sympathise with Hotspur and find Mortimer weak and naive?
166-7. *profited . . . concealments:* most knowledgeable in the secret art of magic.

To any well-deserving friend;
But in the way of bargain, mark ye me,
I'll cavil on the ninth part of a hair.   140
Are the indentures drawn? Shall we be gone?
Glendower
The moon shines fair; you may away by night;
I'll haste the writer, and withal
Break with your wives of your departure hence.
I am afraid my daughter will run mad,   145
So much she doteth on her Mortimer.
                              Exit

Mortimer
Fie, cousin Percy! how you cross my father!
Hotspur
I cannot choose. Sometime he angers me
With telling me of the moldwarp and the ant,
Of the dreamer Merlin and his prophecies,   150
And of a dragon and a finless fish,
A clip-wing'd griffin and a moulten raven,
A couching lion and a ramping cat,
And such a deal of skimble-skamble stuff
As puts me from my faith. I tell you what: 155
He held me last night at least nine hours
In reckoning up the several devils' names
That were his lackeys. I cried 'hum' and 'well, go to'
But mark'd him not a word. O, he is as tedious
As a tired horse, a railing wife;   160
Worse than a smoky house; I had rather live
With cheese and garlic in a windmill, far,
Than feed on cates and have him talk to me
In any summer house in Christendom.
Mortimer
In faith, he is a worthy gentleman,   165
Exceedingly well read, and profited
In strange concealments; valiant as a lion,
And wondrous affable; and as bountiful
As mines of India. Shall I tell you, cousin?

149

170-2. 'He thinks a great deal of you and keeps a tight check on his words and behaviour when you clash with him'.

174. *tempted:* provoked.

175. 'Without suffering the dangerous consequences of his anger'.

176. *do . . . oft:* 'don't make a habit of it'.

177-89. Having said so little, Worcester possibly feels that he should go through the motions of being the stern uncle and deliver a few well-chosen words.

177. *too wilful-blame:* too much to blame on account of your head-strong nature.

179. *To put . . . patience:* to make him loose his patience completely.

181. *blood:* noble birth.

182. 'and that's the greatest benefit it brings you'.

183. *doth present:* is a sign of.

184. *Defect of manners:* Lack of courtesy.
want of government: lack of self-control.

185. *opinion:* conceit.

187. *Loseth . . . hearts:* loses popular support. Worcester wants Hotspur to learn the qualities of toleration and moderation, not for their own sake, but because, as organizer of a rebellion, he is well aware of the importance of public opinion.

189. *Beguiling . . . commendation:* 'depriving them of men's good opinion'.

190. 'Well, I am humbled by that little lecture: may good manners bring us success!' Hotspur, of course, is sarcastic.

192-226. The two marriages, of Mortimer and Lady Mortimer, of Hotspur and Lady Percy, are remarkably contrasted. The first gives us an extreme picture of romantic infatuation, almost a parody through the comedy inherent in the husband's and wife's total inability to understand each other. Set against this is the affectionate foolery of Hotspur and Kate, partners in a marriage which for all its lack of ceremony we have already seen to be solidly founded on love.

192. *deadly spite:* mean trick of fate.

197. *in your conduct:* among your followers.

He holds your temper in a high respect,   *170*
And curbs himself even of his natural scope
When you come 'cross his humour; faith, he does.
I warrant you that man is not alive
Might so have tempted him as you have done
Without the taste of danger and reproof;   *175*
But do not use it oft, let me entreat you.

Worcester

In faith, my lord, you are too wilful-blame;
And since your coming hither have done enough
To put him quite besides his patience.
You must needs learn, lord, to amend this fault;   *180*
Though sometimes it show greatness, courage, blood—
And that's the dearest grace it renders you—
Yet oftentimes it doth present harsh rage,
Defect of manners, want of government,
Pride, haughtiness, opinion, and disdain;   *185*
The least of which, haunting a nobleman,
Loseth men's hearts, and leaves behind a stain
Upon the beauty of all parts besides,
Beguiling them of commendation.

Hotspur

Well, I am school'd: good manners be your speed! *190*
Here come our wives, and let us take our leave.

          Re-enter GLENDOWER, *with* LADY MORTIMER
                    and LADY PERCY

Mortimer

This is the deadly spite that angers me:
My wife can speak no English, I no Welsh.

Glendower

My daughter weeps: she'll not part with you;
She'll be a soldier too, she'll to the wars.   *195*

Mortimer

Good father, tell her that she and my aunt Percy
Shall follow in your conduct speedily.

          GLENDOWER *speaks to her in Welsh, and she answers
                    him in the same*

198. *a . . . harlotry:* a moody, obstinate little minx.

200. *Welsh:* tears, i.e. expression of Welsh emotion.

201. *swelling heavens:* eyes swollen by weeping.

202. *I . . . in:* 'I understand only too well'. Mortimer says that, although he does not understand her words, he understands only too well her grief that he has to leave her.

202-3. *and, . . . thee:* 'and, except that my manhood makes me ashamed to do it, I also would weep with grief at the prospect of leaving you'.

203. *parley:* speech.

205. *And . . . disputation:* 'and that's how we converse through our feelings (since we cannot through words)'.

208. *highly penn'd:* written in a noble style.

210. *With ravishing division:* to an irresistible tune.

211. *melt:* weep.

213. *wanton:* green, fresh. Rushes were used as floor-coverings.

216. 'and soothe you to sleep'.

217-21. Glendower says that his daughter will lull Mortimer to sleep so gradually that he will hardly know the difference between sleeping and waking. This state will resemble the hour before sun-rise which is neither night nor day.

220. *heavenly-harness'd team:* the sun, which in classical legend was believed to be a team of horses and chariot driven across the sky by Phoebus.

223. *our book:* document of agreement.

Glendower

    She is desperate here; a peevish, self-will'd harlotry,
one that no persuasion can do good upon.
The LADY speaks in Welsh

Mortimer

    I understand thy looks: that pretty Welsh   *200*
Which thou pourest down from these swelling heavens
I am too perfect in; and, but for shame,
In such a parley should I answer thee.
The LADY speaks again in Welsh
I understand thy kisses, and thou mine,
And that's a feeling disputation;   *205*
But I will never be a truant, love,
Till I have learnt thy language; for thy tongue
Makes Welsh as sweet as ditties highly penn'd,
Sung by a fair queen in a summer's bow'r,
With ravishing division, to her lute.   *210*

Glendower

    Nay, if you melt, then will she run mad.
The LADY speaks again in Welsh

Mortimer

    O, I am ignorance itself in this!

Glendower

    She bids you on the wanton rushes lay you down,
And rest your gentle head upon her lap,
And she will sing the song that pleaseth you,   *215*
And on your eyelids crown the god of sleep,
Charming your blood with pleasing heaviness,
Making such difference 'twixt wake and sleep
As is the difference betwixt day and night
The hour before the heavenly-harness'd team   *220*
Begins his golden progress in the east.

Mortimer

    With all my heart I'll sit and hear her sing;
By that time will our book, I think, be drawn.

Glendower

    Do so;

227. Glendower summons the music apparently by magic. Where do you think the musicians would be placed in an Elizabethan theatre?

228. Hotspur has probably been watching the Mortimers. What have his feelings about them been? Do you find the situation between them moving and beautiful, or rather ridiculous?
thou . . . down: 'you're a naturally lazy devil'. Notice how in pretending to make romantic love to his wife Hotspur mocks the Mortimers.

231. Hotspur feigns astonishment at the playing of the musicians whom he cannot see. Therefore, he argues, it must be magic!
232. 'No wonder the devil is such a peculiar character (if he bothers to learn Welsh)'.

234-5. *for . . . humours:* 'for you are a thoroughly moody person'.
235. *thief:* rogue.

237. 'I'd rather hear Lady, my wolfhound bitch, wail in her most mournful way'.

241. 'I don't want to lie still either; that's a woman's typical weakness (when she ought to be working).'

244. 'What did you say?' She has heard really, of course.

And those musicians that shall play to you   *225*
Hang in the air a thousand leagues from hence,
And straight they shall be here; sit, and attend.

Hotspur
Come, Kate, thou art perfect in lying down. Come,
quick, quick, that I may lay my head in thy lap.

Lady Percy
Go, ye giddy goose.   *230*

The music plays

Hotspur
Now I perceive the devil understands Welsh;
And 'tis no marvel he is so humorous.
By'r lady, he is a good musician.

Lady Percy
Then should you be nothing but musical, for you are
altogether govern'd by humours. Lie still, ye thief, *235*
and hear the lady sing in Welsh.

Hotspur
I had rather hear Lady, my brach, howl in Irish.

Lady Percy
Wouldst thou have thy head broken?

Hotspur
No.

Lady Percy
Then be still.   *240*

Hotspur
Neither; 'tis a woman's fault.

Lady Percy
Now God help thee!

Hotspur
To the Welsh lady's bed.

Lady Percy
What's that?

Hotspur
Peace! she sings.   *245*

Here the LADY *sings a Welsh song*

247. *in good sooth.* An expression common at the time among the lower classes of society when attempting to appear well-bred.

248-57. Hotspur scolds his wife for using such 'common' language and this again shows up his narrow-mindedness, his almost snobbish insistence on class. It contrasts strongly with Hal's deliberate policy of mixing with all classes of society.
248. *Heart!:* sweetheart, probably.
249. *comfit-maker's wife:* confectioner's wife.
252. 'and swear in such an over-elegant, pseudo-ladylike way'.
253. *Finsbury:* Finsbury Fields was a favourite recreation spot for the citizens of London.
254-5. *Swear me . . . oath:* 'When you swear, swear properly and wholeheartedly'.
254. *lady:* lady of breeding and quality.
256. *protest . . . gingerbread:* weak exclamations.
257. 'to common folk in their Sunday best.'

260-1. *'Tis . . . teacher:* Hotspur laughs at his wife by saying that singing is the best way to become a tailor or singing-tutor to a robin.

262. *and so . . . will:* 'come and see me (to say good-bye) if and when you feel like it'.

265. *we'll but seal:* 'we only have to sign and seal'.

SCENE II

This is the critical scene of the play. Immediately following a scene in which we saw the harmony among the leaders of the rebellion threatened by temperamental differences, we now see the King and the Prince of Wales reach an understanding that will seriously menace the rebels' chances of success.
At the beginning of the scene, Henry IV and Hal should enter and stand in a way that will emphasize their estrangement. Throughout, Henry should take up positions on the stage which will allow the audience to see him shrewdly calculating the effect of his words on his son.

Hotspur

Come, Kate, I'll have your song too.

Lady Percy

Not mine, in good sooth.

Hotspur

Not yours, in good sooth! Heart! you swear like a
comfit-maker's wife. 'Not you, in good sooth' and
'As true as I live' and 'As God shall mend me' and   *250*
'As sure as day'.
And givest such sarcenet surety for thy oaths
As if thou never walk'st further than Finsbury.
Swear me, Kate, like a lady as thou art,
A good mouth-filling oath; and leave 'in sooth'   *255*
And such protest of pepper-gingerbread
To velvet-guards and Sunday-citizens.
Come, sing.

Lady Percy

I will not sing.

Hotspur

'Tis the next way to turn tailor, or be redbreast   *260*
teacher. An the indentures be drawn, I'll away within
these two hours; and so come in when ye will.

Exit

Glendower

Come, come, Lord Mortimer; you are as slow
As hot Lord Percy is on fire to go.
By this our book is drawn; we'll but seal,   *265*
And then to horse immediately.

Mortimer   With all my heart.

Exeunt

SCENE II—*London. The palace*

Enter the KING, *the* PRINCE OF WALES *and* LORDS

King

Lords, give us leave; the Prince of Wales and I
Must have some private conference; but be near at hand,

157

3. *presently:* very soon. This word and also 'anon' have become weakened in the course of time.

4-17. Henry IV speaks to his son, with carefully chosen words, as a father but also as a king who badly needs his son's political support. We therefore see in his speeches the same mixture of sincerity and calculation we noticed earlier, and he opens the interview in forceful terms designed to shock Hal into an awareness of his duty.

5. Possibly wishing to arouse Hal's pity, Henry carefully ignores his own past actions – the usurping of the crown, indirect responsibility for the murder of Richard II, as punishment for which Shakespeare sees the troubles of Henry's reign. This is clever of the King – he wishes, of course, to make Hal feel guilty.

6. *doom:* judgement.

out of my blood: in my own family.

7. *scourge:* torment.

8. *passages:* way.

10. *the rod of heaven:* This is a symbol of God's punishment.

11. *mistreadings:* sins.

11-17. *Tell . . . heart?* 'If this were not so, how could you, with your background of high birth and noble rank, find pleasure in the low life which you lead?'

12. *inordinate:* uncontrolled.

13. *lewd:* degraded.

attempts: activities.

14. *rude:* rough.

15. *As . . . to:* 'as you have lowered yourself to join'. Is Henry deliberately exaggerating the vileness of his son's life, or is he genuinely shocked?

16. *the . . . blood:* the nobility of your family background.

18-28. Stung by his father's attack, as the King intended that he should be, Hal tries to free himself of blame for at least some of the stories that Henry may have heard.

18. *would:* wish.

19-21. 'acquit myself of *all* faults with as clear a conscience as I am sure I can acquit myself of many of them'.

22. *extenuation:* lessening of blame.

23. *in reproof of:* by showing to be false.

devis'd: invented, false.

24. *needs must hear:* can't help hearing.

25. *smiling pick-thanks:* cringing flatterers.

base newsmongers: contemptible spreaders of rumours.

26-8. 'I may beg your forgiveness truly for those sins which, I admit, I have committed in my wild and irregular youth'.

28. *on . . . submission:* as a result of my sincere repentance.

29. *God pardon thee!* Henry IV finds it hard to forgive his son. He is less interested in Hal's moral guilt than in the practical, political consequences of his behaviour.

30-1. 'at your inclinations and interests which are totally different from those of your ancestors'. (The image is of a single bird breaking away from a flock.) This is ironical in two ways. Hal is to emerge as the great victor of Agincourt and in any case how 'noble' were his *ancestors*?

For we shall presently have need of you.

Exeunt LORDS

I know not whether God will have it so,
For some displeasing service I have done,   *5*
That, in his secret doom, out of my blood
He'll breed revengement and a scourge for me;
But thou dost in thy passages of life
Make me believe that thou art only mark'd
For the hot vengeance and the rod of heaven   *10*
To punish my mistreadings. Tell me else,
Could such inordinate and low desires,
Such poor, such bare, such lewd, such mean attempts,
Such barren pleasures, rude society,
As thou art match'd withal and grafted to,   *15*
Accompany the greatness of thy blood
And hold their level with thy princely heart?

Prince
So please your Majesty, I would I could
Quit all offences with as clear excuse,
As well as I am doubtless I can purge   *20*
Myself of many I am charg'd withal;
Yet such extenuation let me beg,
As, in reproof of many tales devis'd,
Which oft the ear of greatness needs must hear,
By smiling pick-thanks and base newsmongers,   *25*
I may, for some things true, wherein my youth
Hath faulty wander'd and irregular,
Find pardon on my true submission.

King
God pardon thee! Yet let me wonder, Harry,
At thy affections, which do hold a wing   *30*
Quite from the flight of all thy ancestors.
Thy place in council thou hast rudely lost,

159

33. Henry aims a deliberate blow at Hal's pride.

34. *alien:* stranger.

36-8. 'Your behaviour has destroyed any hope of your becoming a successful king, and everybody inwardly feels that y ur downfall is inevitable.'

39-84. Continuing to stress the political disadvantages of Hal's behaviour, the King contrasts it with his own policy when seeking the crown and tries to show how Richard II also was doomed by making himself cheap in the eyes of the people.

40. *common-hackney'd:* cheap through familiarity.

41. *vulgar company:* common crowd.

42. *Opinion:* public support.

43. 'would have continued to remain loyal to the existing king (Richard II)'.

44. *in reputeless banishment:* as a disregarded exile.

45. 'a fellow of no importance and no prospects of success'.

46. *stir:* appear in public.

48. *That:* so that.

50-1. 'And then (seeing my opportunity) I deliberately behaved to the people as graciously and humbly as possible'. Hal, as a result of his meeting with the barmen in Act II, Scene iv, also congratulated himself on having *sounded the very base string of humility* and on being accepted as the *king of courtesy.*

50. *stole.* Henry was, of course, a usurper, and this word suggests the illegality of what he was doing.

52. *pluck.* This word indicates Henry's deliberate stealing of popular support from Richard.

56. *like a robe pontifical:* like the richly decorated ceremonial robe of a bishop.

57-9. *and so . . . solemnity:* 'and therefore my few but splendid formal appearances before the public were welcomed by them as a treat and gained for me the people's loyalty just because of their rareness'. Compare with this Hal's policy expressed in Act I, Scene ii, lines 192-205.

60. *skipping:* frivolous. An apt word to describe Richard II's approach to his duties.

61-2. *rash . . . burnt:* 'superficial young men who had nothing of any permanent value to offer the king'.

61. *shallow:* petty.

bavin: firewood, particularly brushwood which ignites easily and soon burns out.

62. *carded his state:* cheapened his dignity.

64. 'found his royal title debased by the scornful laughter of fools'.

65-7. 'and allowed himself, at the cost of great loss of dignity, to laugh at boys' jokes at his expense and to be despised by every conceited young puppy who amused himself by mocking the king'.

69. *Enfeoff'd . . . popularity:* 'committed himself to the gaining of popularity'.

Which by thy younger brother is supplied,
And art almost an alien to the hearts
Of all the court and princes of my blood.   *35*
The hope and expectation of thy time
Is ruin'd, and the soul of every man
Prophetically do forethink thy fall.
Had I so lavish of my presence been,
So common-hackney'd in the eyes of men,   *40*
So stale and cheap to vulgar company,
Opinion, that did help me to the crown,
Had still kept loyal to possession
And left me in reputeless banishment
A fellow of no mark nor likelihood.   *45*
By being seldom seen, I could not stir
But, like a comet, I was wonder'd at;
That men would tell their children 'This is he';
Others would say 'Where, which is Bolingbroke?'
And then I stole all courtesy from heaven,   *50*
And dress'd myself in such humility
That I did pluck allegiance from men's hearts,
Loud shouts and salutations from their mouths,
Even in the presence of the crowned King.
Thus did I keep my person fresh and new,   *55*
My presence, like a robe pontifical,
Ne'er seen but wonder'd at, and so my state,
Seldom but sumptuous, show'd like a feast
And won by rareness such solemnity.
The skipping King, he ambled up and down   *60*
With shallow jesters and rash bavin wits,
Soon kindled and soon burnt; carded his state,
Mingled his royalty with cap'ring fools;
Had his great name profaned with their scorns,
And gave his countenance, against his name,   *65*
To laugh at gibing boys and stand the push
Of every beardless vain comparative;
Grew a companion to the common streets,
Enfeoff'd himself to popularity;

70-3. 'so that they (the public) soon had too much of a good thing'.

76. *not regarded:* ignored.

77. *blunted:* bored.
community: over-familiarity.

78-80. 'pay none of the special, respectful attention that dignified kings are honoured wit   when they make their infrequent appearances'.

82-3. *and render'd . . . adversaries:* 'scowled in the way that discontented men look at their enemies'.

85-7. *And . . . participation.* These are the key lines to which Henry has been leading, a direct comparison of Hal's and Richard's behaviour, with the implication of a common fate. Do you think Hal's present attitude justifies such an uncomplimentary comparison?

87. *vile participation:* 'taking part in the lives of ignorant, useless people'.

89-91. It is hard to know how much of this is sincere, how much it is an 'act', yet another part of the King's campaign to win his son's support.

89. *Save:* except.

92-3. The Prince's reply is very short, formal. Is this because the Prince is too ashamed of himself to be able to say more, or because he is becoming increasingly annoyed at the assumptions that his father's attack is making?

93-128. *For all . . . degenerate.* The next phase of Henry's tactics is to contrast Hal with Hotspur (see Act I, Scene i) in order to arouse Hal's anger and envy, and finally to insult his son by suggesting that he is capable of treason.

94. *to this hour:* in relation to today's circumstances.

97. *to boot:* as well.

98-99. 'his nobility and courage give him a far better claim to the throne than you have through simply being my eldest son'. Henry seems to be warning Hal that this is a world in which 'Might is Right'. (Compare his own succession.)

100. 'for, with no legal claim, nor even any outward appearance of legality'.

101. *harness:* armed troops.

102. *lion's:* king's.

103. 'And, being no older than you are'.

That, being daily swallowed by men's eyes,   *70*
They surfeited with honey and began
To loathe the taste of sweetness, whereof a little
More than a little is by much too much.
So, when he had occasion to be seen,
He was but as the cuckoo is in June,   *75*
Heard, not regarded, seen, but with such eyes
As, sick and blunted with community,
Afford no extraordinary gaze,
Such as is bent on sun-like majesty
When it shines seldom in admiring eyes;   *80*
But rather drowz'd and hung their eyelids down,
Slept in his face, and render'd such aspect
As cloudy men use to their adversaries,
Being with his presence glutted, gorg'd, and full.
And in that very line, Harry, standest thou;   *85*
For thou hast lost thy princely privilege
With vile participation. Not an eye
But is aweary of thy common sight,
Save mine, which hath desir'd to see thee more;
Which now doth that I would not have it do—   *90*
Make blind itself with foolish tenderness.

Prince

I shall hereafter, my thrice-gracious lord,
Be more myself.

King   For all the world
As thou art to this hour was Richard then
When I from France set foot at Ravenspurgh;   *95*
And even as I was then is Percy now.
Now, by my sceptre and my soul to boot,
He hath more worthy interest to the state
Than thou the shadow of succession;
For of no right, nor colour like to right,   *100*
He doth fill fields with harness in the realm;
Turns head against the lion's armed jaws;
And, being no more in debt to years than thou,
Leads ancient lords and reverend bishops on

163

105. *bruising arms:* harmful war.

107. *high deeds:* famous exploits.

108. *hot excursions:* violent attacks.

109-11. 'makes him acknowledged by all soldiers to be the greatest warrior and general throughout Christendom'.

112. *Mars . . . clothes:* infant Mars. Mars was the Roman god of war.

113. *enterprises:* campaigns.

114. *Discomfited:* defeated.
ta'en: captured.

115. *Enlarged:* set free.

116-17. 'in order to complete the ranks of great lords and generals who wish to defy me and destroy the security of my position as king'.

120. 'form an alliance against me and take up arms'. (*Capitulate* now has the almost opposite meaning of 'surrender').

123. '(you) who are my closest and most bitter enemy'.

124-8. Does Henry IV really believe in the likelihood of Hal's treachery, or is this a final, desperate attempt to shame or anger Hal into joining his father?

124. *through vassal fear:* 'through the cowardice that one expects of a slave'.

125. *Base inclination:* the instinct to act contemptibly.
start of spleen: fit of bad temper.

127. *dog:* cower at.

129-59. The Prince's reply is exactly what Henry IV wanted to hear and is the turning-point of the play. The picture he paints of himself is formidable; he emphasizes blood and violence, and suggests an almost mechanical efficiency in his will to win. We sense that here is too strong an antagonist for Hotspur.

132. The King's speeches have convinced Hal that the moment for clear-cut decision has arrived. In Act 1, Scene ii Hal announced his intention of *redeeming time when men think least I will*; now he promises his father to redeem his mis-spent youth by killing Hotspur.

135. *a garment all of blood.* This is a biblical image associated with the coming of the Redeemer to take vengeance on his enemies. It also, together with the *bloody mask*, presents a picture of cruel ferocity and power.

136. 'stain my face with blood'.

137. *scour:* remove (a stain).

138. *lights:* dawns.

139-40. *child . . . renown, gallant, all-praised.* From what we have seen in Act II, Scene iv, it is unlikely that Hal would regard these adjectives as an acceptable description of Hotspur. Probably he either says them sarcastically, or pretends to be serious in order to gratify his father's obvious respect and admiration for Hotspur.

his great reputation in arms

To bloody battles and to bruising arms.   105
What never-dying honour hath he got
Against renowned Douglas! whose high deeds,
Whose hot incursions, and great name in arms,
Holds from all soldiers chief majority
And military title capital   110
Through all the kingdoms that acknowledge Christ.
Thrice hath this Hotspur, Mars in swathling clothes,
This infant warrior, in his enterprises
Discomfited great Douglas; ta'en him once,
Enlarged him and made a friend of him,   115
To fill the mouth of deep defiance up
And shake the peace and safety of our throne.
And what say you to this? Percy, Northumberland,
The Archbishop's Grace of York, Douglas, Mortimer,
Capitulate against us and are up.   120
But wherefore do I tell these news to thee?
Why, Harry, do I tell thee of my foes,
Which art my nearest and dearest enemy?
Thou that art like enough, through vassal fear,
Base inclination, and the start of spleen,   125
To fight against me under Percy's pay,
To dog his heels, and curtsy at his frowns,
To show how much thou art degenerate.

Prince

Do not think so; you shall not find it so;
And God forgive them that so much have sway'd   130
Your Majesty's good thoughts away from me!
I will redeem all this on Percy's head,
And in the closing of some glorious day
Be bold to tell you that I am your son,
When I will wear a garment all of blood,   135
And stain my favours in a bloody mask,
Which, wash'd away, shall scour my shame with it;
And that shall be the day, whene'er it lights,
That this same child of honour and renown,
This gallant Hotspur, this all-praised knight,   140

165

To increase the shouting of defiance

This speech reads that up Harry's to stirs of us

mad) means I love you because you are my son but you Hotspur are my enemy.

142-6. The Prince wishes that Hotspur's good reputation and honour and his own bad reputation and sin were much greater still so that when Hal defeats him in battle he will gain even more from his death.

142. *helm:* helmet.

145. *exchange.* This will please the King who in Act I, Scene i had wished that he could exchange sons with Northumberland.

146. *His glorious deeds.* It is probable that Hotspur's achievements and reputation don't matter at all to Hal for their own sake. He does not intend to adopt Hotspur's view of life. The point is that the Prince, as politically shrewd as his father, knows tha t certain things are necessary for the sake of outward appearances – one of these is the killing of Hotspur to add popularly approved glamour and lustre to his own reputation.

147. *factor:* agent.

148. *engross up:* collect (rather in the way that one can collect medals, badges of honour, etc.).

149. *call . . . account:* challenge him so fiercely and kill him.

151. *worship of his time:* honour paid him during his life.

152. *tear . . . heart.* The savage strength of Hal's determination is obvious in this line.

154-6. 'If I fulfil the vows that I make here, I beg that you will forget the pain I have caused you by my wild way of life'.

155. *salve:* heal.

157. 'If I don't fulfil my vows, it will be because I have died in the attempt'.

cancels all bands: ends all contracts and obligations.

159. *parcel:* part.

160. The King's delight makes him echo the Prince's words in line 158.

161. *charge . . . trust:* a high position of command fitting your status as a future king.

Although the interview ends so successfully, it i s worth noticing that Henry still does not understand the reasons for Hal's past behaviour which were made clear to the audience in Act I, Scene ii and in Act II, Scene iv. Henry's concern is simply that he wishes to win the coming battle.

162. *How . . . Blunt.* Henry is now in the best of spirits.

Thy . . . speed: 'You look like a man in a hurry.'

163. 'The news I bring demands speedy action.'

164. *Lord Mortimer of Scotland.* Not the Mortimer in this play, obviously. Shakespeare, in fact, confused two people, assuming that the Scottish and English Earls of March had the same surname. This is the Earl of March who fought for Henry IV at Shrewsbury.

168. Notice the suggestion of doubt concerning the rebels' strength.

172. *advertisement:* news. As in Ac t I, Scene i, Henry IV seems to have the knack of knowing important information before anyone else does.

And your unthought-of Harry chance to meet.
For every honour sitting on his helm,
Would they were multitudes, and on my head
My shames redoubled! For the time will come
That I shall make this northern youth exchange   *145*
His glorious deeds for my indignities.
Percy is but my factor, good my lord,
To engross up glorious deeds on my behalf;
And I will call him to so strict account
That he shall render every glory up,   *150*
Yea, even the slightest worship of his time,
Or I will tear the reckoning from his heart.
This, in the name of God, I promise here;
The which if He be pleas'd I shall perform,
I do beseech your Majesty may salve   *155*
The long-grown wounds of my intemperature.
If not, the end of life cancels all bands;
And I will die a hundred thousand deaths
Ere break the smallest parcel of this vow.

King
A hundred thousand rebels die in this: *160*
Thou shalt have charge and sovereign trust herein.

Enter SIR WALTER BLUNT

How now, good Blunt! Thy looks are full of speed.

Blunt
So hath the business that I come to speak of.
Lord Mortimer of Scotland hath sent word
That Douglas and the English rebels met   *165*
The eleventh of this month at Shrewsbury.
A mighty and a fearful head they are,
If promises be kept on every hand,
As ever offer'd foul play in a state.

King
The Earl of Westmoreland set forth to-day,   *170*
With him my son, Lord John of Lancaster;
For this advertisement is five days old.

167

176-7. *by . . . valued:* 'according to my calculation and if I have correctly worked out the amount of business to be seen to in the meantime'.

179. *Our . . . of business:* 'We have a great deal to do.'

180. 'Every moment that we delay gives greater advantage to the rebels.'

SCENE III

In this, the last of the inn scenes, there seems to be a considerable change in Falstaff. He seems to be more depressed and to have lost much vitality. Whereas, before, he seemed almost to revel in his occasional bad moods and fits of repentance, now there is much less feeling of enjoyment, and his apparent attempt to cheat the Hostess is emphasized. It is as though he is overawed by the ominous ending (for him) of Act II, Scene iv, as though he senses that his hold on the Prince is slipping away. His movements and general demeanour should emphasize the contrast with the earlier scene.

1. *am I . . . away:* 'haven't I got thinner (and, possibly, gone into a decline)?'
1-2. *this last action:* the robbery.
2. *bate:* lose weight.
4. *apple-john:* old and shrivelled apple.
5. *suddenly:* at once.
while . . . liking: 'while I am in the mood for it'.
6. *out of heart:* in despair.
8. *peppercorn:* another shrivelled object.
9. *brewer's horse:* an old horse only fit for turning the stones used to grind malt.
9-10. *Company . . . of me.* This is a flash of Falstaff's wit. He is, of course, referring to the Prince.
11. *fretful:* upset.
12. *there is it:* 'you're quite right'.
13-14. *I . . . to be:* 'I used to be as good as a prosperous citizen needed to be'.
14-18. *swore . . . compass:* Falstaff is making fun of the easy-going morality that men adopt in order to lead a 'good life'.
14. *dic'd:* gambled.
15. *bawdy-house:* brothel.
17-18. *in good compass:* in moderation.

[handwritten: myself the King]

On Wednesday next, Harry, you shall set forward;
On Thursday we ourselves will march. Our meeting
Is Bridgenorth. And, Harry, you shall march   175
Through Gloucestershire; by which account,
Our business valued, some twelve days hence
Our general forces at Bridgenorth shall meet.
Our hands are full of business. Let's away.
Advantage feeds him fat while men delay.   180

Exeunt

[handwritten: means we got lots to do]

SCENE III—*Eastcheap. The Boar's Head Tavern*

[handwritten: The final scene in the Tavern]

Enter FALSTAFF *and* BARDOLPH

Falstaff

Bardolph, am I not fall'n away vilely since this last
action? Do I not bate? Do I not dwindle? Why, my
skin hangs about me like an old lady's loose gown;
I am withered like an old apple-john. Well, I'll repent,
and that suddenly, while I am in some liking; I shall   5
be out of heart shortly, and then I shall have no
strength to repent. An I have not forgotten what the
inside of a church is made of, I am a peppercorn, a
brewer's horse. The inside of a church! Company,
villainous company, hath been the spoil of me.   10

Bardolph

Sir John, you are so fretful you cannot live long.

[handwritten: means throw the dice,]

Falstaff

Why, there is it; come, sing me a bawdy song, make
me merry. I was as virtuously given as a gentleman
need to be; virtuous enough: swore little, dic'd not
above seven times a week, went to a bawdy-house not   15
above once in a quarter— of an hour, paid money that
I borrowed—three or four times, lived well, and in *[handwritten: gambling]*
good compass; and now I live out of all order, out
of all compass.

169

[handwritten: other people has corrupted me.]

21. *out of all compass:* far too big round the middle.

23. *Do . . . life:* 'When you do something to improve that red face of yours, I'll see about improving my life.'
24. *admiral:* flagship.
25-6. *Knight . . . Lamp:* Falstaff mocks the titles given to knights in the romances, which were a type of story popular at that time.

29. *death's head:* skull.
memento mori: reminder of death.

31. This is a reference to the parable in Luke (chapter 16) of the rich man *Dives* who was condemned to burn in hell for his lack of charity towards the beggar, Lazarus.
32-3. *If thou . . . virtue:* 'if you were a good man'.

35. *given over:* wicked.
36. *son . . . darkness:* a devil.

38. *ignis fatuus:* will o' the wisp. *is a small fiery light*
39. *there's no . . . money:* 'money is worthless'.

41. *links:* torches made of pitch and cheap fibres.

44. *as good cheap:* as cheap.
45. *chandler's:* a chandler was a seller of candles and torches.
46. *salamander:* a lizard which was supposed to live on fire. (The fire here is, of course, Bardolph's face.)

49. *be heart-burnt:* have indigestion.

Bardolph

Why, you are so fat, Sir John, that you must needs   20
be out of all compass—out of all reasonable compass,
Sir John.

Falstaff

Do thou amend thy face, and I'll amend my life.
Thou art our admiral, thou bearest the lantern in the
poop, but 'tis in the nose of thee; thou art the Knight   25
of the Burning Lamp.

Bardolph

Why, Sir John, my face does you no harm.

Falstaff

No, I'll be sworn; I make as good use of it as many a
man doth of a death's head or a memento mori: I
never see thy face but I think upon hell-fire, and   30
Dives that lived in purple; for there he is in his robes,
burning, burning. If thou wert any way given to virtue, I would swear by thy face: my oath should be
'By this fire, that's God's angel'. But thou art altogether given over, and wert indeed, but for the light   35
in thy face, the son of utter darkness. When thou
ran'st up Gadshill in the night to catch my horse, if I
did not think thou hadst been an ignis fatuus or a ball
of wildfire, there's no purchase in money. O, thou art
a perpetual triumph, an everlasting bonfire light!   40
Thou hast saved me a thousand marks in links and
torches, walking with thee in the night betwixt tavern
and tavern; but the sack that thou hast drunk me
would have bought me lights as good cheap at the
dearest chandler's in Europe. I have maintained that   45
salamander of yours with fire any time this two and
thirty years; God reward me for it!

Bardolph

'Sblood, I would my face were in your belly!

Falstaff

God-a-mercy! so should I be sure to be heart-burnt.

Enter HOSTESS

50. *Dame Partlet:* a name for a hen at that time. The Hostess is a good-natured, fussy creature.
50-1. *Have . . . pocket?* Falstaff refers to the time when he was asleep behind the arras in Act II, Scene iv. What did he have in his pocket worth stealing?

55. *The . . . hair:* the smallest thing.

59. *a woman:* a loose woman, trollop.

62. 'Don't deny it, I know your type well enough.'

65. *beguile:* cheat.
64-5. *and now . . . it.* Is the Hostess right?

67. *Dowlas:* cheap linen.
68. *bolters:* flour sieves made of cloth.

69. *holland:* a superior quality of linen.
70. *ell:* a measure of forty-five inches (no longer used).
71. *diet:* meals.
by-drinkings: drinks between meals.

76. *Let . . . cheeks.* Being so red, it is as if they could be transformed into gold.

How, now Dame Partlet the hen! Have you inquir'd   50
yet who pick'd my pocket?

Hostess

Why, Sir John, what do you think, Sir John? Do you
think I keep thieves in my house? I have search'd, I
have inquired, so has my husband, man by man, boy
by boy, servant by servant. The tithe of a hair was   55
never lost in my house before.

Falstaff

Ye lie, hostess: Bardolph was shav'd and lost many a
hair, and I'll be sworn my pocket was pick'd. Go to,
you are a woman, go.

Hostess

Who, I? No, I defy thee. God's light, I was never   60
call'd so in mine own house before.

Falstaff

Go to, I know you well enough.

Hostess

No, Sir John, you do not know me, Sir John. I know
you, Sir John: you owe me money, Sir John; and now
you pick a quarrel to beguile me of it. I bought you a   65
dozen of shirts to your back.

Falstaff

Dowlas, filthy dowlas! I have given them away to
bakers' wives; they have made bolters of them.

Hostess

Now, as I am a true woman, holland of eight shillings
an ell. You owe money here besides, Sir John, for   70
your diet and by-drinkings, and money lent you, four
and twenty pound.

Falstaff

He had his part of it; let him pay.

Hostess

He? Alas, he is poor; he hath nothing.

Falstaff

How! poor? Look upon his face: what call you rich?   75
Let them coin his nose, let them coin his cheeks. I'll

77. *denier:* A French coin of little value.
younker: young wastrel.

83. *Jack:* rogue.
sneak-cup: petty thief.
84-5. *if . . . so:* 'if he insisted that my ring was copper'.

Stage Direction. *Enter the Prince:* In view of the approaching war, Hal and Poins enter pretending to be soldiers. Falstaff joins in the fun with something like his old gusto.

86. *Is . . . door:* 'So it's to be war, is it?'

88. *Newgate fashion.* Newgate prisoners were chained together in pairs. Bardolph gloomily comments on the probability of their being killed in battle.

93. *let her alone:* 'don't listen to her'.

98. Hal assumes an innocent expression as he asks this question.

99. *bonds:* documents promising to pay sums of money to Falstaff.

not pay a denier. What, will you make a younker of me? Shall I not take mine ease in mine inn but I shall have my pocket pick'd? I have lost a seal-ring of my grandfather's worth forty mark.   80

Hostess

O Jesu, I have heard the Prince tell him, I know not how oft, that that ring was copper!

Falstaff

How! the Prince is a Jack, a sneak-cup. 'Sblood, an he were here, I would cudgel him like a dog if he would say so.   85

    Enter the PRINCE *marching, with* PETO; *and* FALSTAFF
    meets him, playing upon his truncheon like a fife

Falstaff

How now, lad! Is the wind in that door, i' faith? Must we all march?

Bardolph

Yea, two and two, Newgate fashion.

Hostess

My lord, I pray you hear me.

Prince

What say'st thou, Mistress Quickly? How doth thy   90
husband? I love him well; he is an honest man.

Hostess

Good my lord, hear me.

Falstaff

Prithee, let her alone, and list to me.

Prince

What say'st thou, Jack?

Falstaff

The other night I fell asleep here behind the arras and   95
had my pocket pick'd; this house is turn'd bawdy-house; they pick pockets.

Prince

What didst thou lose, Jack?

Falstaff

Wilt thou believe me, Hal? Three or four bonds of

102. *eight-penny:* trivial.

110. *stewed prune:* loose woman, because prunes were often served in brothels and low taverns.
111. *drawn fox.* A trick for catching foxes was to drag over the ground a piece of bacon rind soaked in a mixture largely composed of the entrails of a vixen on heat. Male foxes could not resist following the scent.
111-13. *and . . . to thee:* 'as far as womanhood is concerned, that disreputable character, Maid Marian, is thoroughly respectable compared with you'.
115. *a thing . . . on.* Unwilling to be drawn into detail, Falstaff produces a vague phrase that could be either compliment or insult.

116. *I am . . . on.* Not as clever as Falstaff, the Hostess assumes an insult and, in trying to put him in his place, says that she is *no thing* (nothing).

forty pound a-piece and a seal-ring of my grand- *100*
father's.

Prince

A trifle, some eight-penny matter.

Hostess

So I told him, my lord; and I said I heard your Grace
say so; and, my lord, he speaks most vilely of you,
like a foul-mouth'd man as he is, and said he would *105*
cudgel you.

Prince

What! he did not?

Hostess

There's neither faith, truth, nor womanhood, in me
else.

Falstaff

There's no more faith in thee than in a stewed prune; *110*
nor no more truth in thee than in a drawn fox; and for
womanhood, Maid Marian may be the deputy's wife
of the ward to thee. Go, you thing, go.

Hostess

Say, what thing? what thing?

Falstaff

What thing! Why, a thing to thank God on. *115*

Hostess

I am no thing to thank God on, I would thou shouldst
know it; I am an honest man's wife; and setting thy
knighthood aside, thou art a knave to call me so.

Falstaff

Setting thy womanhood aside, thou art a beast to say
otherwise. *120*

Hostess

Say, what beast, thou knave, thou?

Falstaff

What beast! Why, an otter.

Prince

An otter, Sir John! Why an otter?

H.IV.I—G

177

125. *where to have her.* Falstaff deliberately uses an ambiguous phrase. It can mean: (a) where you stand with her, (b) how to take advantage of her as a woman.

127. *where to have me.* The men laugh when the Hostess uses the same phrase, as it sounds as though she intends meaning (b).

131. *ought:* owed.

134. *Thy . . . million:* 'Having me as your close friend is worth a million pounds to you'. Another example of Falstaff's skill in slipping out of an awkward situation. (Is there any truth in Falstaff's statement *thou owest me thy love?*)

143-4. *but . . . whelp.* This is a similar evasion to the one in Act II, Scene iv, lines 258-64. Yet somehow it lacks the humour of the original joke.

Falstaff

    Why, she's neither fish nor flesh: a man knows not
    where to have her.   *125*

Hostess

    Thou art an unjust man in saying so: thou or any
    man knows where to have me, thou knave, thou!

Prince

    Thou say'st true, hostess; and he slanders thee most
    grossly.

Hostess

    So he doth you, my lord; and said this other day you *130*
    ought him a thousand pound.

Prince

    Sirrah, do I owe you a thousand pound?

Falstaff

    A thousand pound, Hal! A million.
    Thy love is worth a million: thou owest me thy love.

Hostess

    Nay, my lord, he call'd you Jack, and said he would *135*
    cudgel you.

Falstaff

    Did I, Bardolph?

Bardolph

    Indeed, Sir John, you said so.

Falstaff

    Yea, if he said my ring was copper.

Prince

    I say 'tis copper. Darest thou be as good as thy word *140*
    now?

Falstaff

    Why, Hal, thou knowest, as thou art but man, I dare;
    but as thou art prince, I fear thee as I fear the roaring
    of the lion's whelp.

Prince

    And why not as the lion?   *145*

Falstaff

    The King himself is to be feared as the lion. Dost

148. *I . . . break:* 'may I be called a liar'.
girdle: belt, midriff.

149-52. *O, if . . . midriff.* Hal, as before, cannot resist dwelling on the most revolting aspects of Falstaff's fatness.

154. *emboss'd:* bloated.

157-8. *if . . . but these:* 'if you had anything in your pocket of more value than this'.

159-60. *And yet . . . wrong:* 'And yet you will insist that you were robbed; you will not admit that you are a liar and the one who robs (by not paying your bills)'.

161-2. *state of innocency:* as in the Garden of Eden.

163. *days of villainy:* the present day. Falstaff protests that he can't be expected to be better than Adam.

167-70. *Hostess . . . still.* Falstaff, now in a good mood, adopts a lordly, forgiving air.

169-70. *tractable . . . reason:* a reasonable man when treated fairly.

170. *pacified still:* always ready to behave peacefully.
170-1. *Nay . . . gone.* The Hostess is naturally not satisfied. He has neither apologized for accusing her wrongly, nor paid her the money he owes.

172. *how . . . answered?:* 'how is that business settled?'

173. *I . . . . to thee:* 'I always have to protect you from the law'.

174. *the money . . . again.* Hal had assured the sheriff that it would be, but he also gave his word to the sheriff that Falstaff would be brought before the representatives of the law: he seems to have forgotten this.
175. *double labour:* double effort (of taking it and giving it back again).

thou think I'll fear thee as I fear thy father? Nay, an
I do, I pray God my girdle break.

Prince

O, if it should, how would thy guts fall about thy
knees! But, sirrah, there's no room for faith, truth, *150*
nor honesty, in this bosom of thine—it is all fill'd up
with guts and midriff. Charge an honest woman with
picking thy pocket! Why, thou whoreson, impudent,
emboss'd rascal, if there were anything in thy pocket
but tavern-reckonings, memorandums of bawdy- *155*
houses, and one poor penny-worth of sugar-candy
to make thee long-winded—if thy pocket were en-
rich'd with any other injuries but these, I am a villain.
And yet you will stand to it, you will not pocket-up
wrong. Art thou not ashamed? *160*

Falstaff

Dost thou hear, Hal? Thou knowest in the state of
innocency Adam fell; and what should poor Jack
Falstaff do in the days of villainy? Thou seest I have
more flesh than another man, and therefore more
frailty. You confess, then, you pick'd my pocket? *165*

Prince

It appears so by the story.

Falstaff

Hostess, I forgive thee. Go make ready breakfast,
love thy husband, look to thy servants, cherish thy
guests. Thou shalt find me tractable to any honest
reason. Thou seest I am pacified still. Nay, prithee, *170*
be gone. [*Exit* HOSTESS] Now, Hal, to the news at
court: for the robbery, lad, how is that answered?

Prince

O, my sweet beef, I must still be good angel to thee:
the money is paid back again.

Falstaff

O, I do not like that paying back; 'tis a double labour. *175*

Prince

I am good friends with my father, and may do

181

179. *with unwash'd hands:* immediately, i.e. without pausing even to wash his hands.

181. *a charge of foot:* the position of officer of a troop of infantry.

182-7. *Where . . . praise them.* Falstaff's natural reaction to the civil war is that of a profiteer. Like all such men, he cares nothing for the political aspect of things but is merely glad of the chance of plunder. This continues the tendency of this scene to emphasize the disruptive, self-seeking aspect of Falstaff that tends to drag the Prince down.
184-5. *heinously unprovided:* disgracefully ill-equipped.
186. *they . . . virtuous:* 'the only people they hurt are the good men (because the rebels destroy the peace and national prosperity)'.
laud: praise.

188-99. Notice the Prince's brisk, business-like way of giving orders now that the time for action has arrived. From line 176 to the end of the scene, he either ignores Falstaff or speaks to him in short, detached sentences. It is as though he sees Falstaff as irrelevant in the present situation; his interest in him is confined to fulfilling his earlier promise to cause him discomfort by making him an infantry officer.

196. *thy charge:* who your troops are to be.

197. *order . . . furniture:* instructions concerning their equipment. As Falstaff's troops were not regular soldiers they would have to be provided with equipment by their officer.

200-1. Falstaff, left alone, is probably sarcastic in this comment on the Prince's military flourish in lines 198-9. He does not want to fight nobly and consoles himself by ordering his breakfast, wishing that the inn could be the only scene of his campaigns (i.e., eating and drinking).

anything.

Falstaff

Rob me the exchequer the first thing thou doest, and
do it with unwash'd hands too.

Bardolph

Do, my lord.   *180*

Prince

I have procured thee, Jack, a charge of foot.

Falstaff

I would it had been of horse. Where shall I find one
that can steal well? O for a fine thief, of the age of
two and twenty or thereabouts! I am heinously unprovided. Well, God be thanked for these rebels— *185*
they offend none but the virtuous; I laud them, I
praise them.

Prince

Bardolph!

Bardolph

My lord?

Prince

Go bear this letter to Lord John of Lancaster,   *190*
To my brother John; this to my Lord of Westmoreland.

Exit BARDOLPH

Go, Peto, to horse, to horse; for thou and I
Have thirty miles to ride yet ere dinner-time.

Exit PETO

Jack, meet me to-morrow in the Temple Hall
At two o'clock in the afternoon;   *195*
There shalt thou know thy charge, and there receive
Money and order for their furniture.
The land is burning; Percy stands on high;
And either we or they must lower lie.

Exit

Falstaff

Rare words! brave world! Hostess, my breakfast, come! *200*
O, I could wish this tavern were my drum!

ACT FOUR

SCENE I

The last two acts of the play take place either at Shrewsbury, near it, or on roads leading to it. This scene shows the increasing weakness of the rebel movement. Notice the reactions of the leaders to their deteriorating situation.

1-13. As he becomes involved in the political scene, greater weaknesses and superficiality appear in Hotspur. Claiming to be above flattery, he in fact flatters Douglas in a fulsome and hollow-sounding way; both men seem embarrassed and ill at ease.

1-5. *If . . . world:* 'If, in this so-called civilized age of ours, a man were not immediately suspected of insincerity the moment he praises anyone, I would insist that no soldier of this time should be given as much widespread recognition for his great achievements as you.'

3. *attribution:* praise.

6-7. *I do . . . soothers:* 'I despise men who flatter others'.

7-8. *but . . . yourself:* 'but I admire no-one's courage as much as yours'.

9. *task . . . word:* 'put my words to the proof'.

approve me: 'test my sincerity'.

11. *potent:* mighty.

12. *beard:* challenge.

13. *I can . . . you.* Hotspur weakly acknowledges Douglas's praise.

14-85. Hotspur's reaction to the news of his father's sickness is at first sensible as he instinctively realizes the seriousness of his absence. Almost at once, however, he swings to the opposite extreme. His bravery is undoubted but his logic absurd, and his forced optimism reveals the uncertainty and fear inside himself which he dare not recognize.

16. *grievous:* seriously.

17-18. *how . . . time ?* An instinctive reaction in Hotspur's best manner. It shows vividly the active, healthy man's intolerance of sickness.

18. *justling:* busy, critical. (It also suggests the pushing and shoving of self-seekers.)

19. *government:* command.

[handwritten: Hotspur admires Douglas because Douglas is a Warrior]

ACT FOUR

SCENE I—*The rebel camp near Shrewsbury*

Enter HOTSPUR, WORCESTER *and* DOUGLAS

Hotspur
    Well said, my noble Scot. If speaking truth
    In this fine age were not thought flattery,
    Such attribution should the Douglas have
    As not a soldier of this season's stamp
    Should go so general current through the world.   5
    By God, I cannot flatter; I do defy
    The tongues of soothers; but a braver place
    In my heart's love hath no man than yourself.
    Nay, task me to my word; approve me, lord.
Douglas
    Thou art the king of honour: 10
    No man so potent breathes upon the ground
    But I will beard him.
Hotspur   Do so, and 'tis well.
    Enter a MESSENGER *with letters*
    What letters hast thou there?—I can but thank you.
Messenger
    These letters come from your father.
Hotspur
    Letters from him! Why comes he not himself?   15
Messenger
    He cannot come, my lord, he is grievous sick.
Hotspur
    Zounds! how has he the leisure to be sick
    In such a justling time? Who leads his power?
    Under whose government come they along?

185

[handwritten: Who's bringing up his army]

20. *bears his mind:* contains the information. Hotspur is too impatient to read the letters.

24. 'his doctors were most concerned about him'.

25-6. 'I wish he could have waited until we had won before falling sick'.

27. *better worth:* of more value. Worcester's shrewd mind at once grasps the danger.

28-30. Stunned by the news, Hotspur is in despair too – for the time being. 'This sickness (of my father's) is a fatal blow and will infect the morale of the troops in camp.'

31. *inward sickness:* sickness of the mind. Northumberland's illness seems to have been caused by his fear concerning the rebellion. Does Hotspur's realization of this explain why he stops reading in mid-sentence?

32-5. 'and that his troops couldn't be called up quickly enough by his deputizing officers; and he didn't think he should ask anyone outside their small circle to take on such responsibility'. Northumberland seems to give as many reasons for the absence of his troops as possible. What does this suggest?

36. *bold advertisement:* advice to carry on courageously.

37. *conjunction:* united army.

on: proceed.

39. *there is no quailing now:* 'we can't feebly go back on our intentions now'.

40. *possess'd:* informed.

41. *What . . . it?* For once, Hotspur is at a loss for words.

42. *maim:* very serious loss. To go into battle without Northumberland and his army will be like a man trying to fight without an arm or a leg.

44. *And yet . . . not:* After a moment's silence Hotspur's mood changes to one of over-optimism.

44-5. *His . . . find it:* 'His absence is not as crippling as it seems.'

45-8. 'Is it a good idea to risk all our fortunes at one time and gamble with everything we have in one chancy battle?' Despite himself, Hotspur is forced to admit that a gamble is involved (*cast, set* and *hazard* are all gambling terms).

49-52. This new-found awareness is very different from his earlier extravagant love of danger, especially as expressed in Act I, Scene iii, lines 194-8.

49. *read:* see, understand.

Messenger
  His letters bears his mind, not I, my lord.   **20**
Worcester
  I prithee tell me, doth he keep his bed?
Messenger
  He did, my lord, four days ere I set forth;
  And at the time of my departure thence
  He was much fear'd by his physicians.
Worcester
  I would the state of time had first been whole   **25**
  Ere he by sickness had been visited:
  His health was never better worth than now.
Hotspur
  Sick now! droop now! This sickness doth infect
  The very life-blood of our enterprise;
  'Tis catching hither, even to our camp.   **30**
  He writes me here that inward sickness—
  And that his friends by deputation could not
  So soon be drawn; nor did he think it meet
  To lay so dangerous and dear a trust
  On any soul remov'd, but on his own.   **35**
  Yet doth he give us bold advertisement
  That with our small conjunction we should on,
  To see how fortune is dispos'd to us;
  For, as he writes, there is no quailing now,
  Because the King is certainly possess'd   **40**
  Of all our purposes. What say you to it?
Worcester
  Your father's sickness is a maim to us.
Hotspur
  A perilous gash, a very limb lopp'd off.
  And yet, in faith, it is not. His present want
  Seems more than we shall find it. Were it good   **45**
  To set the exact wealth of all our states
  All at one cast? To set so rich a main
  On the nice hazard of one doubtful hour?
  It were not good; for therein should we read

50. 'the final result of all our hopes'.

51. *list:* extreme fate.
bound: limit.

52-6. Douglas eagerly catches on to Hotspur's argument.

53. *sweet reversion:* welcome second line of attack to fall back on. A *reversion* is a legacy, which explains the meaning of lines 54 and 55.

56. 'It is good to know that we shall have further support if we need it.' (Strictly, a comfortable place to retire to.)

58. *mischance:* bad luck.
look big: threaten.
59. *maidenhead:* first stage.

60-75. Worcester's intelligence refuses to be weakened by the illogical arguments of men naively trying to comfort themselves. He is forced to admit that the illegality of their rebellion makes it inevitable that public support will only be retained if the facts are kept hidden. The fact that Worcester, having perceived the truth, remains implacable shows him to be a ruthless adventurer, aiming to overthrow the king to make himself powerful.
61-2. *The . . . division:* 'The character of our attack on the king will not safely allow us to divide our forces or give any outward sign of disagreement.'
66-8. 'and think how such thoughts could lose us the support of our more half-hearted, timid allies and raise doubts concerning the justice of our cause'.
69-72. 'for you know very well that, as the aggressors, we cannot allow people to judge our motives fairly. We must close up every chink of weakness through which ordinary people (who normally know that the right and reasonable policy for a citizen is to support the king) may be able to pry into our affairs'.
70. *arbitrement:* judgement.
71. *loop:* loop-hole.
73-5. 'The common people may see through the gap left by your father's absence the presence of fear in our ranks, something that previously they never thought possible in us.' Worcester's image is that of a tightly shuttered and curtained house in which the rebels must live in order to stop outsiders observing them.
75. *You . . . far:* 'You are making a lot of fuss about nothing.'
77. *lustre:* glamour.
more great opinion: nobler reputation.
79. *men must think.* Although his logic is wrong, Hotspur has become as aware as everyone else in the play (except Falstaff) of the importance of public opinion.

The very bottom and the soul of hope,   *50*
The very list, the very utmost bound
Of all our fortunes.
Douglas   Faith, and so we should;
Where now remains a sweet reversion.   → *means inheritance*
We may boldly spend upon the hope of what
Is to come in.   *55*
A comfort of retirement lives in this.

Hotspur
A rendezvous, a home to fly unto,
If that the devil and mischance look big
Upon the maidenhead of our affairs.   → *beginning of our Affairs*

Worcester
But yet I would your father had been here.   *60*
The quality and hair of our attempt
Brooks no division. It will be thought
By some, that know not why he is away,
That wisdom, loyalty, and mere dislike
Of our proceedings, kept the earl from hence;   *65*
And think how such an apprehension
May turn the tide of fearful faction   → *means of the timid rebellion*
And breed a kind of question in our cause;
For well you know we of the off'ring side
Must keep aloof from strict arbitrement,   *70*
And stop all sight-holes, every loop from whence
The eye of reason may pry in upon us.
This absence of your father's draws a curtain
That shows the ignorant a kind of fear
Before not dreamt of.
Hotspur   You strain too far.   → *you are taxing things to far*   *75*
I rather of his absence make this use:
It lends a lustre and more great opinion,
A larger dare to our great enterprise,
Than if the earl were here; for men must think,
If we, without his help, can make a head   *80*
To push against a kingdom, with his help
We shall o'erturn it topsy-turvy down.

189

close all sight-holes

83. Hotspur contradicts line 43. His love of danger and honour makes him ignore good sense and his lack of right-thinking is also betrayed by his rejoicing in the prospect of turning the state *topsy-turvy down* just as Falstaff revels in the thought of evil becoming good.

84-5. Foolish as he is, Douglas is undoubtedly brave. And he cannot be condemned in the way that Worcester and Hotspur can – he is a Scotsman and Scotland was a separate country and a traditional enemy of England. It is civil war and rebellion that is unforgivable.

92. *intended:* plans to set out.

95. *nimble-footed:* cowardly. Hotspur describes Hal in much the same way that Henry IV described Richard II in Act III, Scene ii.

96-7. *daff'd . . . pass:* 'ignored the serious matters of life and wasted their time'.

97-110. This remarkable speech describes the Prince in rich terms that celebrate his recent determination to do his duty. He is pictured as the perfect image of a Renaissance ruler – *eagles, gold, sun, Mercury* are all images of royalty and godliness. Even Vernon, a rebel, is overwhelmed by Hal's power and magnificence. He is a symbol of the united forces of the king contrasted with the increasingly divided rebel troops.

97. *furnish'd:* equipped.

98-9. A difficult passage but probably it means 'all of them wearing large ostrich-like plumes that fluttered in the wind like the feathers of eagles fresh from bathing'. Old stories told of eagles renewing their youth by bathing in a fountain and preening themselves in the sun.

99. *Bated:* fluttered.

100. *images.* A reference to the rich vestments with which statues of saints in churches were decked. This word brings out religious ideas of spiritual rebirth. (Remember the frequent use of the word *redeem*.)

102. Hal now resembles the sun, which indicates the working of his plan (see Act I, Scene ii, line 85-91).

gorgeous: glorious in rich attire.

103. *Wanton:* lively.

104. *beaver:* helmet.

105. *cushes:* cuisses, pieces of thigh armour.

106. *feathered Mercury.* The messenger god of the Romans is always shown as a young man with wings on his helmet and sandals.

109. *turn, wind:* manage, control. Pegasus was a winged horse of ancient Greek and Roman legend.

110. *witch:* bewitch, dazzle.

Yet all goes well, yet all our joints are whole.
Douglas
  As heart can think; there is not such a word
  Spoke of in Scotland as this term of fear.   *85*
                    Enter SIR RICHARD VERNON

Hotspur
  My cousin Vernon! welcome, by my soul.
Vernon
  Pray God my news be worth a welcome, lord.
  The Earl of Westmoreland, seven thousand strong,
  Is marching hitherwards; with him Prince John.
Hotspur
  No harm; what more?
Vernon   And further, I have learn'd   *90*
  The King himself in person is set forth,
  Or hitherwards intended speedily,
  With strong and mighty preparation.
Hotspur
  He shall be welcome too. Where is his son,
  The nimble-footed madcap Prince of Wales,   *95*
  And his comrades that daff'd the world aside
  And bid it pass?
Vernon   All furnish'd, all in arms;
  All plum'd like estriges, that with the wind
  Bated like eagles having lately bath'd;
  Glittering in golden coats, like images;   *100*
  As full of spirit as the month of May
  And gorgeous as the sun at midsummer;
  Wanton as youthful goats, wild as young bulls.
  I saw young Harry with his beaver on,
  His cushes on his thighs, gallantly arm'd,   *105*
  Rise from the ground like feathered Mercury,
  And vaulted with such ease into his seat
  As if an angel dropp'd down from the clouds
  To turn and wind a fiery Pegasus,
  And witch the world with noble horsemanship.   *110*

111-23. Hearing the news of the change in Prince Hal, Hotspur writhes with anger and jealousy. His repetition of *No more* is an agonized cry and he now talks of the coming battle in a blood-thirsty way, quite different from his earlier attitude to it. But his speech is melodramatic in its viciousness, suggesting that yet again Hotspur is trying to convince himself, and is consequently less impressive than the passage (Act III, Scene ii, lines 132-7) which showed us the ruthless efficiency of Hal's attitude to his struggle with Hotspur.

111-12. 'This praise makes me shudder worse than fevers spread by the March sun'. It was a common belief that diseases were caused by fogs which the sun sucked up from fens and marshes.

112. *Let . . . come:* Hotspur is now recklessly defiant.

113. *like . . . trim:* like victims adorned for sacrifice.

114. *fire-ey'd . . . war:* Bellona, the Roman goddess of war.

116. *mailed:* armoured.

Mars: the Roman god of war.

118. *reprisal:* reward, prize.

nigh: close at hand.

119. *taste:* feel the power of.

120. *thunderbolt.* According to the ancient Greek legends the gods on Olympus used the thunderbolt as a weapon to punish the earth and Hotspur sees himself in the service of the pagan gods, Bellona and Mars. In Act III, Scene ii, line 153, the Prince had, by contrast, appealed to the Christian God.

123. *corse:* corpse.

126. 'He cannot raise his army within the fortnight'. One might wonder after Hotspur's attitude to him, how hard, in fact, Glendower has tried.

128. *frosty:* chilling, ominous.

129. 'How large is the King's army likely to be?'

130. *Forty . . . be:* 'Let's say forty.'

131-2. 'Although my father and Glendower are absent, our combined forces may be adequate to deal with the situation'. Dismayed at the news of Glendower's defection, Hotspur cannot produce his usual optimism.

133. *take a muster:* 'assemble the troops to check our numbers'.

134. *Doomsday:* the day of fate, of doom.

die . . . merrily: Hotspur is resolved to fight bravely, but a feeling of pessimism, of inevitable defeat and death, runs through this line.

135-6. Douglas alone will not yield to the general feeling of despair.

Hotspur
No more, no more; worse than the sun in March,
This praise doth nourish agues. Let them come.
They come like sacrifices in their trim,
And to the fire-ey'd maid of smoky war
All hot and bleeding will we offer them.   *115*
The mailed Mars shall on his altar sit
Up to the ears in blood. I am on fire
To hear this rich reprisal is so nigh
And yet not ours. Come, let me taste my horse,
Who is to bear me like a thunderbolt   *120*
Against the bosom of the Prince of Wales.
Harry to Harry shall, hot horse to horse,
Meet, and ne'er part till one drop down a corse.
O that Glendower were come!
Vernon   There is more news.
I learn'd in Worcester, as I rode along,   *125*
He cannot draw his power this fourteen days.
Douglas
That's the worst tidings that I hear of yet.
Worcester
Ay, by my faith, that bears a frosty sound.
Hotspur
What may the King's whole battle reach unto?
Vernon
To thirty thousand.
Hotspur   Forty let it be: *130*
My father and Glendower being both away,
The powers of us may serve so great a day.
Come, let us take a muster speedily.
Doomsday is near; die all, die merrily.
Douglas
Talk not of dying; I am out of fear   *135*
Of death or death's hand for this one half year.
                            Exeunt

193

SCENE II

Falstaff's tired plodding to Shrewsbury at the head of his troop of soldiers provides some comedy, but the emphasis in this scene is on the real victims of civil war, the misery caused by the actions of politicians and taken advantage of by men such as Falstaff himself. There does not seem much honour left in the campaign about which Hotspur once spoke so excitedly.

1. *get thee before:* go on ahead.
2. *through:* through Coventry without stopping.

5. *Lay out:* pay for it out of the funds.

6. 'This bottle of sack will bring your debts up to ten shillings.'

8. *I'll . . . coinage:* 'I'll see that the money is provided'.
11-48. Falstaff has made use of his authority as an officer, typically, to make money for himself. By the power of *the King's press*, an officer had the right to enlist his soldiers by force (a kind of compulsory call-up). Falstaff, in the first place, has enlisted wealthy men prepared to pay in order to be released from service. Falstaff then made up his complement of soldiers by enlisting criminals, tramps and the derelicts of society. Hence the appalling poverty and beggary of his troops' appearance.
11-12. *sous'd gurnet:* pickled gurnard (a kind of fish).
12. *damnably:* unforgivably.
14-15. *good . . . sons.* They would not wish to leave their farms and property uncared-for in time of war.
15-17. *contracted . . . banns:* engaged man due to be married in a couple of weeks' time.
17. *commodity . . . slaves:* collection of wealthy cowards.
17-18. *as had as lief:* 'who would rather'.
19. *caliver:* musket, an old type of gun.
struck fowl: wounded bird.
20. *toasts-and butter:* soft creatures ('sissies').
22. *bought . . . services:* 'paid me in order to be excused military service'.
22-31. *and now . . . ancient.* Falstaff may mean here that the officers serving under him are only the most junior in rank, lacking ability to gain promotion, having only joined the army because they had failed to make a success of their peace-time careers.
22-3. *my whole charge:* all my officers.
23. *ancients:* ensigns, the lowest rank of commissioned officers.
24-6. *slaves . . . sores.* Pictures of Lazarus in his rags were common in Elizabethan times.

SCENE II—*A public road near Coventry*

Enter FALSTAFF *and* BARDOLPH

Falstaff

Bardolph, get thee before to Coventry; fill me a bottle
of sack. Our soldiers shall march through; we'll to
Sutton Co'fil' to-night.

Bardolph

Will you give me money, Captain?

Falstaff

Lay out, lay out.   5

Bardolph

This bottle makes an angel.

Falstaff

An if it do, take it for thy labour; and if it make
twenty, take them all; I'll answer the coinage. Bid
my lieutenant Peto meet me at town's end.

Bardolph

I will, Captain; farewell.

Exit   10

Falstaff

If I be not ashamed of my soldiers, I am a sous'd gurnet. I have misused the King's press damnably. I have
got, in exchange of a hundred and fifty soldiers, three
hundred and odd pounds. I press me none but good
householders, yeomen's sons; inquire me out con-   15
tracted bachelors, such as had been ask'd twice on the
banns; such a commodity of warm slaves as had as
lief hear the devil as a drum; such as fear the report
of a caliver worse than a struck fowl or a hurt wild-
duck. I press'd me none but such toasts-and-butter,   20
with hearts in their bellies no bigger than pins' heads,
and they have bought out their services; and now my
whole charge consists of ancients, corporals, lieuten-
ants, gentlemen of companies—slaves as ragged as

27. *discarded . . . serving-men:* nobleman's servants dismissed for dishonesty.
27-8. *younger . . . brothers.* Since the wealth and title of a family passed from eldest son to eldest son, these men, although educated to lead the leisurely life of a gentleman, had no money of their own to live on.
28. *revolted tapsters:* runaway apprentices to inn-keepers.
29. *ostlers trade-fall'n:* out-of-work ostlers.
29-30. *cankers . . . peace:* the dregs of society that people ignore in time of peace.
30. *dishonourable:* dishonourably.
31. *old-fac'd ancient:* tattered old flag.
31-48. Falstaff now seems to be talking about the ordinary soldiers themselves.
32. *rooms:* ranks.
34-5. *Prodigals . . . husks.* A reference to the parable of the Prodigal Son (Luke chapter 15) who left home and squandered his share of his father's wealth. As a result, he lived in great poverty for a time.
draff: pig-slops.
36. *gibbets:* way-side gallows for hanging criminals.
39-40. *march . . . legs:* 'march with their legs wide apart'.
40. *gyves:* fetters.
41. *out of prison.* Prisoners could be released for service in the army in wartime.

47. *that's . . . one:* 'that doesn't matter'.
47-8. *linen . . . hedge:* washing left out to dry which they can steal.

49. *blown . . . quilt:* Two terms once again referring to Falstaff's fatness.

50-3. Falstaff is taken by surprise, first by Hal, then by Westmoreland. Notice how on seeing the latter, he quickly changes his language to that of an educated and humble courtier. Why?
52. *I . . . mercy:* I beg your pardon (for not seeing you before).

56. *looks . . . all:* 'expects us all eagerly'.
56-7. *away all night:* march all night.

Lazarus in the painted cloth, where the Glutton's   *25*
dogs licked his sores; and such as indeed were never
soldiers, but discarded unjust serving-men, younger
sons to younger brothers, revolted tapsters, and
ostlers trade-fall'n; the cankers of a calm world and a
long peace; ten times more dishonourable ragged   *30*
than an old-fac'd ancient. And such have I, to fill up
the rooms of them as have bought out their services,
that you would think that I had a hundred and fifty
tattered Prodigals lately come from swine-keeping,
from eating draff and husks. A mad fellow met me   *35*
on the way, and told me I had unloaded all the gibbets
and press'd the dead bodies. No eye hath seen such
scarecrows. I'll not march through Coventry with
them, that's flat. Nay, and the villains march wide
betwixt the legs, as if they had gyves on; for indeed I   *40*
had the most of them out of prison. There's not a
shirt and a half in all my company; and the half shirt
is two napkins tack'd together and thrown over the
shoulders like a herald's coat without sleeves; and
the shirt, to say the truth, stol'n from my host at   *45*
Saint Albans, or the red-nose innkeeper of Daventry.
But that's all one; they'll find linen enough on every
hedge.

Enter the PRINCE OF WALES *and* WESTMORELAND

Prince

How now, blown Jack! how now, quilt!

Falstaff

What, Hal! how now, mad wag! What a devil dost   *50*
thou in Warwickshire? My good Lord of Westmoreland, I cry you mercy; I thought your honour had
already been at Shrewsbury.

Westmoreland

Faith, Sir John, 'tis more than time that I were there,
and you too; but my powers are there already. The   *55*
King, I can tell you, looks for us all; we must away all
night.

58. *never fear me:* 'don't worry about me'.
vigilant: alert and eager.

61. *made thee butter:* Falstaff will be perspiring freely after all the marching.

63. *Mine.* Falstaff now pretends to be proud of his troops to try to convince Hal and Westmoreland what a devoted officer he is.

65-7. *good . . . men:* This apparently casual, unfeeling reply may partly be intended to show Falstaff's heartlessness. But he is so fond of life himself that this may not be Shakespeare's main intention. Falstaff is probably satirizing the official attitude of kings, noblemen and generals, to their troops as 'cannon-fodder'. By pretending to hold the same view, Falstaff shows up this attitude in all its hideousness. Certainly Westmoreland in his next speech seems more worried by their wretched appearance than by the fact that they will probably die.
65. *to toss:* to be killed by pikes and spears.
powder: gun-powder.
66. *they'll . . . better:* 'they will die just as well as their betters'.
67. *mortal men:* 'all men must die'.
69. *bare:* raggedly clothed.
71. *bareness:* leanness.

73-4. *three . . . ribs:* three fingers' width of flesh covering the ribs.

79-80. 'To arrive at a battle when it is over and when the feasting is about to begin suits a reluctant soldier and hearty eater like me.' It is remarks like this, so typical of Falstaff, that suggest that he cannot seriously mean what he says in lines 65-7.
How will Falstaff organize the departure of himself and his troops?

Falstaff

Tut, never fear me; I am as vigilant as a cat to steal
cream.

Prince

I think, to steal cream indeed; for thy theft hath   60
already made thee butter. But tell me, Jack, whose
fellows are these that come after?

Falstaff

Mine, Hal, mine.

Prince

I did never see such pitiful rascals.

Falstaff

Tut, tut; good enough to toss; food for powder, food   65
for powder; they'll fill a pit as well as better: tush,
man, mortal men, mortal men.

Westmoreland

Ay, but, Sir John, methinks they are exceeding poor
and bare—too beggarly.

Falstaff

Faith, for their poverty, I know not where they had   70
that; and for their bareness, I am sure they never
learn'd that of me.

Prince

No, I'll be sworn; unless you call three fingers in the
ribs bare. But, sirrah, make haste; Percy is already in
the field.   75

Exit

Falstaff

What, is the King encamp'd?

Westmoreland

He is, Sir John: I fear we shall stay too long.

Exit

Falstaff

Well,
To the latter end of a fray and the beginning of a feast
Fits a dull fighter and a keen guest.   80

Exit

SCENE III

As the battle approaches, the relative weakness of the rebels cannot prevent the leaders arguing about when the battle should be fought. The quarrel is a symptom of nervousness and tension – and Hotspur's reaction to the King's offer of a parley to settle grievances is most revealing.

1-7. The short, snappy speeches suggest the agitated state of mind of these men.

1. Perhaps more important than the reasons Hotspur gives for wishing to fight at once is his restlessness and hatred of inaction.

It . . . be: 'It isn't possible.'

2. *Not a whit:* 'Not a scrap.'

3. *supply:* reinforcements.

[handwritten: reinforcement are Hal and Falstaff]

6. *counsel well:* give good advice.

6-7. Douglas's only answer to being thwarted is to become insulting.

9. 'and I will stake my life on it'.

10-12. 'in any carefully thought-out and honourable action I am as little of a coward as you or any other living Scotsman'.

14. *Content:* 'Right, we shall see.'

16. *I . . . much:* 'I am very surprised'.

17. *of . . . leading:* so experienced in generalship.

18-19. 'that you don't realise the obstacles to our successfully fighting the battle at once'.

horse: cavalry.

SCENE III—*The rebel camp near Shrewsbury*

    Enter HOTSPUR, WORCESTER, DOUGLAS *and* VERNON

Hotspur
  We'll fight with him to-night.

Worcester   It may not be.

Douglas
  You give him, then, advantage.

Vernon   Not a whit.

Hotspur
  Why say you so? looks he not for supply?

Vernon
  So do we.

Hotspur   His is certain, ours is doubtful.

Worcester
  Good cousin, be advis'd, stir not to-night.   5

Vernon
  Do not, my lord.

Douglas   You do not counsel well;
  You speak it out of fear and cold heart.

Vernon
  Do me no slander, Douglas; by my life,
  And I dare well maintain it with my life,
  If well-respected honour bid me on,   10
  I hold as little counsel with weak fear
  As you, my lord, or any Scot that this day lives;
  Let it be seen to-morrow in the battle
  Which of us fears.

Douglas   Yea, or to-night.

Vernon   Content.

Hotspur
  To-night, say I.   15

Vernon
  Come, come, it may not be. I wonder much,
  Being men of such great leading as you are,
  That you foresee not what impediments

22-4. 'And now through tiredness they lack so much of their spirit that none can be worth more than a quarter of its real value'.

26. *journey-bated:* exhausted by the journey.

27. *better part:* majority. Which set of arguments do you think sounds the more sensible?

31. *vouchsafe:* grant.

30-7. Blunt's straightforwardness and sense of honour arouse respect among the rebels as Hotspur admits, and his presence here emphasizes the wastage and futility involved in the rebellion. Men such as Blunt will never rebel; for them the only rational course is to remain loyal to the King and thus to England as a whole.

32-3. *and . . . determination:* 'how I wish you were on our side'.

35-6. 'admire and envy your loyalty and high reputation in not joining our party'. This unselfish tribute shows the potential greatness of Hotspur and makes his entanglement in such an unworthy cause all the more deplorable.

38. *defend:* forbid.

still: always.

39. *out . . . rule:* 'in opposition to your duty of loyalty to the government'.

40. *anointed:* legally crowned. Blunt firmly reminds the rebels that, although Henry IV is a usurper, he was nevertheless ceremonially crowned and accepted as king.

42. *griefs:* grievances.

means Thes have not got as much Courage and pride anymore. They are tired.

Drag back our expedition: certain horse
Of my cousin Vernon's are not yet come up;
Your uncle Worcester's horse came but to-day;   *20*
And now their pride and mettle is asleep,
Their courage with hard labour tame and dull,
That not a horse is half the half of himself.

Hotspur

So are the horses of the enemy   *25*
In general, journey-bated and brought low;
The better part of ours are full of rest.

Worcester

The number of the King exceedeth ours.
For God's sake, cousin, stay till all come in.

The trumpet sounds a parley
Enter SIR WALTER BLUNT

Blunt

I come with gracious offers from the King,   *30*
If you vouchsafe me hearing and respect.

Hotspur

Welcome, Sir Walter Blunt; and would to God
You were of our determination!
Some of us love you well; and even those some
Envy your great deservings and good name,
Because you are not of our quality,   *35*
But stand against us like an enemy.

Blunt

And God defend but still I should stand so,
So long as out of limit and true rule
You stand against anointed majesty!   *40*
But, to my charge. The King hath sent to know
The nature of your griefs; and whereupon

We are reluctant to give you our qualities because your not on our side

203

42-5. 'and why you unnaturally destroy the peace of the land, forcing normally obedient citizens to fight cruel wars'.

43. *conjure:* raise by witchcraft. This word stresses the evil of the rebels' cause.

45-51. The King's offer sounds fine and generous – but we are in the world of subtle politics again. Henry IV knows very well what the rebels' complaints are, but the need for good publicity makes him pretend to be an innocent, honest ruler who is being harshly treated. Blunt, too, must know this – but his duty is to serve the King and, here, act as his mouthpiece.

47. 'which he admits are numerous'.

51. *Herein:* in this matter.

suggestion: influence and example.

52-105. *The King is kind.* Hotspur's sarcastic opening sets the tone for the second long account of how Henry IV became king. He has learned most of the details from his father and uncle, as he was too young at the time; some details are absurdly false in making the King too corrupt and the Percy family too innocent. Hotspur's purpose is to show the King to be a hypocrite, a liar, utterly ungrateful and unreliable. The interesting but difficult question to answer is how much does Hotspur himself believe what he says?

kind: gracious.

56. *not . . . strong:* supported by fewer than twenty-six men.

57. *Sick . . . regard:* down-and-out in the eyes of the public.

58. *unminded:* unnoticed.

outlaw. He had been banished by Richard II.

sneaking. Richard II was fighting rebels in Ireland at the time.

61. *Duke of Lancaster.* His dead father's title, which Richard II had refused to allow him to inherit.

62. *To . . . livery:* claim his inheritance.

beg his peace: 'offer homage to the King, begging forgiveness for having returned to England illegally'.

63. *With . . . innocency.* This phrase raises the difficult question of when exactly Bolingbroke decided to try to get the crown. Hotspur argues that Henry was a hypocrite from the beginning.

terms of zeal: earnest words of loyalty.

64. *in kind . . . mov'd.* This description of Northumberland certainly does not ring true. In *Richard II*, one senses him to be rather unscrupulous, supporting Bolingbroke in the hope of rewards for himself and his family.

68. *The . . . less:* both the nobility and the lower classes.

with cap and knee: 'kneeling to him with cap in hand'.

70. *stood in lanes:* stood in rows on either side of his route.

72. *heirs as pages.* It was common practice for sons of trading, middle-class men to be sent to the houses of noblemen to attend on them as pages.

73. *golden:* rejoicing in Bolingbroke's success.

74. *as . . . itself:* 'as he realised the power that he wielded'.

75. 'begins to act in a more ambitious way than could be justified by his promise'.

77. *naked:* deserted (when there were no crowds to welcome him).

You conjure from the breast of civil peace
Such bold hostility, teaching his duteous land
Audacious cruelty. If that the King   45
Have any way your good deserts forgot,
Which he confesseth to be manifold,
He bids you name your griefs, and with all speed
You shall have your desires with interest,
And pardon absolute for yourself and these   50
Herein misled by your suggestion.

Hotspur

The King is kind; and well we know the King
Knows at what time to promise, when to pay.
My father and my uncle and myself
Did give him that same royalty he wears;   55
And when he was not six and twenty strong,
Sick in the world's regard, wretched and low,
A poor unminded outlaw sneaking home,
My father gave him welcome to the shore;
And when he heard him swear and vow to God   60
He came but to be Duke of Lancaster,
To sue his livery and beg his peace,
With tears of innocency and terms of zeal,
My father, in kind heart and pity mov'd,
Swore him assistance, and perform'd it too.   65
Now when the lords and barons of the realm
Perceiv'd Northumberland did lean to him,
The more and less came in with cap and knee;
Met him in boroughs, cities, villages;
Attended him on bridges, stood in lanes,   70
Laid gifts before him, proffer'd him their oaths,
Gave him their heirs as pages, followed him
Even at the heels in golden multitudes.
He presently—as greatness knows itself—
Steps me a little higher than his vow   75
Made to my father, while his blood was poor,
Upon the naked shore at Ravenspurgh;

78. *forsooth:* indeed, what is more.
78-80. *takes . . . commonwealth:* 'decides to alter certain laws and harsh regulations that oppressed the country too severely'. (i.e., Bolingbroke began to act like a king).
81. *Cries . . . abuses:* 'denounces injustice'.
seems. Notice how this word suggests Henry's hypocrisy.
82. *by this face:* 'as a result of this false outward appearance'.
83. *seeming . . . justice:* apparent concern for justice.
84. *angle for:* entice (as an angler entices his prey).
87. *In deputation:* as deputies during his absence.
88. *personal in:* actually present at.
89. *Tut . . . this.* This is past history and does not give a list of their grievances. However, Hotspur's account does lead naturally up to them in lines 92-101.
92. *in the neck of that:* 'as soon as that was done'.
task'd: taxed.
93. *suffer'd:* allowed.
94. *well plac'd:* in legal possession of his own property.
95. *engag'd:* held as prisoner.
96. *forfeited:* abandoned.
97. *Disgrac'd me:* discredited me – Holmedon, for example.
98. *Sought . . . intelligence:* 'tried to trap me into speaking treason by sending spies to talk to me'. This, presumably, is Hotspur's recent interpretation of the incident of the *certain lord* in Act I, Scene iii, lines 30-69.
99. *Rated:* 'ordered bad-temperedly'. This is a reference to Act I, Scene iii, lines 15-21.

100. See Act I, Scene iii, lines 122-4.

103. *head of safety:* self-protection through strength.
withal: in addition.
103-4. *to pry . . . title:* 'to examine carefully his claim to the throne'.
104-5. *the which . . . continuance:* 'which we find too weak (since he does not claim it by direct descent) to justify his remaining king any longer'. Does this justify the rebellion? Are Hotspur's accusations against the King true as they stand or has he over-simplified the issues in order to give the rebels an outwardly good cause?
107. *Not so.* A surprising reply at the conclusion of Hotspur's outburst. For all his violence of speech, he is learning caution and prudence.
108-9. *and . . . return again:* 'and let hostages be arranged so that no harm can come to the messengers'.

And now, forsooth, takes on him to reform
Some certain edicts, and some strait decrees
That lie too heavy on the commonwealth;   *80*
Cries out upon abuses, seems to weep
Over his country's wrongs; and by this face,
This seeming brow of justice, did he win
The hearts of all that he did angle for;
Proceeded further; cut me off the heads   *85*
Of all the favourites that the absent King
In deputation left behind him here,
When he was personal in the Irish war.

means He Went further

Blunt
  Tut, I came not to hear this.
Hotspur   Then to the point
  In short time after, he depos'd the King;   *90*
  Soon after that depriv'd him of his life;
  And in the neck of that, task'd the whole state;
  To make that worse, suffer'd his kinsman March—
  Who is, if every owner were well plac'd,
  Indeed his king—to be engag'd in Wales,   *95*
  There without ransom to lie forfeited;
  Disgrac'd me in my happy victories;
  Sought to entrap me by intelligence;
  Rated mine uncle from the council-board;
  In rage dismiss'd my father from the court;   *100*
  Broke oath on oath, committed wrong on wrong;
  And in conclusion drove us to seek out
  This head of safety, and withal to pry
  Into his title, the which we find
  Too indirect for long continuance.   *105*
Blunt
  Shall I return this answer to the King?
Hotspur
  Not so, Sir Walter; we'll withdraw awhile.
  Go to the King; and let there be impawn'd
  Some surety for a safe return again,
  And in the morning early shall mine uncle   *110*

111. *purposes:* proposals.

This short scene provides a breathing-space before hostilities commence in Act V. It sums up the political situation, provides a comment on the likely outcome of the struggle, and indicates that Henry IV's troubles will not end if he is successful at Shrewsbury. In this way it links up with the next play *Henry IV Part II*, which continues to show that as a usurper Henry's fate is never to know the peace for which he hankers.

1. *Hie:* hurry. The entry of these two men and their conversation should be agitated and anxious.
brief: document.
2. *Lord Marshal:* The Earl of Norfolk, who joined the rebels later.
5. *How . . . import:* 'how important they are'.

7. *I . . . tenour:* 'I can guess their contents'.

10. *bide the touch:* be put to the test.

13. *Lord Harry:* Hotspur.

15. *in . . . proportion:* of very great strength.

17. *a rated sinew:* a powerful ally on whom they relied.
18. *o'errul'd by prophecies:* persuaded against fighting by dismal omens. This gives another reason for Glendower's absence. Does it sound a likely one?
20. 'To fight (successfully) an immediate battle against the King'.

means I wish you would accept our grace and love

Bring him our purposes. And so, farewell.

Blunt

I would you would accept of grace and love.

Hotspur

And may be so we shall.

Blunt   Pray God you do.

Exeunt

This is the last we hear of Glendower in the play

SCENE IV—*York. The Archbishop's palace*

Enter the ARCHBISHOP OF YORK *and* SIR MICHAEL

Archbishop

Hie, good Sir Michael; bear this sealed brief

With winged haste to the Lord Marshal;

This to my cousin Scroop; and all the rest

To whom they are directed. If you knew

How much they do import, you would make haste.   *5*

Sir Michael

My good lord,

I guess their tenour.

Archbishop   Like enough you do.

To-morrow, good Sir Michael, is a day

Wherein the fortune of ten thousand men

Must bide the touch; for, sir, at Shrewsbury,   *10*

As I am truly given to understand,

The King with mighty and quick-raised power

Meets with Lord Harry; and I fear, Sir Michael,

What with the sickness of Northumberland,

Whose power was in the first proportion,   *15*

And what with Owen Glendower's absence thence,

Who with them was a rated sinew too

And comes not in, o'errul'd by prophecies,

I fear the power of Percy is too weak

To wage an instant trial with the King.   *20*

means we have been told of Glendower's delay for two weeks

24. *Mordake:* See Act I, Scene i, lines 71-2.

28. *special head:* greatest men.

31. *moe corrivals:* more warriors of equal rank.
31-2. *dear . . . arms:* men valuable for their military reputation and experience of leadership.

35. *prevent:* forestall.

37. *he . . . us:* 'he intends to punish us'.
38. *confederacy:* negotiations with the other rebels.

Sir Michael
  Why, my good lord, you need not fear;
  There is Douglas and Lord Mortimer.
Archbishop
  No, Mortimer is not there.
Sir Michael
  But there is Mordake, Vernon, Lord Harry Percy,
  And there is my Lord of Worcester, and a head   *25*
  Of gallant warriors, noble gentlemen.
Archbishop
  And so there is; but yet the King hath drawn
  The special head of all the land together:
  The Prince of Wales, Lord John of Lancaster,
  The noble Westmoreland, and warlike Blunt;   *30*
  And many moe corrivals and dear men
  Of estimation and command in arms.
Sir Michael
  Doubt not, my lord, they shall be well oppos'd.
Archbishop
  I hope no less, yet needful 'tis to fear;
  And, to prevent the worst, Sir Michael, speed;   *35*
  For if Lord Percy thrive not, ere the King
  Dismiss his power, he means to visit us—
  For he hath heard of our confederacy—
  And 'tis but wisdom to make strong against him;
  Therefore make haste. I must go write again   *40*
  To other friends; and so farewell, Sir Michael.
              Exeunt severally

ACT FIVE

SCENE I

Worcester's account of Henry's gaining of the crown, the King's offer of peace, the Prince's challenge to Hotspur – each of these is important in defining the attitudes of some of the play's leading characters. And at the end of the scene, the 'rat-race' and, to him, the futility of politics and honour are brilliantly exposed by Falstaff who believes in life at all costs.

1-6. The weather is shown to be disturbed as the day of battle dawns. Often in Shakespeare the weather provides an appropriate background for events.

1. *bloodily:* This word suggests both the possibility of a storm and of bloodshed.

peer: The sun seems reluctant to rise on such a day.

2. *busky:* wooded.

2-3. *The day . . . distemp'rature:* The dawn looks grey and bleak in keeping with the sun's threatening appearance.

3-4. *The southern . . . purposes.* The fact that the wind is from the south indicates (acts as a herald for) the weather we can expect.

7-8. 'Then the stormy weather will match the fortunes of the losers, for success will be all that matters to the winners.' This defiant remark may be covering up the King's anxiety at such omens.

9-21. Henry's speech to Worcester again demonstrates his mastery of politics. Appearing innocent and hurt by the opposition of the Percy family, he contrives to put Worcester in the wrong. The problem is more complex than Henry's simplification of the issues indicates.

12-13. Notice the King's effective image of substituting civilian clothes for armour.

12. *doff:* take off.

13. *crush . . . limbs.* Henry's picture of himself as an old man longing for peace is certainly sincere, but also politically clever in its claim for pity.

15-16. *Will . . . war:* 'Will you return to the simple ways of peace?'

churlish knot: violent tangle.

all-abhorred: utterly loathed.

17-21. 'And become once again an obedient subject, supporting order and prosperity, instead of a rebel, arousing fear and bringing disaster to the future of this country'.

Henry IV again refers to meteors as images of disorder as he did in Act I, Scene i. Stars and planets move in regulated paths, *orbs*, round the sun (king) while *meteors* are erratic in the speed and direction of their movements (rebels).

20. *A . . . fear:* sign of alarm.

21. *broached mischief:* active evil.

ACT FIVE

SCENE I—*The King's camp near Shrewsbury*

Enter the KING, *the* PRINCE OF WALES, PRINCE JOHN
OF LANCASTER, SIR WALTER BLUNT *and* SIR JOHN
FALSTAFF

King
  How bloodily the sun begins to peer
  Above yon busky hill! The day looks pale
  At his distemp'rature.
Prince   The southern wind
  Doth play the trumpet to his purposes,
  And by his hollow whistling in the leaves   5
  Foretells a tempest and a blust'ring day.
King
  Then with the losers let it sympathize,
  For nothing can seem foul to those that win.

  The trumpet sounds. Enter WORCESTER *and* VERNON

  How now, my Lord of Worcester! 'Tis not well
  That you and I should meet upon such terms   10
  As now we meet. You have deceiv'd our trust,
  And made us doff our easy robes of peace
  To crush our old limbs in ungentle steel;
  This is not well, my lord, this is not well.
  What say you to it? Will you again unknit   15
  This churlish knot of all-abhorred war,
  And move in that obedient orb again
  Where you did give a fair and natural light,
  And be no more an exhal'd meteor,
  A prodigy of fear, and a portent   20
  Of broached mischief to the unborn times?

213

22-71. Worcester's reaction to the King's challenging speech is typical of the man. Starting on the defensive, claiming that he, too, is an old man wishing for peace, he quickly attacks, using outwardly accurate historical detail to accuse the King of ingratitude, perjury, hypocrisy and political trickery. In fact, Worcester, as did Hotspur in Act IV, Scene i, unconsciously reveals the enormous pressures on Bolingbroke to become king, and thus condemns the rebels.

26. 'I have not deliberately caused this quarrel'.

28. Falstaff's remark is both funny and brilliantly true, exposing the hollowness of Worcester's argument. No matter how afraid of the king the Percy family may be, the fact remains that they have destroyed the peace by rebelling. Possibly Falstaff should be slightly apart from the others, almost as an observer, to enable the full force of his remark to be felt by the audience.

29. *chewet:* jackdaw, a noisy bird. The sense of the phrase is 'Shut up, you chatterbox!'

30. *It . . . Majesty.* Notice Worcester's polite sarcasm.

31. *house:* family.

32. *remember:* remind.

34. *my . . . break:* I resigned my position (as Steward of the Household).

35. *posted:* rode.

37-8. 'when you were much less powerful than I was'.

40. *brought you home:* brought you back to England and made you successful.

43-5. 'That you had no intention of taking the crown but merely claimed your title of Duke of Lancaster'. What Worcester says is true as far as it goes; what is equally obvious in *Richard II* is that the Percy family, especially Northumberland, hoped from the beginning to replace Richard II with Bolingbroke.

44. *new-fall'n:* John of Gaunt, Bolingbroke's father, had died.

45. *seat:* estates.

46-57. Worcester himself lists a remarkable number of circumstances favouring Henry's success. How much can Henry be blamed for following what must have seemed to be his destiny?

46. *in short space:* in a short time.

47-8. 'Good luck, prosperity and power came your way'.

49. *absent King:* absence of the King.

50. *injuries . . . time:* abuses resulting from bad government.

51. *seeming . . . borne:* apparent injustices that you had had to suffer.

52. *contrarious:* unfavourable.

Worcester
  Hear me, my liege:
  For mine own part, I could be well content
  To entertain the lag-end of my life
  With quiet hours; for I protest   25
  I have not sought the day of this dislike.
King
  You have not sought it! How comes it then?
Falstaff
  Rebellion lay in his way, and he found it.
Prince
  Peace, chewet, peace!
Worcester
  It pleas'd your Majesty to turn your looks   30
  Of favour from myself and all our house;
  And yet I must remember you, my lord,
  We were the first and dearest of your friends.
  For you my staff of office did I break
  In Richard's time, and posted day and night   35
  To meet you on the way and kiss your hand,
  When yet you were in place and in account
  Nothing so strong and fortunate as I.
  It was myself, my brother, and his son,
  That brought you home, and boldly did outdare   40
  The dangers of the time. You swore to us—
  And you did swear that oath at Doncaster—
  That you did nothing purpose 'gainst the state,
  Nor claim no further than your new-fall'n right,
  The seat of Gaunt, dukedom of Lancaster;   45
  To this we swore our aid. But in short space
  It rain'd down fortune show'ring on your head;
  And such a flood of greatness fell on you,
  What with our help, what with the absent King,
  What with the injuries of a wanton time,   50
  The seeming sufferances that you had borne,
  And the contrarious winds that held the King
  So long in his unlucky Irish wars

54. *That:* with the result that.

56-7. 'you allowed yourself to be quickly persuaded to seize the crown'. By whom?

59-66. *And . . . sight:* 'And, as a result of our support, you became so powerful and threatened us to such an extent that we were forced to combine with each other in self-defence'. Worcester likens Henry's action to that of the cuckoo which, having been hatched in a smaller bird's nest, grows much bigger than its foster-parents and terrorizes them.

63-4. *even . . . swallowing:* we were afraid of being persecuted despite our loyalty.

67-8. 'so that the reasons for our opposition are of your own creation'.

69. *unkind usage:* harsh treatment. There is no evidence in *Richard II* of the oppression of which Worcester complains.

dangerous countenance: hostile behaviour.

70. 'and by your breaking of all your oaths'.

71. *in . . . enterprise:* at the time of your early ambition.

72-82. The King's reply accuses Worcester of using false arguments, common to those who wish to justify rebellion. He also claims that the Percy rebellion, in contrast to the widespread support that he received, is only supported by riff-raff.

72. *articulate:* made public. Notice the King's constant awareness of the value (and danger) of propaganda and public opinion.

73. *market-crosses.* Stone or wooden crosses were often erected in market squares, popular meeting-places of townsfolk.

74-5. 'in order to make your rebellion attract the support'. The image is of the use of brightly-coloured material to disguise the shoddy workmanship of a piece of clothing.

76. *fickle changelings:* people easily swayed by fashionable opinions.

discontents: discontented men.

77-8. 'who stare in amazement and are delighted with any new ideas that cause disorder'.

79-80. 'And rebellions have always been made to look attractive by means of such false arguments'. Notice the image of painting.

want: lack.

81-2. 'nor have rebellions lacked the support of wretched beggars, longing to take advantage of general confusion in order to make a living'. Notice that this statement also condemns Falstaff, who has lined his own pocket.

83-100. Hal is perhaps aware of the hopeless atmosphere of mistrust; perhaps he also realizes that, although more right than wrong, his father is not guiltless. Whatever the reason, Hal changes the subject. Why does he challenge Hotspur in this way and why does he praise him so freely?

84. *full dearly:* with their deaths.

85. *trial:* battle.

87. *By my hopes:* on my honour.

88-92. 'apart from his error in supporting this rebellion I do not think there is anyone living who has contributed more by his honour, courage and energy to the achievements of this present period of history'.

That all in England did repute him dead;
And from this swarm of fair advantages   55
You took occasion to be quickly woo'd
To gripe the general sway into your hand;
Forgot your oath to us at Doncaster;
And being fed by us you us'd us so
As that ungentle gull, the cuckoo's bird,   60
Useth the sparrow—did oppress our nest,
Grew by our feeding to so great a bulk
That even our love durst not come near your sight
For fear of swallowing; but with nimble wing
We were enforc'd, for safety sake, to fly   65
Out of your sight, and raise this present head;
Whereby we stand opposed by such means
As you yourself have forg'd against yourself,
By unkind usage, dangerous countenance,
And violation of all faith and troth   70
Sworn to us in your younger enterprise.

King

These things, indeed, you have articulate,
Proclaim'd at market-crosses, read in churches,
To face the garment of rebellion
With some fine colour that may please the eye   75
Of fickle changelings and poor discontents,
Which gape and rub the elbow at the news
Of hurlyburly innovation;
And never yet did insurrection want
Such water-colours to impaint his cause,   80
Nor moody beggars, starving for a time
Of pellmell havoc and confusion.

Prince

In both your armies there is many a soul
Shall pay full dearly for this encounter,
If once they join in trial. Tell your nephew   85
The Prince of Wales doth join with all the world
In praise of Henry Percy. By my hopes,
This present enterprise set off his head,

94. 'I have neglected to lead a life of glory and honour'.

95. 'And I hear that he shares the poor opinion that I have of myself'.

96. *Yet this:* Yet I will declare this.

97. *take the odds:* have the advantage.

98. *estimation:* reputation.

101-14. Why does the King refuse his son's offer? Does he fear that Hal will be defeated or that such gestures will settle nothing? Perhaps he needs the political advantage to be gained from acting mercifully if the rebels accept his offer of peace.

101. *so . . . thee.* He has no doubt of Hal's ability to win such a contest.

102. *Albeit:* however.

103. *Do . . . it:* argue against it.

105. 'who are misled in supporting your nephew (Hotspur)'.

106. *And . . . take:* and if they will accept.

grace: forgiveness.

111. 'The power of defeating and punishing you severely lies in my hands'. Impressively Henry reminds the rebels that he, as King, is the representative of God on earth and must be obeyed.

112. *And . . . office:* and I shall use that power.

114. *fair:* sincerely.

take . . . advisedly: you will be wise to accept our offer.

118. *charge:* duty as an officer. The King does not expect his offer to be accepted. What has he gained from this interview?

I do not think a braver gentleman,
More active-valiant or more valiant-young,   *90*
More daring or more bold, is now alive
To grace this latter age with noble deeds.
For my part, I may speak it to my shame,
I have a truant been to chivalry;
And so I hear he doth account me too.   *95*
Yet this before my father's majesty—
I am content that he shall take the odds
Of his great name and estimation,
And will, to save the blood on either side,
Try fortune with him in a single fight.   *100*

King

And, Prince of Wales, so dare we venture thee,
Albeit considerations infinite
Do make against it. No, good Worcester, no,
We love our people well; even those we love
That are misled upon your cousin's part;   *105*
And will they take the offer of our grace,
Both he and they and you, yea, every man
Shall be my friend again, and I'll be his.
So tell your cousin, and bring me word
What he will do. But if he will not yield,   *110*
Rebuke and dread correction wait on us,
And they shall do their office. So, be gone;
We will not now be troubled with reply.
We offer fair; take it advisedly.
             Exeunt WORCESTER *and* VERNON

Prince

It will not be accepted, on my life: *115*
The Douglas and the Hotspur both together
Are confident against the world in arms.

King

Hence, therefore, every leader to his charge;
For, on their answer, will we set on them;
And God befriend us, as our cause is just!   *120*
             Exeunt all but the PRINCE *and* FALSTAFF

121-2. *bestride me:* stand over me to defend me.
so: good.
123. *colossus.* In ancient times, the Colossus was an enormous statue at the entrance of the harbour of the Greek island of Rhodes. It was wrongly believed by the Elizabethans and others that ships sailed under its legs on their way into dock.
125. *bed-time:* the proper time for saying prayers. Falstaff wishes the battle were over.
126. Hal has no time to joke with Falstaff and leaves him quickly with the grim reminder that he must die sometime.
127-41. This speech is Falstaff's brilliant answer to the 'honour-and-glory boys'. He argues that no cause is worth dying for since honour is no use to dead, or living, men. More than ever, Falstaff stands out as the man in the play most concerned with the enjoyment of, and respect for life. Despite all his disreputable activities, the politicians and soldiers, with their longing for power and glory, seem second-rate by comparison with him.
127. *Tis . . . yet:* God does not want me to die yet.
loath: unwilling.
128-9. *What . . . on me:* Why should I be eager to die when my death is not required?
129-30. *honour . . . on:* honour spurs me on (to fight bravely). With this remark Falstaff begins a mock-conversation with himself, debating whether he ought to risk dying or not.
130. *prick me off:* kills me.
131. *set . . . leg:* mend a broken leg.
132. *grief:* pain.
134. *A word:* just a name, a sound without substance.
135. *A trim reckoning!* What a comforting conclusion!
137. *insensible:* unable to be felt or enjoyed.
139. *Detraction . . . it:* 'Even if you manage to stay alive after fighting honourably, other people's jealousy of your reputation will make them belittle your achievements'. (Is Falstaff thinking of Hal's mockery of Hotspur earlier in the play?)
139-40. *Therefore . . . it:* therefore I'll have nothing to do with it.
140. *mere scutcheon:* simply the heraldic design on your shield that is displayed at your funeral.
141. *catechism:* in Christian teaching, a course of instruction by question and answer. This speech therefore fits in with Falstaff's habit of using religious language to justify his independent attitudes.

SCENE II

Henry IV's and Hal's belief that the offer of peace will be rejected proves to be correct, though not for the reasons they stated. From this point Worcester has to accept the main share of blame for the battle; the scene concludes with Hotspur's brave but rather desperate speeches as the fighting commences.
1-2. Vernon, who remained silent throughout the previous scene, has apparently been attempting to persuade Worcester of the advisability of making peace.
2. *liberal:* generous. Is Worcester being sarcastic?

Falstaff

    Hal, if thou see me down in the battle, and bestride
    me, so; 'tis a point of friendship.

Prince

    Nothing but a colossus can do thee that friendship.
    Say thy prayers, and farewell.

Falstaff

    I would 'twere bed-time, Hal, and all well.   *125*

Prince

    Why, thou owest God a death.

                                       Exit

Falstaff

    'Tis not due yet; I would be loath to pay him before
    his day. What need I be so forward with him that
    calls not on me? Well, 'tis no matter; honour pricks
    me on. Yea, but how if honour prick me off when I *130*
    come on? How then? Can honour set to a leg? No.
    Or an arm? No. Or take away the grief of a wound?
    No. Honour hath no skill in surgery, then? No.
    What is honour? A word. What is in that word?
    Honour. What is that honour? Air. A trim reckoning! *135*
    Who hath it? He that died o' Wednesday. Doth he
    feel it? No. Doth he hear it? No. 'Tis insensible,
    then? Yea, to the dead. But will it not live with the
    living? No. Why? Detraction will not suffer it. There-
    fore I'll none of it. Honour is a mere scutcheon. And *140*
    so ends my catechism.

                                         Exit

SCENE II—*The rebel camp*

                Enter WORCESTER *and* VERNON

Worcester

    O, no, my nephew must not know, Sir Richard,
    The liberal and kind offer of the King.

3. *undone:* ruined.

4-5. The basic impossibility for each side to trust the other suggests that Worcester's comment here may be true. Nevertheless, Worcester, by refusing to pass on the King's offer, clearly puts himself in the wrong. And perhaps Worcester's personal dislike of the King (remember Act I, Scene iii) is a strong motive for his decision.

6. *still:* always.

6-7. *and find . . . faults:* and make other disagreements between us in the future an excuse for punishing us for our opposition now.

8. A difficult line but it may mean 'All our lives the King will imagine that we are being disloyal to him'. It certainly suggests extreme suspicion.

9-11. 'Since a one-time traitor is trusted no more than the fox who, no matter how domesticated he apparently becomes, will always revert to the savage behaviour of his kind'.

12-13. 'Our attitude to the King will be misinterpreted, whether we behave loyally or irresponsibly'.

12. *or sad or merrily:* either seriously or cheerfully.

14-15. 'and we shall be treated like cattle, fed well in order to be fattened up for killing'.

16. *trespass:* offence.

well: easily.

17. *heat of blood:* fiery temperament.

18. 'and his nickname makes you expect such things from him'.

19. *hare-brained:* rash.

governed . . . spleen: ruled by outbursts of passion.

20. *live . . . head:* are blamed on me.

21. *we . . . on:* we encouraged him in his opposition to the King.

22-3. 'and because we are the ones from whom he learned to be a traitor we shall be the ones who suffer for it'.

25. *In . . . case:* whatever happens.

26. 'Say what you like, I'll back you up.' Has Worcester convinced Vernon that he is being reasonable or is Vernon too afraid of Worcester to stand up to him?

29. *Deliver up:* Set free. Westmoreland had been held as a hostage.

31. *bid:* offer.

32. 'Let Westmoreland carry back our message of defiance.'

Vernon
  'Twere best he did.
Worcester   Then are we all undone.
  It is not possible, it cannot be,
  The King should keep his word in loving us;   5
  He will suspect us still, and find a time
  To punish this offence in other faults;
  Supposition all our lives shall be stuck full of eyes,
  For treason is but trusted like the fox,
  Who, never so tame, so cherish'd, and lock'd up,   10
  Will have a wild trick of his ancestors.
  Look how we can, or sad or merrily,
  Interpretation will misquote our looks,
  And we shall feed like oxen at a stall,
  The better cherish'd still the nearer death.   15
  My nephew's trespass may be well forgot;
  It hath the excuse of youth and heat of blood,
  And an adopted name of privilege—
  A hare-brain'd Hotspur, govern'd by a spleen.
  All his offences live upon my head   20
  And on his father's: we did train him on;
  And, his corruption being ta'en from us,
  We, as the spring of all, shall pay for all.
  Therefore, good cousin, let not Harry know,
  In any case, the offer of the King.   25
Vernon
  Deliver what you will, I'll say 'tis so.
  Here comes your cousin.

                Enter HOTSPUR *and* DOUGLAS

Hotspur   My uncle is return'd:
  Deliver up my Lord of Westmoreland.
  Uncle, what news?   30
Worcester
  The King will bid you battle presently.
Douglas
  Defy him by the Lord of Westmoreland.

37. *gently.* Is this true?

38. *which . . . thus:* 'which he made excuses for in the following way'. Worcester, trying to rouse Hotspur's anger against the King, is very sarcastic.

39. 'by denying that he ever broke any oaths'.

40. *scourge:* punish.

41. *hateful name:* hated name of 'traitor'.

44. *engag'd:* kept here as a hostage.

45. 'which is bound to make him attack us quickly'.

48-50. Now that the time for politics, which brought out the worst characteristics of Hotspur, is past, Shakespeare's purpose seems to be to portray him once again as the brave, chivalrous soldier.

49. *draw short breath:* exhaust himself by fighting.

51. 'How did he challenge me? Was it in a contemptuous way?' Hotspur is so anxious that his reputation shall be respected, even by a man he despises.

52-69. As in Act IV, Scene i, Vernon's admiration of Hal is obvious. What is the dramatic effect of having Hal praised by one of the rebels?

54-5. 'unless in the way a man challenges his brother to a friendly contest'.

56. *duties:* qualities.

57. *Trimm'd up:* elegantly spoken.

58. 'listed your good points'.

Hotspur
  Lord Douglas, go you and tell him so.
Douglas
  Marry, and shall, and very willingly.
                    Exit
Worcester
  There is no seeming mercy in the King.   *35*
Hotspur
  Did you beg any? God forbid!
Worcester
  I told him gently of our grievances,
  Of his oath-breaking; which he mended thus,
  By now forswearing that he is forsworn.
  He calls us rebels, traitors, and will scourge   *40*
  With haughty arms this hateful name in us.
                Re-enter DOUGLAS
Douglas
  Arm, gentlemen, to arms! for I have thrown
  A brave defiance in King Henry's teeth—
  And Westmoreland, that was engag'd, did bear it—
  Which cannot choose but bring him quickly on.   *45*
Worcester
  The Prince of Wales stepp'd forth before the King,
  And, nephew, challeng'd you to single fight.
Hotspur
  O, would the quarrel lay upon our heads;
  And that no man might draw short breath to-day
  But I and Harry Monmouth! Tell me, tell me,   *50*
  How show'd his tasking? Seem'd it in contempt?
Vernon
  No, by my soul, I never in my life
  Did hear a challenge urg'd more modestly,
  Unless a brother should a brother dare
  To gentle exercise and proof of arms.   *55*
  He gave you all the duties of a man;
  Trimm'd up your praises with a princely tongue;
  Spoke your deservings like a chronicle;

59-60. 'saying that no praise could do justice to your virtues'.

61. *which . . . indeed:* which was indeed princely behaviour on his part.

62. 'He made embarrassed comments about himself'.

63-5. 'and the honesty with which he showed that he was ashamed of his wild youth gave the impression that he has the ability both of teaching goodness in life and of learning from his own mistakes at the same time'.

67. *envy:* hostility.

68-9. 'England has never had so promising an heir to the throne nor one who has been so misunderstood because of his wild behaviour'.

70-2. Compare Hotspur's reaction to Vernon's praise of the Prince to that of Act IV, Scene i, lines 111-12. There his response was an agonized and bewildered cry. Here, although his pride will not let him accept Vernon's account of Hal, he seems almost pleased to hear the Prince's good points described. Perhaps, having emerged from the despair caused by politics, Hotspur is delighted to find Hal a worthy opponent. Or is he just being sarcastic?

70-1. 'Cousin, I think you have fallen in love with his silly ways.'

72. *liberty:* libertine.

74-5. 'I will fight him so fiercely that he will retreat as quickly as he can'. What is the effect of *embrace, arm, courtesy*?

77-9. 'It will be better if you think over your duties in the coming battle than if I, who am no gifted speaker, attempt to rouse your courage'. Is Hotspur so obsessed now with his coming fight with Hal that he cannot think any longer of the battle as a whole?

82-7. Hotspur now seems very conscious of death. Does he feel instinctively that in Hal he will meet his match?

83-5. 'Even if life only lasted one hour, it would still be too long if we lived in an ignoble manner.'

86. *An if:* if.

87. *If die, brave death:* 'If we die, it's a fine death . . .'

88-9. 'Now, for the peace of our consciences, a battle is honourable when our reasons for fighting it are just.' Does Hotspur believe this or is he trying to convince himself? A possible interpretation of Hotspur's state of mind is that he has lost faith in their cause, that he feels doomed and that, despite this, he intends to live up as well as he can to his principles of honour.

Making you ever better than his praise,
By still dispraising praise valued with you;   *60*
And, which became him like a prince indeed,
He made a blushing cital of himself,
And chid his truant youth with such a grace
As if he master'd there a double spirit,
Of teaching and of learning instantly.   *65*
There did he pause; but let me tell the world—
If he outlive the envy of this day,
England did never owe so sweet a hope,
So much misconstrued in his wantonness.

Hotspur

Cousin, I think thou art enamoured   *70*
On his follies. Never did I hear
Of any prince so wild a liberty.
But be he as he will, yet once ere night
I will embrace him with a soldier's arm,
That he shall shrink under my courtesy.   *75*
Arm, arm with speed! and, fellows, soldiers, friends,
Better consider what you have to do
Than I, that have not well the gift of tongue,
Can lift your blood up with persuasion.

Enter a MESSENGER

Messenger

My lord, here are letters for you.   *80*

Hotspur

I cannot read them now.
O gentlemen, the time of life is short!
To spend that shortness basely were too long,
If life did ride upon a dial's point,
Still ending at the arrival of an hour.   *85*
An if we live, we live to tread on kings;
If die, brave death, when princes die with us!
Now, for our consciences, the arms are fair,
When the intent of bearing them is just.

Enter another MESSENGER

92. *For . . . talking.* In fact he does a great deal of it.

94. *temper:* hardened metal.

95. *best blood:* blood of the highest-born men.

97. *Esperance:* the motto of the Percy family ('Hope'.)

98-101. The sounds of the trumpets, the farewells, possibly some marching of troops with banners should in their impressive pomp merge into and finally conflict with the realities of the battle that we see in the next scene.

SCENE III

This and the following scene provide a complete unit – the battle itself. Battle scenes on stage present a problem, partly because a cast is usually very limited in its number. However, as far as possible, the incidents depicted in these scenes should be seen against the movements, fighting and death of ordinary troops, the 'food for powder' of which Falstaff spoke and who for various reasons do not have the facilities of the King or Falstaff for escaping death. Occasional trumpet calls and banners too can provide the contrast with the pomp of the court scenes and the glitter of the rebel camp before the battle.

1-13. The death of Blunt shows how civil war often brings about the loss of a country's most loyal servants. And the fact that Henry IV has many noblemen fighting in his colours poses a question. Even if this tactic can be defended as politically sensible, does it detract from the King's 'kingliness' that he should allow such sacrifices to be made in this way?

1. *What is thy name.* Knights at that time would not have been readily recognizable because of their helmets.

2. *Thou crossest me:* you challenge me.

3. *Upon . . . head:* by my death.

7-8. *The . . . likeness:* The Lord of Stafford has paid dearly for looking like you.

Messenger
My lord, prepare; the King comes on apace.   *90*
Hotspur
I thank him that he cuts me from my tale,
For I profess not talking; only this—
Let each man do his best. And here draw I
A sword, whose temper I intend to stain
With the best blood that I can meet withal   *95*
In the adventure of this perilous day.
Now, Esperance! Percy! and set on.
Sound all the lofty instruments of war,
And by that music let us all embrace;
For, heaven to earth, some of us never shall   *100*
A second time do such a courtesy.
          They embrace. The trumpets sound. Exeunt

SCENE III—*A plain between the camps*

          The KING *passes across with his power. Alarum to
                    the battle*
          Then enter DOUGLAS *and* SIR WALTER BLUNT
Blunt
What is thy name, that in battle thus
Thou crossest me? What honour dost thou seek
Upon my head?
Douglas
Know, then, my name is Douglas;
And I do haunt thee in the battle thus
Because some tell me that thou art a king.   *5*
Blunt
They tell thee true.
Douglas
The Lord of Stafford dear to-day hath bought
Thy likeness; for instead of thee, King Harry,
This sword hath ended him. So shall it thee.
Unless thou yield thee as my prisoner.   *10*

229

12. 'shall find (me) a king . . .'

15. *upon:* over.

16-18. These short lines suggest Douglas's delight and Hotspur's excitement.

19. Hotspur lifts Blunt's visor and recognizes him.

21. *Semblably furnish'd like:* clad in similar armour to.

22-8. Douglas's fury at discovering his mistake is grimly amusing. The most straightforward of all the characters in the battle, he hates deception and feels cheated.
22. 'May the title of fool accompany your soul wherever it goes' (spoken to the dead Blunt).

29. *stand . . . day:* are in courageous mood for the battle.
30-8. Falstaff, alone on stage, provides through his comments a strong contrast to the tragic heroics of Blunt. As always, he will try to stay alive at all costs.
30. *shot-free:* both 'without a bullet in me' and 'without paying my bill'.
31. *here's . . . pate:* the only accounts kept here concern the number of wounds in your head.
Soft! A cry of alarm. Falstaff is scared of the sight of a soldier even though he seems dead!

Blunt

I was not born a yielder, thou proud Scot;
And thou shalt find a king that will revenge
Lord Stafford's death.

They fight. DOUGLAS *kills* BLUNT
Enter HOTSPUR

Hotspur

O Douglas, hadst thou fought at Holmedon thus,
I never had triumph'd upon a Scot.   *15*

Douglas

All's done, all's won; here breathless lies the King.

Hotspur

Where?

Douglas

Here.

Hotspur

This, Douglas? No: I know this face full well;
A gallant knight he was, his name was Blunt;   *20*
Semblably furnish'd like the King himself.

Douglas

A fool go with thy soul whither it goes!
A borrowed title hast thou bought too dear;
Why didst thou tell me that thou wert a king?

Hotspur

The King hath many marching in his coats.   *25*

Douglas

Now, by my sword, I will kill all his coats;
I'll murder all his wardrobe, piece by piece,
Until I meet the King.

Hotspur   Up, and away!
Our soldiers stand full fairly for the day.

Exeunt
Alarum. Enter FALSTAFF, *solus*

Falstaff

Though I could scape shot-free at London, I fear the   *30*
shot here: here's no scoring but upon the pate. Soft!
who are you? Sir Walter Blunt. There's honour for

32-3. *There's . . . vanity!:* 'There's honour and no mistake!'

35-8. *1 . . . life.* The callousness of Falstaff can be glimpsed here as he has led his troops to the thickest part of the battle and then retired, leaving them to be slaughtered. At the same time he shows an awareness of the miserable fate of the survivors and his comments have a touch of pity that is lacking in the thoughts of the leading politicians.

37-8. *they . . . life:* made beggars because of wounds. Even Falstaff's surviving men are probably crippled and therefore bound to be beggars. Beggars were punished by the authorities and they therefore kept to the outskirts of the towns

45. *Turk Gregory.* If this is a reference to Pope Gregory XIII, it would be very popular with Shakespeare's audiences since Falstaff talks of the Pope who wished to have the Protestant Queen Elizabeth I murdered, as if he were a pagan.

46. *paid:* killed.

47. *sure:* safe.

52. *is . . . case?* is it still in its holster?

53. *'tis hot.* Falstaff pretends that he has put it back in its case to cool down.

54. Notice Hal's annoyance with Falstaff's jokes.

55-7. *If he . . . of me:* If he comes across me, that's that; if he doesn't, I'll be hanged if I'll go looking for him.

you! Here's no vanity! I am as hot as molten lead, and as heavy too. God keep lead out of me! I need no more weight than mine own bowels. I have led my ragamuffins where they are pepper'd; there's not three of my hundred and fifty left alive, and they are for the town's end, to beg during life. But who comes here? 35

Enter the PRINCE OF WALES

Prince

What, stand'st thou idle here? Lend me thy sword.
Many a nobleman lies stark and stiff 40
Under the hoofs of vaunting enemies,
Whose deaths, are yet unreveng'd. I prithee lend me
thy sword.

Falstaff

O Hal, I prithee give me leave to breathe awhile.
Turk Gregory never did such deeds in arms as I have 45
done this day. I have paid Percy, I have made him
sure.

Prince

He is, indeed, and living to kill thee. I prithee lend
me thy sword.

Falstaff

Nay, before God, Hal, if Percy be alive, thou get'st 50
not my sword; but take my pistol, if thou wilt.

Prince

Give it me. What, is it in the case?

Falstaff

Ay, Hal; 'tis hot, 'tis hot; there's that will sack a city.
The PRINCE *draws it out, and finds it to be a bottle of sack*

Prince

What, is it a time to jest and dally now?

He throws the bottle at him.
Exit

Falstaff

Well, if Percy be alive, I'll pierce him. If he do come 55
in my way, so; if he do not, if I come in his willingly,

57. *carbonado:* a piece of pork with its skin sliced.

59-60. *if not . . . end:* if I can't save my life, I'll be a dead hero without seeking it, and that's the end of it. Although he is still amusing, Falstaff, as he desperately tries to avoid any action, becomes rather a pathetic figure. He is now caught up in the political and military world, where he is lost; he lacks some of his original vitality since he can no longer manipulate life to suit him.

SCENE IV

Stage Direction. *Excursions:* movements of soldiers. Between this and the preceding scene which ended with Falstaff's cautious exit, fighting probably takes place before the royal group enters away from the main area of the battle.

2. *thou . . . much.* A sign that Hal has been in the thick of the fighting. Notice Henry's concern for the safety of his sons.

5. *beseech:* beg.
5-6. *make . . . friends:* 'go back to the battle to prevent your retiring from it causing panic among your troops'. Has the King come out of the danger-zone through fear?

12. *field:* battle-field.
13. *stain'd:* blood-stained.
13-14. At this stage it seems as though the rebels are gaining the upper hand: Falstaff has already described the fate of his men.

15. *breathe:* pause for breath.

let him make a carbonado of me. I like not such
grinning honour as Sir Walter hath. Give me life,
which if I can save, so; if not, honour comes un-
look'd for, and there's an end.   60

Exit

SCENE IV—*Another part of the field*

Alarums. Excursions. Enter the KING, *the* PRINCE
OF WALES, PRINCE JOHN OF LANCASTER *and* WEST-
MORELAND

King
  I prithee,
  Harry, withdraw thyself; thou bleedest too much;
  Lord John of Lancaster, go you with him.
Prince John
  Not I, my lord, unless I did bleed too.
Prince
  I beseech your Majesty, make up,   5
  Lest your retirement do amaze your friends.
King
  I will do so.
  My Lord of Westmoreland, lead him to his tent.
West
  Come, my lord, I'll lead you to your tent.
Prince
  Lead me, my Lord? I do not need your help;   10
  And God forbid a shallow scratch should drive
  The Prince of Wales from such a field as this,
  Where stain'd nobility lies trodden on,
  And rebels' arms triumph in massacres!
Prince John
  We breathe too long. Come, cousin Westmoreland,   15
  Our duty this way lies; for God's sake, come.

Exeunt PRINCE JOHN *and* WESTMORELAND

18. 'I did not think you had so much courage'.

21. *at the point:* at sword-point.
22. *lustier maintenance:* greater power of resistance.
23. *Of:* in.

24. *Lends mettle:* gives determination. Hal's reconciliation with Prince John who had taken his place on the Council completes his peace-making with his family.

25. *Hydra's heads:* according to the ancient Greek legends the Hydra was a many-headed snake eventually killed by Hercules. Its heads grew as fast as they were cut off.

28. *counterfeit'st:* pretends to be.

30. 'That you have met so many wearing my colours'. Douglas, of course, has killed them.

34. *assay:* attack, test.

36. *thou . . . king:* 'you have the manner of a king'. Henry IV is still presented in an ambiguous way. On the one hand, he retreats from the battle and needs to be persuaded by his son to return; on the other hand, his manner is regal and authoritative (which impresses Douglas) and he fights bravely when challenged. As a much younger man it is natural that Douglas should be the more powerful fighter of the two.

Prince

By God, thou hast deceiv'd me, Lancaster!
I did not think thee lord of such a spirit;
Before, I lov'd thee as a brother, John,
But now I do respect thee as my soul.   *20*

King

I saw him hold Lord Percy at the point
With lustier maintenance than I did look for
Of such an ungrown warrior.

Prince   O, this boy
Lends mettle to us all!

Exit

Enter DOUGLAS

Douglas

Another king! They grow like Hydra's heads.   *25*
I am the Douglas, fatal to all those
That wear those colours on them. What art thou,
That counterfeit'st the person of a king?

King

The King himself, who, Douglas, grieves at heart
So many of his shadows thou hast met,   *30*
And not the very King. I have two boys
Seek Percy and thyself about the field;
But, seeing thou fall'st on me so luckily,
I will assay thee; so, defend thyself.

Douglas

I fear thou art another counterfeit;   *35*
And yet, in faith, thou bearest thee like a king;
But mine I am sure thou art, who'er thou be,
And thus I win thee.

They fight, the KING *being in danger*
Re-enter the PRINCE

Prince

Hold up thy head, vile Scot, or thou art like
Never to hold it up again. The spirits   *40*
Of valiant Shirley, Stafford, Blunt, are in my arms;
It is the Prince of Wales that threatens thee,

237

43. *pay:* honour that promise, i.e., kill. Compare this line with Act I, Scene ii, line 197. The time has now come for Hal to put into operation the plan that he stated in his speech at the end of Act I, Scene ii.

45. *succour:* reinforcements.

48. Just as Hal is now intent on paying *the debt he never promised*, so in the process he redeems his lost reputation. This is the culmination of the theme of redemption in the play.
opinion: reputation.
49. *mak'st some tender of:* have some concern for.
50. *fair:* timely.
51-7. Although Henry IV and his son are now reconciled there seems little affection or real bond between them. Their conversation is formal, rather chilling in fact. One wonders how much they really understand each other even now.
51. *they.* These are the people whom in Act III, Scene ii, Hal accused of spreading false reports of him.
52. *hearken'd for:* listened to plots aimed at.
54. *insulting:* threatening.
55. *in your end:* in bringing about your death.

59-110. The confrontation between Hal and Hotspur is the climax of both the battle and the play. Hal's earlier contests, and especially that with Douglas, served to bring out his military prowess and to prepare us for this triumph. The main contest is parodied by the Douglas-Falstaff duel and the honour gained by Hotspur's real death is mocked by the mock-death of Falstaff.
60. How has Hotspur presumably spoken to make the Prince answer in this way?

63. *Prince of Wales.* Hal gives his official title. Why?

65. 'It is impossible for you and me to exist in the same country'. The image used is that of two stars, which cannot travel in the same orbit. Each star has its own path round the sun.
66. *brook:* endure.

Who never promiseth but he means to pay.

They fight; DOUGLAS *flies*

Cheerly, my lord: how fares your Grace?
Sir Nicholas Gawsey hath for succour sent,   *45*
And so hath Clifton. I'll to Clifton straight.
King
Stay, and breathe awhile.
Thou hast redeem'd thy lost opinion;
And show'd thou mak'st some tender of my life,
In this fair rescue thou hast brought to me.   *50*
Prince
O God, they did me too much injury
That ever said I hearken'd for your death!
If it were so, I might have let alone
The insulting hand of Douglas over you,
Which would have been as speedy in your end   *55*
As all the poisonous potions in the world,
And sav'd the treacherous labour of your son.
King
Make up to Clifton, I'll to Sir Nicholas Gawsey.

Exit
Enter HOTSPUR

Hotspur
If I mistake not, thou art Harry Monmouth.
Prince
Thou speak'st as if I would deny my name.   *60*
Hotspur
My name is Harry Percy
Prince   Why, then I see
A very valiant rebel of the name.
I am the Prince of Wales; and think not, Percy,
To share with me in glory any more.
Two stars keep not their motion in one sphere,   *65*
Nor can one England brook a double reign
Of Harry Percy and the Prince of Wales.

70. *name in arms:* military reputation. Why does Hotspur have this wish?

72-3. Hal deliberately uses taunting language in order to make Hotspur angry.
72. *budding honours:* growing and flourishing plumes. The feathers of Hotspur's equipment are possibly seen as symbols of his reputation.
74. *vanities:* foolish boasting.

75. *Well said:* Well done.

Stage Direction. Falstaff's fight with Douglas will naturally be a very short-lived affair. How can it best be staged to contrast with the main bout that is going on at the same time?

77-86. Faced with death Hotspur speaks fatalistically. Although he begins by stating a view of life utterly opposed to Falstaff's, one wonders whether in his last moments he comes to realize the futility of his ideas of honour and glory.
78. 'I would rather lose my life . . .'

81-3. *But . . . stop:* 'But thoughts and life itself, both of which are controlled by time, must finally come to an end; even time, which controls all existence and activity, must one day come to an end'. This seems an unusually profound thought for Hotspur to have.
83. *prophesy:* tell you much about the nature of life (now that I am dying).
84. *But that:* if it weren't for the fact that.

87. *worms.* Is this what Hotspur was going to say?
87-110. Compare the two speeches which Hal makes about Hotspur and the apparently dead Falstaff. The first is a formal and generous tribute to the reputation of his enemy. The second is informal, even somewhat playful in its use of language. But is there more affection in it or is Hal callously dismissing his former companion?
88. *Ill-weav'd:* misguided. Poorly woven cloth was liable to shrink.
89. *When that:* when.
89-90. 'When you were alive, an entire country was too small to satisfy your ambition'.

Hotspur

Nor shall it, Harry, for the hour is come
To end the one of us; and would to God
Thy name in arms were now as great as mine!   *70*

Prince

I'll make it greater ere I part from thee,
And all the budding honours on thy crest
I'll crop to make a garland for my head.

Hotspur

I can no longer brook thy vanities.
                    They fight
                Enter FALSTAFF

Falstaff

Well said, Hal! to it, Hal! Nay, you shall find no   *75*
boy's play here, I can tell you.
    Re-enter DOUGLAS; *he fights with* FALSTAFF, *who*
    falls down as if he were dead; DOUGLAS *withdraws.*
        HOTSPUR *is wounded and falls*

Hotspur

O, Harry, thou hast robb'd me of my youth!
I better brook the loss of brittle life
Than those proud titles thou hast won of me:
They wound my thoughts worse than thy sword my
    flesh;   *80*
But thoughts, the slaves of life, and life, time's fool,
And time, that takes survey of all the world,
Must have a stop. O, I could prophesy,
But that the earthy and cold hand of death
Lies on my tongue. No, Percy, thou art dust   *85*
And food for—
                    Dies

Prince

For worms, brave Percy. Fare thee well, great heart!
Ill-weav'd ambition, how much art thou shrunk!
When that this body did contain a spirit,
A kingdom for it was too small a bound;   *90*
But now two paces of the vilest earth

93. *stout:* courageous.

94-5. 'If you were able to hear my praise, I could not let myself show my grief for your death so openly'. This remark illustrates the point made by Falstaff that the demands of politics will not allow a man of honour to enjoy his reputation unchallenged while he is alive. *Detraction will not suffer it.*

96. *favours.* Perhaps a cloak or some piece of his equipment bearing his colours.

97-8. 'and I'll accept the thanks that I know you would have wished to express to me for paying you these compliments to your honour'.

100. *ignominy:* shame (for being a rebel).

105-6. 'I should miss you a very great deal if I were deeply attached to the foolish life we led together.'

108. *dearer:* of greater value. What is the effect of this word after *deer* in line 107?

109. *Embowell'd:* prepared for embalming by removing the entrails.

111-65. Falstaff's mock-death, his reaction to the dead Hotspur and his subsequent account to Hal constitute a final great comic triumph for Falstaff, although there is grimness in it as well. But it is as though the threat to his life provides the necessary action which once again brings out magnificent powers of fantasy and comic invention similar to those that he displayed at and after the Gadshill robbery.

112. *powder:* pickle (Hal has likened Falstaff to a fat deer).

114. *counterfeit:* pretend to be dead. Compare Falstaff's counterfeiting to that of the King. Is there any real difference in the measures they take to stay alive?

114-15. *termagant:* ferocious.

115. *paid . . . lot:* finished me off. The term *scot and lot* meant dues demanded, for example by the parish authorities.

116-20. *I lie . . . indeed.* This is Falstaff's attitude in a nutshell. He argues that since the main business of a man is to stay alive it is the dead who are 'counterfeit' since, while still looking like men, they have lost the power of living for which they were created.

118-20. *but to counterfeit . . . indeed:* but to save your life by pretending to be dead is not to be false, but to show that you have the greatest possible respect for the unique value of life itself.

120-1. *The . . . discretion:* Bravery, if not regulated by commonsense, is simply foolhardiness.

121-2. *in . . . life:* in using my commonsense I have been truly brave since I have saved my life.

123-4. *how . . . rise?* Falstaff is suddenly struck by the terrifying thought that Hotspur, too, might be shamming death!

Is room enough. This earth that bears thee dead
Bears not alive so stout a gentleman.
If thou wert sensible of courtesy,
I should not make so dear a show of zeal;   95
But let my favours hide thy mangled face,
And, even in thy behalf, I'll thank myself
For doing these fair rites of tenderness.
Adieu, and take thy praise with thee to heaven!
Thy ignominy sleep with thee in the grave,   100
But not remember'd in thy epitaph!

He spieth FALSTAFF *on the ground*

What, old acquaintance! Could not all this flesh
Keep in a little life? Poor Jack, farewell!
I could have better spar'd a better man.
O, I should have a heavy miss of thee,   105
If I were much in love with vanity!
Death hath not struck so fat a deer to-day,
Though many dearer, in this bloody fray.
Embowell'd will I see thee by and by;
Till then in blood by noble Percy lie.   110
Exit

Falstaff [*Rising up*]
Embowell'd! If thou embowel me to-day, I'll give you
leave to powder me and eat me too to-morrow.
'Sblood, 'twas time to counterfeit, or that hot termagant Scot had paid me scot and lot too. Counter-   115
feit? I lie, I am no counterfeit: to die is to be a
counterfeit; for he is but the counterfeit of a man who
hath not the life of a man; but to counterfeit dying,
when a man thereby liveth, is to be no counterfeit,
but the true and perfect image of life indeed. The   120
better part of valour is discretion; in the which better
part I have saved my life. Zounds, I am afraid of this
gunpowder Percy, though he be dead; how if he
should counterfeit too, and rise? By my faith, I am
afraid he would prove the better counterfeit. There-   125

126. *make . . . sure:* make sure he is dead.

127-8. *Nothing . . . sees me:* only witnesses can prove that I didn't kill him, and there aren't any.

Stage Direction. *stabbing him.* Is this action merely comic or is there a certain grimness in Falstaff's joke as well?

131-2. *full . . . sword:* you have fought extremely well in your first battle. *flesh'd:* blooded.

136. *fantasy:* a ghost, our imagination.

139. *double man:* (a) a ghost. (b) two men (he is carrying Hotspur's body on his back).
140. *Jack:* knave.
141-2. *will . . . honour:* will give me some material reward (not Hotspur's abstract honour).
143. *look:* expect.

145-8. *Lord . . . clock.* Brilliant Falstaffian lines; they have the quality of genius in their audacity and detail.

150-1. *I'll . . . death:* I swear.

fore I'll make him sure; yea, and I'll swear I kill'd him.
Why may not he rise as well as I? Nothing confutes
me but eyes, and nobody sees me. Therefore, sirrah
[*stabbing him*], with a new wound in your thigh, come
you along with me.   *130*

He takes up HOTSPUR *on his back*
Re-enter the PRINCE OF WALES *and* PRINCE JOHN OF
LANCASTER

Prince
Come, brother John, full bravely hast thou flesh'd
Thy maiden sword.
Prince John   But, soft! whom have we here?
Did you not tell me this fat man was dead?
Prince
I did; I saw him dead,
Breathless and bleeding on the ground. Art thou
    alive?   *135*
Or is it fantasy that plays upon our eyesight?
I prithee speak; we will not trust our eyes
Without our ears: thou art not what thou seem'st.
Falstaff
No, that's certain: I am not a double man; but if I
be not Jack Falstaff, then am I a Jack. There is Percy *140*
[*throwing the body down*]; if your father will do me any
honour, so; if not, let him kill the next Percy himself.
I look to be either earl or duke, I can assure you.
Prince
Why, Percy I kill'd myself, and saw thee dead.
Falstaff
Didst thou? Lord, Lord, how this world is given to *145*
lying! I grant you I was down and out of breath, and
so was he; but we rose both at an instant, and fought
a long hour by Shrewsbury clock. If I may be believ'd,
so; if not, let them that should reward valour bear
the sin upon their own heads. I'll take it upon my *150*

156. *your luggage:* Hotspur's body.

157-8. 'As far as I am concerned, if you want to gain rewards as the result of a lie, I'll back up your story as successfully as I can.' Is Hal amused by Falstaff's trickery or is he merely contemptuous of him now? Hal does not care about personally losing the honour to be gained from Hotspur's death.

159. *the day is ours:* we are victorious.

160. *highest:* highest part (so that we can survey the battleground).

163-5. Do these lines suggest that Falstaff intends to reform if he becomes a nobleman?
163. *grow great:* become a great man.
163-4. *grow less:* become thinner.
164. *purge:* (a) confess my sins; (b) take laxatives.
The end of the scene is rather sad. Falstaff, for all his ambition, is now quite isolated: Hal, reconciled with his family, seems no longer interested in him.

SCENE V

A ceremonial entry of the King, his nobles and the prisoners should open this scene. Although the play ends with the victory of the royal party, the references to the other, undefeated enemies strike an inconclusive, slightly threatening note. Just as the opening scene linked this play firmly with its predecessor, *Richard II*, so its concluding one leads into *Henry IV Part II* and thence to the final play of the series, *Henry V*. To understand the overall pattern that Shakespe re finds in these three reigns, you should read the Introduction and Summing-up in this volume.
1. 'Thus has rebellion always been punished in the end.'
2. *Ill-spirited:* malevolent.
grace: offer of forgiveness.
4. *turn . . . contrary:* deliberately prevent our offer being accepted.
5. 'abuse the trus t placed in you by your nephew Hotspur'.

death, I gave him this wound in the thigh; if the man
were alive, and would deny it, zounds, I would make
him eat a piece of my sword.

Prince John

This is the strangest tale that ever I heard.

Prince

This is the strangest fellow, brother John.   *155*
Come, bring your luggage nobly on your back.
For my part, if a lie may do thee grace,
I'll gild it with the happiest terms I have.

A retreat is sounded

The trumpet sounds retreat; the day is ours.
Come, brother, let us to the highest of the field,   *160*
To see what friends are living, who are dead.

Exeunt the PRINCE *and* PRINCE JOHN OF LANCASTER

Falstaff

I'll follow, as they say, for reward. He that rewards
me, God reward him! If I do grow great, I'll grow
less; for I'll purge, and leave sack, and live cleanly,
as a nobleman should do.   *165*

Exit

SCENE V—*Another part of the field*

The Trumpets sound. Enter the KING, *the* PRINCE
OF WALES, PRINCE JOHN OF LANCASTER, WESTMORE-
LAND, *with* WORCESTER *and* VERNON *prisoners*

King

Thus ever did rebellion find rebuke.
Ill-spirited Worcester! did not we send grace,
Pardon and terms of love to all of you?
And wouldst thou turn our offers contrary?
Misuse the tenour of thy kinsman's trust?

6. *upon:* of.

8. *Had been:* would have been.

10. *intelligence:* information.

11-13. Worcester is defiant to the end and refuses to sue for pardon. Vernon, too, is executed for his complicity in Worcester's deception.

15. *pause upon:* wait before we make a decision.

16. 'What is the state of affairs on the battle-field?'

20. *Upon . . . fear:* fleeing in panic.

24. *I . . . him:* I may decide his fate.

26. *honourable bounty:* honourable and generous action.
27. *deliver:* release.

29-31. 'His great courage against us has taught us to value brave exploits even when carried out by our enemies'. Would you agree that Douglas's part in the battle merits this high praise, or should we suspect that, with an eye to the future, Hal is making a political decision, hoping to make a friend and ally of Douglas?

32. *high courtesy:* noble gesture of respect.
33. *give away:* put into practice.

Three knights upon our party slain to-day,
A noble earl, and many a creature else,
Had been alive this hour,
If like a Christian thou hadst truly borne
Betwixt our armies true intelligence.   *10*

Worcester
What I have done my safety urg'd me to;
And I embrace this fortune patiently,
Since not to be avoided it falls on me.

King
Bear Worcester to the death, and Vernon too;
Other offenders we will pause upon.   *15*

   Exeunt WORCESTER *and* VERNON *guarded*
How goes the field?

Prince
The noble Scot, Lord Douglas, when he saw
The fortune of the day quite turn'd from him,
The noble Percy slain, and all his men
Upon the foot of fear, fled with the rest;   *20*
And falling from a hill, he was so bruis'd
That the pursuers took him. At my tent
The Douglas is; and I beseech your Grace
I may dispose of him.

King   With all my heart.

Prince
Then, brother John of Lancaster, to you   *25*
This honourable bounty shall belong:
Go to the Douglas, and deliver him
Up to his pleasure, ransomless and free;
His valours shown upon our crests to-day
Have taught us how to cherish such high deeds   *30*
Even in the bosom of our adversaries.

Prince John
I thank your Grace for this high courtesy,
Which I shall give away immediately.

King
Then this remains—that we divide our power.

36. *bend you:* direct your march.
dearest: greatest.

41-2. 'One more decisive battle such as today's will destroy the power of the rebels finally'.

43-5. 'And since we have achieved so much already, let us complete the task and become sole master of our own country'. A final ceremony with music and banners ends the play.

You, son John, and my cousin Westmoreland,   *35*
Towards York shall bend you with your dearest speed
To meet Northumberland and the prelate Scroop,
Who, as we hear, are busily in arms.
Myself, and you, son Harry, will towards Wales
To fight with Glendower and the Earl of March.   *40*
Rebellion in this land shall lose his sway,
Meeting the check of such another day;
And since this business so fair is done,
Let us not leave till all our own be won.

                  Exeunt

SUMMING UP

'History repeats itself.' As the introduction suggested, Shakespeare tried to show how past events contained lessons for his own time. In his two groups of histories (the *Richard II – Henry V* plays and the series *Henry VI – Richard III*) he was clearly demonstrating how the sins and crimes of rulers were punished by God according to a certain pattern.

The Elizabethans believed in order, not only at the human level where each person had his place in society, but also at the divine and animal levels of creation. One well-established theory saw all creatures as part of a ladder or chain of being. God occupied the topmost rung of the ladder and below him came the precisely graded forms of angelic creation down to the 'ordinary' angels. Just below this point, on the highest rung of human existence was the King, God's representative on Earth, and below him stretched the defined range of human social classes—from the nobility to servants. The last stage of the ladder was occupied by the animal world, headed by the lion and the eagle, and again these were followed by a carefully arranged hierarchy.

It was thought that a peaceful world would result from each part of creation accepting its lot, its place (in the case of human beings) in a static human society. Such perfect order, naturally, was unobtainable; human weaknesses— pride, greed, etc.—have always caused men to rebel against it in the hope of self-advancement. Kings, too, although at the head of society and consequently in theory the best of men, have sinned by governing wrongfully, ambitious noblemen by displacing weak kings. When this occurred, the natural order was upset and God's pattern was destroyed temporarily. These beliefs help to explain the pattern of recurrent events that Shakespeare, in common with his contemporaries, saw in history. The results of a king's crime affected not only himself but also eventually his descendants, although an intervening period, before the final working-out of guilt, could be a period of prosperity.

We see this in Shakespeare's handling of the history of the reigns of Richard II, Henry IV, Henry V, and, in another series, Henry VI. Henry IV, the usurper of Richard II's throne, is punished in two ways during his lifetime. He suffers politically through a reign of constant unrest and revolt, and as a father he suffers from the wild behaviour of his son, whom he sees as an agent of God's punishment. At the beginning of their vital interview he addresses Hal bitterly:

> *I know not whether God will have it so,*
> *For some displeasing service I have done,*
> *That, in his secret doom, out of my blood*
> *He'll breed revengement and a scourge for me;*

> (Act III, Scene ii, lines 4-7)

Despite their reconciliation, he never understands his son. Henry V, as Prince Hall becomes, is, however, guiltless of his father's crime of usurpation and can enjoy a triumphant short reign.

The idea of redemption from sin is therefore a recurrent theme in *Henry IV, Part I*. Early in the play Hal announces his intention of:

> *Redeeming time when men think least I will*

> (Act I, Scene ii, line 205)

To his father, when accused of intending to join the Percy faction he promises:

> *I will redeem all this on Percy's head,*

> (Act III, Scene ii, line 132)

For Henry IV himself no redemption is possible.

It is easy to see from this the special problem posed by kingship. The ideal king is one who combines the efficiency and authority needed to guide a country to internal peace and prosperity (the public virtues) with such qualities as pity, love and religious fear (the private Christian virtues). In practice, the realities of the political world make it impossible for the ideal man-king to exist.

Shakespeare's first group of history plays showed the disasters ensuing from the attempts of Henry VI, a man of saint-like qualities in private life but of utter incompetence in public affairs, to govern England. But what is the value of having a saint as king if civil war follows? Isn't the first duty of a king to provide a peaceful, orderly society? It is a crime to rebel against God's anointed king. Gaunt, asked to revenge on Richard II the death of the Duke of Gloucester, firmly states:

> God's is the quarrel; for God's substitute,
> His deputy anointed in his sight,
> Hath caused his death; the which if wrongfully,
> Let heaven revenge, for I may never lift
> An angry arm against his minister.

But isn't it, perhaps, better in the long run for a usurper to take the crown, even though this is a sin, if the result is the firm government a country needs?

These questions were in Shakespeare's mind when he wrote his second series of history plays, to which *Henry IV, Part I* belongs. It is interesting that Shakespeare makes Worcester, of all people, admit a certain lessening of guilt in Bolingbroke's usurpation of the crown. Giving his account of the process of Bolingbroke's success to the King himself, he states:

> It rain'd down fortune show'ring on your head;
> And such a flood of greatness fell on you,

(Act V, Scene i, lines 47-8)

Certainly it must have seemed to Bolingbroke in those decisive weeks that by becoming king he would be fulfilling his destiny. It was an Elizabethan belief that, if the wheel of Fortune rolled so strongly in a man's favour, it was wrong to ignore the opportunity.

The atmosphere of *Henry IV, Part I*, its cold political tone and the calculations of most of its leading figures suggest very strongly that for the time being Shakespeare had despaired of finding the ideal man-king. A ruler's first duty was to govern efficiently. Such a conclusion certainly assists our understanding of Henry IV and his son, among others.

Henry IV is a complex character, aptly summed up in Hotspur's phrase—*this subtle king*. Shakespeare also presents him to us subtly, so that it is difficult at times to tell when he is being sincere and when hypocritical, when he feels genuine emotion and when he is simply calculating. He is not merely a political contriver. We sense that he wishes fervently to overcome the disadvantage of his usurpation, to be accepted by his subjects as an honoured and trusted king. He is a conventional man, tied to the values of the past. So, apparently, he fails to see Hotspur's limitations, admires him wholeheartedly for his chivalrous career, and in the first scene of the play wishes to exchange this *theme of honour's tongue* for his own son. Aware of his guilt, he seems genuinely to desire forgiveness; his words about the crusade in Act I, Scene i, and his speech to his son at the beginning of Act III, Scene ii, both seem to contain personal grief and at least some religious conviction. His basic qualities and the facts of his past, however, make Henry a natural 'politician'. He frankly admits the element of scheming with which he pursued his goal when once he had made up his mind to oust Richard:

> *And then I stole all courtesy from heaven,*
> *And dress'd myself in such humility*
> *That I did pluck allegiance from men's hearts,*
>
> (Act III, Scene ii, lines 50-2)

He never forgets the vital importance of public opinion, of the outward appearance of things, and this seems uppermost in his mind in his accusation of Hal. Henry feels Hal is making the same mistake as Richard II, debasing himself in the people's eyes, thus losing his *princely privilege with vile participation.*

As king, Henry IV is well served. Westmoreland is ever-reliable and Blunt a devoted servant who dies wearing the royal colours in an attempt to protect his sovereign. Prince John of Lancaster loyally occupies his brother's seat on the Council. Yet despite this loyalty, Henry's policy is self-reliance. He seems unable to trust anybody and makes a point of keeping a personal check on events. In the first scene of the play, he shows that he knows the reason for delaying the Crusade well before it was known to the court. To Blunt at the end of the interview with his son he announces his prior knowledge of the rebels' movements. At Shrewsbury his personal safety precautions are undoubtedly politically sensible but they are hardly king-like in the fullest sense. *The king hath many marching in his coats* and three loyal knights, Blunt, Shirley, and Stafford, all die as a result of the King's counterfeiting. Henry also needs to be reminded by his son of his duty to return to the thick of the battle. However, when confronted by Douglas, he fights as bravely as he can against a stronger opponent.

For all his faults and the ambiguity of much of his speech and action there can be little doubt that Shakespeare sees Henry IV, caught as he is in an insoluble dilemma, as preferable to Richard II. He longs for peace, he has great authority, and his efficiency is such that, if given the chance, he would bring much-needed prosperity to the country.

Prince Hal resembles his father in many ways. He realizes the value of securing public approval and intends to become a strong and efficient ruler. But he will set about doing so in his own way. He will not be the aloof figure his father prided himself on being, nor will he fall into Richard II's trap and allow the public to become finally sickened by his over-familiarity with them. From the beginning of the play he lets the audience into his secret intentions in leading what appears such a wild life. Of Falstaff and his other companions he says:

> *I know you all, and will awhile uphold*
> *The unyok'd humour of your idleness;*
> (Act I, Scene ii, lines 183-4)

Having lost all public confidence he will, when the time comes, reform suddenly and imitate the sun in its habit of emerging unexpectedly from behind clouds. Political calculation is at the root of this:

> *My reformation, glitt'ring o'er my fault,*
> *Shall show more goodly and attract more eyes*
> *Than that which hath no foil to set it off.*
> (Act I, Scene ii, lines 201-3)

Meanwhile he uses his 'mis-spent' youth to learn about the lower-class world of which his father is completely ignorant. His self-imposed education is complete by Act II; his farcical encounter with Francis, the pot-boy on the lowest rung of the social ladder, enables him to declare that he is:

> *now of all humours that have showed themselves humours*
> *since the old days of goodman Adam to the pupil-age of*
> *this present twelve o'clock at midnight.*
> (Act II, Scene iv, lines 90-3)

In this comprehensiveness he contrasts himself with the one-track-mindedness of Hotspur, who is obsessed by the pursuit of honour and glory. In Hal's eyes these are, when given such prominence, out-worn ideals.

But although Hal is in many ways a 'new man' approaching the business of government unhampered by the clutter of age-old conventions, his shrewdness makes him realize the necessity of paying lip-service to these ideals once he has decided to join his father. So, as we learn from Vernon's speech in Act IV, Scene i, he emerges as the glorious image of a Renaissance prince; he publicly expresses his admiration of Hotspur's achievements and reputation and challenges him to single combat. It is unlikely that he has changed his views, but such attitudes are essential if he is to redeem his *lost opinion*.

In the light of this, Hal's relationship with Falstaff becomes easier to understand. Although some critics argue that this shows the sad breakdown of a genuine friendship under the pressures of public duty, what we really see is not two friends merrily wasing their time in idleness but two companions each using the other for what he can get. Falstaff, for all his wit, occasional gaiety, and infectious energy, is an anarchist aiming at the overturning of law and order. He hopes to establish so firm a hold on the prince that, on Hal's accession, he personally will be rewarded with power and wealth, so that life can be shaped to his liking.

> *But, I prithee, sweet wag, shall there be gallows standing in England when thou art king, and resolution thus fubb'd as it is with the rusty curb of old father antic the law?*

(Act I, Scene ii, lines 55-8)

For his part, Hal, though probably not completely lacking in affection for Falstaff, nevertheless sees him as a pastime, as part of his education, as one who will one day have to be rejected. Their relationship, therefore, reveals considerable tension, a concealed struggle for power in which Hal's detachment enables him to gain the upper hand. He delights in taunting Falstaff by talking of the gallows and death, enjoys pointing out the more revolting aspects of Falstaff's physique, and he joins the robbery because he sees this as a

way of playing a practical joke on Falstaff. A more
ominous stage is reached at the end of the mock-interview
in Act II, Scene iv when, in answer to Falstaff's plea that
Hal will not reject him, the Prince's grim rejoinder is *I do,
I will.* From then on, Hal, committed now to his father's
campaign, views Falstaff increasingly as an irrelevance, as
we finally see in his contemptuous acceptance of Falstaff's
lies concerning the killing of Hotspur. Only when Hal
believes Falstaff to be dead do we get a glimpse of the
affection that he has always fought against:

> *Poor Jack, farewell*!
> *I could have better spar'd a better man.*
> (Act V, Scene iv, lines 103-4)

The political calculation characterizing Henry IV and his
son is present in most of the play's leading figures. Westmoreland seems more concerned with the outward appearance of Falstaff's troops than with their poor chances of
surviving the battle, The senior members of the Percy
family, Northumberland and Worcester, view matters in a
totally political light. The former is scheming, crafty, and
also weak. Having encouraged his brother in planning the
rebellion, he absents himself from the battle on the excuse
of a sickness which is obviously the product of fear rather
than anything physical. Worcester, by contrast, is unyielding,
and his ruthlessness and incisive intelligence make him a
formidable enemy. Unlike Hotspur, he has no illusions.
Although he is prepared to use the language of honour in
order to entice his nephew, he knows the utter illegality and
unreasonableness of the rebellion and he reacts to the news
of Northumberland's absence with a devastating admission
of the need to:

> *. . . stop all sight-holes, every loop from whence*
> *The eye of reason may pry in upon us.*
> (Act IV, Scene i, lines 71-2)

He feels strong personal antagonism to Henry IV in addition
to his desire for aggrandisement and his extreme family
pride. His behaviour in certain instances undoubtedly con-
tributes to eventual failure. He seems to put family reputation above the success of the revolt when he rebukes his
nephew in perfunctory fashion for threatening the rebellion's

success by his attitude to Glendower. More damaging still is his refusal to pass on to Hotspur the King's offer of mercy on the eve of battle, a decision of political and personal hatred that justifies his later execution.

The two characters against whom Hal is dramatically set in his process of education for kingship are Hotspur and Falstaff. Each represents an extreme and opposed point of view, a kind of 'temptation' which Hal must resist. It is no coincidence that each of them makes a great appeal to audience and readers and is largely responsible for the play's popularity, for what each possesses in his individual way is a quality of zest for life, of energy and imagination, a capacity for giving and demanding an emotional response to things that we have seen the play's other main characters to lack.

Hotspur, despite his pride in being above *mincing poetry* speaks much of the most fresh and vivid verse in the play. He appears at his best early on, in his account of his conversation with the *certain lord* after the battle of Holmedon, and in his outraged fury at the duplicity of Henry IV's treatment of Mortimer. At this stage he is the straightforward soldier, intolerant of double-dealing, energetic in his pursuit of honour. His open nature contrasts with the 'chess-game' policy of his equals, as does the love that he and his wife feel for each other. But the attractive side of his nature does not obscure his equally pronounced faults. His love of honour is absurd in its naivety. For it he is prepared to go to any lengths, and the beauty and strength of his language should not blind us to this fact:

> *By heaven, methinks it were an easy leap*
> *To pluck bright honour from the pale-fac'd moon;*
> *Or dive into the bottom of the deep,*
> *Where fathom-line could never touch the ground,*
>
> (Act I Scene iii, lines 201-4)

He is narrow-minded, intolerant of any point of view but his own, and he rarely speaks well of anybody. His arrogance towards Glendower threatens to wreck the rebellion before it really begins.

As he becomes entangled in the web of politics, his faults are exaggerated and he becomes a somewhat pathetic figure. His insistence on treating the rebellion as a noble sport prevents him from facing realistically the implications of his father's defection; despite his scorn of flattery he feels constrained to greet Douglas with stilted compliments, and he writhes with anguish on hearing Vernon's praise of his despised rival. His rhetoric becomes bombastic and hollow-sounding. Only at the end of the play, when he cannot ignore any longer persistent doubts concerning the rebellion's success, does he recover something of his early dignity and attractiveness. He becomes more mature, his praise of Blunt is admirable, and his new-found sense of caution makes him consider the King's offer of mercy. In Act V he regrets that the quarrel cannot be settled by single combat between him and Hal, and he enters the battle in a brave but fatalistic frame of mind, possibly sensing his imminent death:

> *O gentlemen, the time of life is short!*
> *To spend that shortness basely were too long,*
> *If life did ride upon a dial's point,*
> *Still ending at the arrival of an hour.*

(Act V, Scene ii, lines 82-5)

In another play, Hotspur could perhaps develop into a tragic hero; in the world of *Henry IV, Part I* he is out of his depth and a figure of futility.

Falstaff's view of life is very different from Hotspur's. If death with honour is, in Hotspur's opinion, preferable to ignoble life, life at all costs is what matters to Falstaff. His philosophy is expressed clearly in his famous 'catechism' on the eve of battle:

> *What is honour? A word. What is in that word? Honour.*
> *What is that honour? Air. A trim reckoning! Who hath*
> *it? He that died o' Wednesday! Doth he feel it? No. Doth*
> *he hear it? No. 'Tis insensible, then? Yea to the dead. But*
> *will it not live with the living? No. Why? Detraction*
> *will not suffer it. Therefore I'll none of it. Honour is a*
> *mere scutcheon. And so ends my catechism.*

(Act V, Scene i, lines 134-41)

The determination to stay alive, to enjoy his life extravagantly and, in so doing, to reject the harshness of political reality with its gallows, wars, and eventual death is at the heart of Falstaffian comedy and largely explains his constant popularity. Despite his vast size and loss of youth, Falstaff's vitality and dexterity make him dwarf all other characters. He is no coward, but he will not *fight longer than he sees reason* and quickly shams death in the battle when confronted by Douglas. To escape the drabness of reality he uses lies to build a world of fantasy in which he is more real than ever, and his absurd account of his feats at Gadshill constitute his greatest triumph. Lies, for Falstaff, are not intended to be believed. They are a means of escape into a world of pretence, the only place in which he can live to his satisfaction. Even at the play's end, when his vitality has been gradually ebbing away as he sees his hold on the Prince to be weakening, he can accomplish another masterpiece of comic invention in his description of his killing of Hotspur, and when Hal claims to have done this himself he can only mutter in stupefaction:

Lord, Lord, how this world is given to lying!
(Act V, Scene iv, lines 145-6)

In asserting the value of life for its own sake and at no matter what cost, Falstaff brings lungfuls of fresh air to the stuffy world of politics.

Falstaff, however, is also *that villainous, abominable misleader of youth, that old whitebearded Satan*—white-bearded because he too adopts an outward pose of respectability when it suits him, and quotes Scripture freely for his own unscrupulous ends. Despite his contempt for politicians, for honour, despite his hatred of war, the triumph of Falstaff would destroy any hope of the order for which Henry IV and his son are looking. He wishes to abolish the rule of law and, in trying to persuade Hal to join in the robbery, hopes that *the true prince will prove a false thief*.

In the second half of the play, Falstaff becomes more depressed, and Shakespeare lays greater emphasis on the predatory aspect of his nature. He refuses to pay his debts and accuses Mistress Quickly of stealing valuable property that in fact amounts to *some eight-penny matter*. He abuses the recruiting system, and at Shrewsbury leads his ragged troops *where they are pepper'd*, having earlier dismissed them as *food for powder*. Even at the moment of his comic success in pretending to have killed Hotspur, his stabbing of Hotspur's dead body in the thigh adds a gruesome

touch, and his lies to Hal about this matter are no longer
for their own sake but in the hope of material reward:

I look to be either earl or duke, I can assure you.

(Act V, Scene iv, line 143)

It is obvious, therefore, that if Hal is to be the king he
plans to be, his eventual rejection of Falstaff is inevitable.
It is a measure of Falstaff's greatness that, while we are
increasingly repelled by aspects of his nature, we also regard
his loss of influence and impending downfall with sadness
and pity. At the end of *Henry IV, Part II*, Falstaff, on
hearing of Henry IV's death, rides furiously from Gloucestershire to London to greet the new king and, as he
hopes, enjoy the rewards that he expects Hal to give him.
Henry V's lines:

I know thee not, old man: fall to thy prayers;
How ill white hairs become a fool and jester.
I have long dream'd of such a kind of man,
So surfeit-swell'd, so old, and so profane;
But being awak'd, I do despise my dream.

provide a moment of dramatic shock. Even then, Falstaff,
outwardly at least, will not accept reality. He turns to his
companions:

Do not you grieve at this; I shall be sent for in private
to him. Look you, he must seem thus to the world.

As one might expect in a play so much involved with
power politics, the ordinary people play a minor role.
Through them we see how England as a whole suffers from
the disorder resulting from the activities of its aristocratic
leaders. The two carriers trust nobody; they lie concerning
their time of travelling and will not lend Gadshill their
lantern. Francis will not dare to end his life of drudgery
by breaking his contract and running away. Falstaff's
commodity of warm slaves buy their way out of the military
service they fear and those who take their place are *food
for powder*.

One of the major achievements of the series of plays
Richard II – Henry V is the broad picture of English society
that it gives. Nearly every class is represented. To achieve
this, Shakespeare makes full use of his unequalled insight
into human situations and character; his mastery of
language, both verse and prose, is constantly put to the

same dramatic purpose. Not only does he use contrasting styles of speech to differentiate between individuals, but recurring images and symbols are carefully integrated to bring out the full meaning of his plays.

Thus, in *Henry IV, Part I* we notice the elaborate, somewhat forced images of the King's speeches at times of stress, contrasting with his more direct language when attending to routine business. Hotspur's manner of speech is brusque, bombastic, imaginative, thoughtful, or strongly colloquial, according to his moods and the situation. The prose of the play is most impressively spoken by Falstaff. As an educated man, he is capable of subtle argument, of quoting proverbs and Biblical sayings, of voicing an endless variety of colloquial phrases frequently used for insult, and of parodying contemporary literary styles. The astonishing flexibility of his speech contrasts with Hal's normally more straightforward expression. Francis's speech catches exactly the mechanical, illiterate thinking of his type; the lively, cynical language of the carriers suggests vividly their way of life.

Finally we note the dramatic effect of key images. There are references to the sun and moon, meteors and stars; to animals, the majority of which describe Falstaff or are mentioned by him; to ill-fitting or tawdry clothing, linked with the rebellion. Such points are, of course, minor when considered separately. It is from the imaginative integration of all these elements—plot, situation, character, poetic speech with its wealth of varied vocabulary and contrasted styles—that the greatness of a Shakespeare play emerges.

THEME INDEX

The main themes of the play, as one would expect, concern public rather than private qualities and centre on political and military concepts such as authority and anarchy, honour, kingship, political intrigue and war. Although glimpses of more private values appear at times in individuals and in some of the relationships, between Hotspur and his wife, for instance, personal warmth is, on the whole, lacking in this play and we can sense Shakespeare's regret at this necessary state of affairs in Falstaff's satirical comments on the 'rat-race' of politics and power.

The list given below is in no way comprehensive, but the inclusion of references to some of the play's main ideas is intended to enable the student to grasp more easily Shakespeare's handling of his material.

Anarchy
This is a state of affairs which threatens for much of the play, largely through the Percy rebellion and in the aims and activities of Falstaff and his cronies. The Percies attempt:

> *To face the garment of rebellion*
> *With some fine colour that may please the eye*
> (V i, 74–5)

while Falstaff begs of Hal:

> *Do not thou, when thou art king, hang a thief.*
> (I ii, 58–9)

Other relevant passages are: I ii 13–29, II i 64–80, II iv 64–74, V i 72–82.

Authority (Law and Order)
This is what Henry IV (although he is a usurper) Westmoreland, Blunt and, essentially, Hal stand for. Henry sums up the outcome of the main plot in the last scene:
> *Thus ever did rebellion find rebuke.*
> (V v, 1)

and

> *Let us not leave till all our own be won.*

(V v 44)

Other examples occur in: I i 100–7, III ii 153–61, V i 104–14.

Honour

For Hotspur this is the dominant ideal in life. For its sake he is prepared to go to all extremes:

> *To pluck bright honour from the pale-fac'd moon;*
> *Or dive into the bottom of the deep.*

(I iii 202–3)

His naïve notions are obsolete in a cynical world, and Hal claims:

> *Percy is but my factor, good my lord,*
> *To engross up glorious deeds on my behalf;*

(III ii 147–8)

And there is Falstaff's acid comment:

> *Detraction will not suffer it. Therefore I'll none of it.*

(V i 139–40)

Other passages of interest in this respect are: I iii 29–69; III i 139–40; IV i 75–83; V i 83–100; V ii 52–69; V iii 1–13; V iv 39–101.

Parodies of honour are to be found in: V i 129–41; V iii 50–60; V iv 75–6 (and Stage Direction); V iv 139–58.

Kingship

The nature of kingship is the main theme of the *Richard II-Henry V* series. In this play the rebels emphasize the illegality of Henry's position (I iii 162–3; IV iii 52–105; V i 30–71) and contrast him with Richard II, *that sweet, lovely rose.* Dramatically, however, the power of Henry's kingship is our dominant impression (I i 100–7; I iii 113–24; V i 101–14; V v), compared with the weakness of that of Richard II, *the skipping king* (III ii 60–84).

Political Intrigue

The rebels, Worcester especially, are masters of this. He is well aware that they:

> *Must keep aloof from strict arbitrement,*
> *And stop all sight-holes, every loop from whence*
> *The eye of reason may pry in upon us.*
>
> (IV i 70–2)

Other passages on the same lines are: I iii 77–92, 259–302; IV i 31–41; IV iv; V ii 1–25.
But the King is also an adept at this (I i 47–74; I iii 113–24, 155–9).

War

The horrors of civil war were all too obvious to Shakespeare and his Elizabethan audiences. In the first scene, Henry IV pleads:

> *The edge of war, like an ill-sheathed knife,*
> *No more shall cut his master.*
>
> (I i 17–18)

He calls on Worcester to:

> *unknit*
> *This churlish knot of all-abhorred war,*
>
> (V i 15–16)

Important passages on this theme are: I i 5–13; I iii 259–90; IV i 112–23; IV ii 11–48; V iii and iv.
Henry's wish to go on a crusade offsets these passages, in I i 18–27. So, to some extent, do the wars against Scotland and Ireland (I i 34–75, I iii 93–112).

Imagery

There is an interesting use of sun and moon images to point the contrast between the forces of law and disorder. The sun is an emblem of royalty. Hal decides to *imitate the sun* (I ii 185) and is seen by Vernon to be *as gorgeous as the sun at midsummer* (IV i 102). The badge of the Percies, on the other hand, is the half-moon, Hotspur wishes to pluck honour from the *pale-faced moon*, and Falstaff describes himself and his highwaymen-associates as *minions of the moon* (I ii 26).
Other recurrent images concern meteors (signifying rebellion) and animals (associated with Falstaff, particularly in I ii).

Character

This play typically illustrates Shakespeare's fascination with the intricacies of human nature. The following references give a guide to some facets of the main characters, but you should not regard them as easy summaries of all that is to be said about each man.

Henry IV

his yearning for peace and sense of insecurity: I i 1–18; I iii 142–4; II iv 349–50.

his (possible) religious sense: I i 18–27; III ii 4–11.

his authority and decisiveness: I i 100–7; I iii 15–21; III ii 170–80; V v.

his political shrewdness: III ii 39–59, 121–8; IV iii 54–105; V iii 25.

Hal

his essential authority: I ii 30–8; II iv 494–514; III ii 22–8, 129–59; V v 25–31.

his self-knowledge: I ii 183–205.

his preparation for kingship: I ii 183–205; II iv 1–109; III ii 11–28, 129–59.

as epitome of Renaissance power and honour: IV i 97–110; V i 83–100; V ii 52–69; V iv 87–101; V v 22–31.

Falstaff

as representative of disorder: I ii 1–29, 55–9.

his vitality and instinct for life: II ii 80–7; II iv 156–274, 363–469; V iv 111–30.

his fear of death: I ii 69–77; V i 121–9; V iv 111–30.

his mock-repentance: I ii 77–93; III iii 1–19.

his self-pity: II iv 111–30.

his insecurity: II iv 455–69, 480–7.

his unscrupulousness: II iv 296–304; IV ii 11–48; V iii 35–8; V iv 139–65.

as commentator on political and military events: V i 28, 129–41; V iii 44–53.

Hotspur

his sense of honour: I iii 93–112, 194–8, 201–8.

his vitality: I iii; V ii 91–101.
his naïveté: I iii 155–86.
his insecurity: II iii 1–34; IV i; V ii 81–101.
his lack of organization: III i 5–6.
his fear and jealousy of Hal: IV i 111–12, 119–23; V ii 70–9.
his hatred of pomp: I iii 29–69; III i 18–190.
his immaturity: I iii; III i; IV i (in various places).

Relationships

We learn much about the characters from their relationships with others. In this play there are two father-son relationships that provide an interesting contrast. The King's attitude to and dealings with his son can be seen in I i 78–90; III ii; V i 83–103; V iv 1–24, 44–57; Northumberland and Hotspur are linked in I i 78–83; I iii; IV i 13–85.

Two marriages are also presented. That between Mortimer and Lady Mortimer is, perhaps, a parody of romantic love (III i 192–227) and contrasts with the down-to-earth, but more moving one between Hotspur and Lady Percy (II iii 35–117; III i 228–62).

The most fully developed relationship in the play is that of Hal and Falstaff. It changes throughout as Hal is drawn more into the world of political duty, but the undercurrent of tension is always present as each attempts to use the other for his own ends. You should particularly look at: I ii 1–49; II iv 110–538; III iii 86–201; V iii 39–54; V iv 137–58.

FURTHER READING

There are several works that give a detailed study of the four linked 'Bolingbroke plays'. Among them, D. A. Traversi's *From Richard II to Henry V* (Hollis and Carter) brings out, as its title suggests, the unity of this series of plays. Its section on *Henry IV* examines the close-knit relationship between the comic and political plots and reveals Falstaff's vital role as commentator on them. E. M. W. Tillyard's section on *Henry IV* in *Shakespeare's History Plays* (Chatto & Windus and Penguin) studies Hal's role as the traditional morality hero with Falstaff and Hotspur as his tempters. According to this view *Part I* shows Hal acquiring the military virtues necessary to the true Prince, while *Part II* proceeds to the completion of his training by similar success in the civil sphere. Tillyard also sees in both plays a picture of the contemporary condition of English life and society.

Other valuable studies are J. Dover Wilson's *The Fortunes of Falstaff* (Cambridge University Press), which traces the plan of the *Henry IV* plays by examining the knight's career, and J. Palmer's *Political Characters in Shakespeare* (Macmillan) whose chapter on Henry of Monmouth forms part of his study of Shakespeare's attitude to politics and presentation of the public man. A sombre view of the play (*Part I*) is given in a few pages of J. F. Danby's *Shakespeare's Doctrine of Nature* (Faber and Faber). The function of the dominant images in revealing character in the drama is discussed in *Shakespeare's Imagery and What It Tells Us* by Caroline Spurgeon (Cambridge University Press).